Writing UNIX® Device Drivers

George Pajari

Addison-Wesley Publishing Company, Inc.

Reading, Massachusetts   Menlo Park, California   New York
Don Mills, Ontario   Wokingham, England   Amsterdam   Bonn
Sydney   Singapore   Tokyo   Madrid   San Juan
Paris   Seoul   Milan   Mexico City   Taipei

Many of the designations used by manufacturers and sellers to distinguish their products are claimed as trademarks. Where those designations appear in this book and Addison-Wesley was aware of a trademark claim, the designations have been printed in initial capital letters.

The authors and publishers have taken care in preparation of this book, but make no expressed or implied warranty of any kind and assume no responsibility for errors or omissions. No liability is assumed for incidental or consequential damages in connection with or arising out of the use of the information or programs contained herein.

Library of Congress Cataloging-in-Publication Data

Pajari, George.
  Writing UNIX device drivers / by George Pajari.
    p.   cm.
  Includes index.
  ISBN 0-201-52374-4
  1. UNIX device drivers (Computer programs)   I. Title.
QA76.76.D49P35   1991
005.4'3—dc20   91-42361

ISBN 0-201-52374-4

Managing Editor: Amorette Pedersen
Set in 11-point New Century Schoolbook by Benchmark Productions

   3 4 5 6 7 8 9-MW-95949392
Third printing, September 1992

This book is dedicated to Carol, who has taken the fun out of being alone.

Acknowledgments

To my colleagues at Driver Design Labs: Jeff Tate, who checked that it made sense and helped make it somewhat understandable; Carolanne Reynolds, who spent many hours reading and revising drafts trying to convert it into something much closer to English; and to Frank Pronk who provided a useful reality check. The unseen corrections and improvements are theirs (many remaining problems and errors are mine).

To Harry Henderson, Mitch Waite, Rebecca Thomas, David Flack, Tom Ward, Ben Smith, and Jane Tazelaar; all of whom have helped with one or more of my previously published works on device drivers.

To Chris Williams and Amy Pedersen who, as editors of this book, exhibited patience and understanding above and beyond the call. No author could ask for more, and aspiring authors of technical books are urged to contact them.

To Jeff Kulick and the Department of Computing and Information Science at Queen's University at Kingston: both gave me the opportunity to play with the UNIX kernel well over a decade ago and both have to take at least some responsibility for all of this.

To Ed Palmer and the organizers of the annual UniForum Conference and Exhibition, where the author has had the pleasure of delivering the *Writing UNIX Device Drivers* tutorial for several years. The course notes for those tutorials formed the basis for this book.

To the Scottish & Newcastle Breweries PLC Edinburgh, whose McEwan's Scotch Malt Liquor had a very enjoyable, if detrimental, effect on the writing of this book.

To my parents and grandparents who have always encouraged and supported me.

And most importantly to my wife, Carolanne Reynolds, for more reasons than there is room in these notes to list.

Table of Contents

Preface

So you want to write a UNIX device driver. Or perhaps you just want to learn a bit more about a topic that has historically been the exclusive domain of systems gurus and programming wizards. In either case, this book is written expressly for you.

Writing UNIX Device Drivers

Writing device drivers is one of the most challenging and interesting types of programming. In contrast to applications programming, the device driver writer has to be concerned with hardware details at the lowest levels as well as the problems of concurrency. These additional complexities not only make device driver programming much more difficult and frustrating, they make it far more interesting and challenging.

Let us consider some of the problems that regularly arise during the development of a device driver—problems which, by the way, rarely if ever affect applications programmers.

Device drivers interface with the kernel using an entirely different set of routines than those used by applications software. This programming interface is all too often incompletely (or incorrectly) documented, frequently leaving the device driver programmer to debug the documentation as well as the driver.

Device drivers usually interface with hardware (i.e., disk drives or tape drives). Not only is this interface almost always incompletely documented, it usually suffers from idiosyncrasies that are very different from software interfaces. Some hardware devices will malfunction if their control registers are written in the wrong order, or if written before being read, or if read before being written, or if written too quickly after being read, etc. and etc.

What adds to the frustration is that these problems are very different from those normally experienced by software developers.

For example, device drivers also have to deal with the problem of concurrent execution. In other words, the driver may be handling one request when another request from some other process arrives. The driver has to make sure that multiple requests can be scheduled and processed without confusion.

Another problem arises with hardware interrupts. Usually when the device is finished with the last request it was given, it will interrupt the computer. This can cause the computer to stop what it is doing and start executing the driver's interrupt handler. Since the interrupt can come at any time, it may arrive while the driver is in the midst of handling another request. The driver must take special steps to prevent data structures from being corrupted in this situation.

These problems do not usually arise in applications programming or with drivers for single-tasking operating systems such as MS-DOS.

Finally, the driver may have to perform certain operations under very tight time constraints. For example, a driver handling an unbuffered serial communications device will experience an interrupt every 500-millionths of a second for a line running at 19,200 baud. The challenge is to handle the data while still allowing the UNIX system to accomplish some other work.

As if the design problems were not enough, testing and debugging drivers is also more difficult than for applications software.

In order to operate as the master control program, the kernel runs with few limitations on its actions. As a result many of the protections for stray pointers and illegal operations provided for applications programs are not available to the kernel and device drivers.

The traditional debugging tools will not work on the kernel, and the kernel usually cannot be breakpointed or single-stepped.

Furthermore, driver problems can be very time-dependent. Interrupts can arrive at any time and a driver may function correctly most of the time only to fail when an interrupt arrives in the middle of a particular operation.

Things can get even more frustrating when one adds *printf* statements to the driver in an attempt to trace the operation of the driver only to find that adding the *printf*s changes the behaviour of the driver.

Yet, as challenging and frustrating device driver writing can be, it can also be particularly rewarding. Developing software that has to cope with all of the problems mentioned and debugging it in the face of limited debugging tools can be very satisfying.

There is also a special feeling of accomplishment that results from writing software that: controls hardware; causes a tape drive to start moving, or sends data across a communications link.

This book will introduce you to the techniques of addressing these problems and enable you to enter this exciting realm of programming.

This Book's Approach

The primary objective of this book is to explain, through the use of source code for working drivers, the issues related to the design and implementation of UNIX device drivers.

The approach is unusual in that most of the book consists of the examination and discussion of the source for more than a dozen device drivers. The source code is complete and unabridged. Every line of C that was compiled during the testing of the drivers appears in this book.

This has several advantages over other approaches. As with any complex subject, some of the concepts and issues related to the design of device drivers can be somewhat abstract and difficult to grasp. In this presentation everything is introduced in the context of an actual driver. This concrete grounding of the material makes understanding easier since their application can be seen immediately. It also helps the reader to organise the subject material and to grasp the relationships between different pieces of information.

Not only does this book provide sample drivers to illustrate the material, it provides the complete source to each driver. Some books and courses only provide excerpts from working drivers. Although useful, what they leave out can be as important as what they include. And it is the unfortunate programmer who, while trying to write his first driver, finds out just how much was left out. Excerpts of drivers are just not enough. To be truly useful, a text on writing device drivers must include the complete source to every driver. This book does just that.

Another advantage is based on the observation that no device driver is ever written from scratch. The approach is to find a device driver that is close to what is required and then to modify it to suit. This book provides copious amounts of raw material from which to draw. With the complete source to about a dozen drivers, any prospective device driver writer is certain to find something close to what is needed.

It is the author's belief that the best way to learn how to write device drivers is to write one, and the second best way is to study someone else's. This book is a useful companion to either endeavour.

This book also provides exercises after most chapters that suggest ways in which the reader can modify the drivers. This can aid in the understanding of the sample drivers and the material itself.

Prerequisites

It is expected that the reader of this book have some experience developing software for the UNIX operating system and be reasonably familiar with the C programming language.

Note that this book is intended to serve as a textbook or self-study guide for those wishing to learn how to write device drivers. It is not a reference manual. There are many details that have had to be omitted in order for the presentation to be clear, concise, and easily understood. These details are more appropriate for a reference manual than the tutorial this book endeavours to be. Before you actually start writing a device driver it essential that you acquire and acquaint yourself with the device driver reference manual for the version of the UNIX operating system you will be using.

One other book that complements the coverage of this book is *The Design of the UNIX Operating System* by Maurice Bach. While a detailed understanding of the UNIX operating system itself is not necessary in order to write device drivers, it certainly would help. The book you are reading will introduce the major concepts of the UNIX operating system as they are encountered, but Bach's book is a most readable account of the internals of the UNIX operating system in their full glory.

Applicability

All of the drivers in this book, except for the STREAMS drivers in Chapters 11 and 12, have been written for AT&T UNIX System V Release 3. In particular, they have been compiled and tested with The Santa Cruz Operation's SCO UNIX System V/386 Release 3.2 on various 386 and 486 computers. These drivers ought to compile and run with little or no change on all Release 3.2 UNIX systems, and with some changes on any Release 3 system that can support the devices described.

The STREAMS drivers and the drivers in Chapter 15 have been written for AT&T UNIX System V Release 4 and were compiled and tested on UHC's Release 4 product running on various 386 and 486 computers.

Chapter 1

What is a Device Driver?

The Grand Design

A device driver is the glue between an operating system and its I/O devices. Device drivers act as translators, converting the generic requests received from the operating system into commands that specific peripheral controllers can understand.

This relationship is illustrated in Figure 1-1. The applications software makes system calls to the operating system requesting services (for example, *write this data to file x*).

The operating system analyzes these requests and, when necessary, issues requests to the appropriate device driver (for example, *write this data to disk 2, block 23654*).

The device driver in turn analyzes the request from the operating system and, when necessary, issues commands to the hardware interface to perform the operations needed to service the request (for example: *transfer 1024 bytes starting at address 235400 to disk 2, cylinder 173, head 7, sector 8*).

FIGURE 1-1

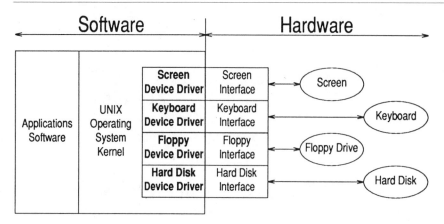

Although this process may seem unnecessarily complex, the existence of device drivers actually simplifies the operating system considerably. Without device drivers, the operating system would be responsible for talking directly to the hardware. This would require the operating system's designer to include support for all of the devices that users might want to connect to their computer. It would also mean that adding support for a new device would mean modifying the operating system itself.

By separating the device driver's functions from the operating system itself, the designer of the operating system can concern himself with issues that relate to the operation of the system as a whole. Furthermore, details related to individual hardware devices can be ignored and generic requests for I/O operations can be issued by the operating system to the device driver.

The device driver writer, on the other hand, does not have to worry about the many issues related to general I/O management, as these are handled by the operating system. All the device driver writer has to do is to take detailed device-independent requests from the operating system and to manipulate the hardware in order to fulfil the request.

Finally, the operating system can be written without any knowledge of the specific devices that will be connected. And the device driver writer can connect any I/O device to the system without having to modify the operating system. The operating system views all hard disks through the same interface, and the device driver writer can connect almost any type of disk to the system by providing a driver so that the operating system is happy.

The result is a clean separation of responsibilities and the ability to add device drivers for new devices without changing the operating system. Device drivers provide the operating system with a standard interface to non-standard I/O devices.

The Details

A UNIX device driver is a collection of functions, usually written in C, that can be called by the UNIX operating system using the standard C function-calling mechanism. These routines are often referred to as *entry points*. The compiled code for the device driver is linked with the code for the operating system itself and the result is a new file containing the bootable operating system with all the device drivers.

In order to understand the relationship between the UNIX operating system and its drivers better, let us examine the result of running a simple UNIX command that references the line printer driver. Consider the result of typing the following command on a UNIX system:

```
echo hello, world > /dev/lp
```

Since we are only interested in the issues related to UNIX device drivers we shall ignore the details of how the shell command interpreter actually processes this input.

The first part of interest occurs when the shell goes to open the file /dev/lp. The C code that is executed is the equivalent of:

```
fileds = open("/dev/lp", O_WRONLY);
```

The UNIX operating system first examines the file /dev/lp and determines that it is, in fact, not a normal data file but a special file. Special files are files that can represent device drivers (among other things). If we were to examine the /dev/lp file using the ls -l command, we would find:

```
crw-------    2 bin    bin    6,   0   Oct 4  1991 /dev/lp
```

There are two things in this display that differ from what we would normally see if /dev/lp had been a normal data file. Note that the first character on the line is *c*. This indicates that this special file represents a character device driver. Character drivers are one of the four different types of drivers (more on the other three shortly). Also note that the numbers *6, 0* appear in the place where we would normally expect to find the size of the file. These are the major (6) and minor (0) device numbers for this special file. The major device number specifies the device driver while the minor device number is used by the driver to distinguish between different devices under the control of a single driver.

When the UNIX operating system goes to process the open system call, it sees that the file being opened is a character special file with major device number 6. It uses the major device number to index into a table of all of the character drivers installed on the system. The declaration of this table looks something like the following:

```
struct cdevsw
{
    int      (*d_open)();
    int      (*d_close)();
    int      (*d_read)();
    int      (*d_write)();
    int      (*d_ioctl)();
    struct tty *d_ttys;
    struct streamtab *d_str;
    char     *d_name;
};

extern int lpopen(), lpclose(), lpread(), lpwrite(), lpioctl();
struct cdevsw cdevsw[] =
{
```

```
    . . .
    lpopen, lpclose, lpread, lpwrite, lpioctl, NULL, NULL, "lp",
    . . .
};
```

This table is defined when a new operating system kernel is configured and built. The kernel is the part of the UNIX operating system that is always resident in memory when the system is running, and which sits between the hardware and the processes. Device drivers are considered part of the kernel.

Every member of the table is a structure containing pointers to each of the five main entry points for each character driver. The remaining three members of the structure are pointers to various data structures that are not used by the line printer driver.

If the kernel has stored the major device number in a variable called *dev_major*, it can invoke the driver's open entry point using the expression *cdevsw[dev_major].d_open(...)*.

Similarly, when the echo utility goes to write the string "hello, world", the UNIX operating system passes the data to the line printer driver by invoking the driver's write routine (e.g., *cdevsw[dev_major].d_write...*).

In this manner, the connection is made between a UNIX process and the device driver.

An important consideration is that the driver's routines (entry points) are linked into the rest of the UNIX kernel and form part of the operating system. One result is device drivers execute with all of the privileges of the operating system and can do things that normal applications software cannot. They also can malfunction in ways never imagined by applications programmers.

The Major Design Issues

To make studying the design of device drivers easier, we have divided the issues to be considered into three broad categories:

1. Operating System/Driver Communications
2. Driver/Hardware Communications
3. Driver Operations

The first category covers all of the issues related to the exchange of information (commands and data) between the device driver and the operating system. It also includes support functions that the kernel provides for the benefit of the device driver.

The second covers those issues related to the exchange of information (commands and data) between the device driver and the device it controls (i.e., the hardware). This also includes issues such as how software talks to hardware—and how the hardware talks back.

The third covers issues related to the actual internal operation of the driver itself. This includes:

- interpreting commands received from the operating system;
- scheduling multiple outstanding requests for service;
- managing the transfer of data across both interfaces (operating system and hardware);
- accepting and processing hardware interrupts; and
- maintaining the integrity of the driver's and the kernel's data structures.

When we proceed to study the actual drivers presented in this book, we shall examine each in the context of these three general design issues.

Types of Device Drivers

UNIX device drivers can be divided into four different types based entirely on differences in the way they communicate with the UNIX operating system. The types are: block, character, terminal, and STREAMS. The kernel data structures that are accessed and the entry points that the driver can provide vary between the various types of drivers. These differences affect the type of devices that can be supported with each interface.

The following sections will describe these differences briefly and the types of devices that each driver can support. As we study the drivers in the remainder of this book we shall examine these differences in detail.

Block Drivers

Block drivers communicate with the operating system through a collection of fixed-sized buffers as illustrated in Figure 1-2. The operating system manages a cache of these buffers and attempts to satisfy user requests for data by accessing buffers in the cache. The driver is invoked only when the requested data is not in the cache, or when buffers in the cache have been changed and must be written out.

FIGURE 1-2

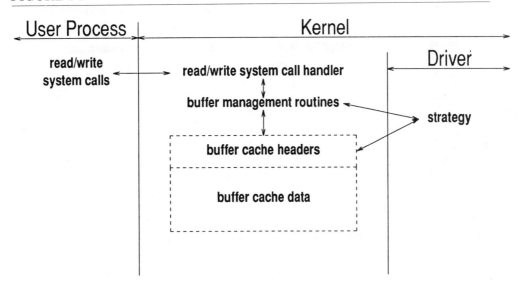

Because of this buffer cache the driver is insulated from many of the details of the users' requests and need only handle requests from the operating system to fill or empty fixed-sized buffers.

Block drivers are used primarily to support devices that can contain file systems (such as hard disks).

Character Drivers

Character drivers can handle I/O requests of arbitrary size and can be used to support almost any type of device. Usually, character drivers are used for devices that either deal with data a byte at a time (such as line printers) or work best with data in chunks smaller or larger than the standard fixed-sized buffers used by block drivers (such as analog-to-digital converters or tape drives).

One of the major differences between block and character drivers is that while user processes interact with block drivers only indirectly through the buffer cache, their relationship with character drivers is very direct. This is shown schematically in Figure 1-3. The I/O request is passed essentially unchanged to the driver to process and the character driver is responsible for transferring the data directly to and from the user process's memory.

FIGURE 1-3

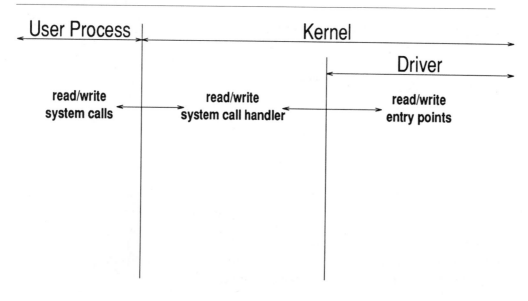

Terminal Drivers

Terminal drivers are really just character drivers specialized to deal with communication terminals that connect users to the central UNIX computer system. Terminal drivers are responsible not only for shipping data to and from users' terminals, but also for handling line editing, tab expansion, and the many other terminal functions that are part of the standard UNIX terminal interface described by the TERMIO manual page. Because of this additional processing that terminal drivers must perform (and the additional kernel routines and data structures that are provided to handle this), it is useful to consider terminal drivers as a separate type of driver altogether. Compare Figure 1-4, which represents the special relationship of a terminal driver with the kernel, with the earlier Figure 1-3 of a prototypical character driver.

FIGURE 1-4

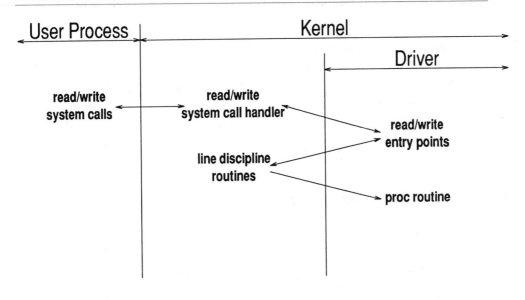

STREAMS Drivers

STREAMS drivers are used to handle high-speed communications devices such as networking adapters that deal with unusual-sized chunks of data and that need to handle protocols. In System V Release 4, STREAMS driveeers are also used to interface terminals.

Versions of UNIX prior to System V Release 3 supported network devices using character drivers. This was unsatisfactory because the character model assumes that a single driver sits between the user process and the device. Remember that with character drivers the user process's request is handed directly to the driver with little intervention or processing by the kernel.

Networking devices, however, usually support a number of layered protocols. The character model essentially required that each layer of the protocol be implemented within the single driver. This lack of modularity and reusability reduced the efficiency of the system.

As a result, Dennis Ritchie of Bell Laboratories (one of the originators of UNIX) developed an extension to the character driver model called STREAMS (in uppercase). This new type of driver was introduced by AT&T in UNIX System V Release 3 and makes it possible to stack protocol processing modules between the user process and the driver. This can be seen on the next page in Figure 1-5. Stacking modules in this way makes it much easier to implement network protocols.

The Gross Anatomy of a Device Driver

Each of the following chapters will present a complete driver for study. But before we turn the page and start considering our first driver, it might be helpful to consider the major components of a driver.

Recall that a driver is a set of entry points (routines) that can be called by the operating system. A driver can also contain: data structures private to the driver; references to kernel data structures external to the driver; and routines private to the driver (i.e., not entry points).

FIGURE 1-5

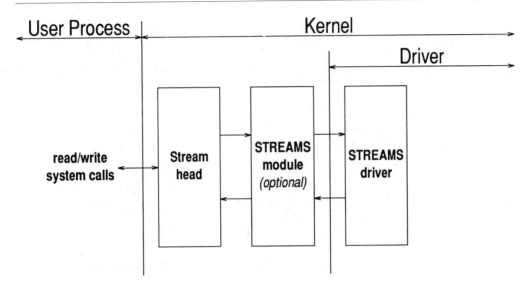

Most device drivers are written as a single source file. The initial part of the driver is sometimes called the *prologue*. The prologue is everything before the first routine and like most C programs contains:

- *#include* directives referencing header files which define various kernel data types and structures;
- *#define* directives that provide mnemonic names for various constants used in the driver (in particular constants related to the location and definition of the hardware registers); and
- declarations of variables and data structures.

The remaining parts of the driver are the entry points (C functions referenced by the operating system) and routines (C functions private to the driver.)

When we examine our drivers we shall consider each of these parts in turn.

General Programming Considerations

As we shall see in the many examples in this book, writing device drivers is somewhat different from writing applications programs in C. While explanation of the subtle differences can wait until we encounter them, it will be helpful to discuss the significant differences now.

As obvious as it sounds, the main difference is that device drivers are part of the kernel and not normal user processes. This means that many of the things that a normal C program can do a driver cannot. For starters, forget about using any of the normal C library functions described in the programmer's reference for your UNIX system. These functions, normally documented in sections 2 and 3 of your manual (or section S if you have an SCO XENIX or UNIX operating system) are not supported by the kernel. The functions that *are* supported by your kernel may be found in the device driver manual for your system. Note that although some of the kernel routines have the same name as standard C library functions (e.g., *printf*) they are somewhat different.

In addition, make frugal use of the stack (do not use recursive functions and do not declare local arrays). The stack space available to the kernel is limited and is not expandable on most UNIX systems. Also, do not use floating-point arithmetic. Although your machine may have a floating-point unit, the kernel does not save the contents of the FPU's registers unless it is planning to switch processes. Therefore using the FPU at best can cause incorrect results both in your code and some poor innocent user's program and at worst can cause the system to crash.

Do not *busy wait* (spin) within your driver waiting for an event to occur unless the expected time to wait is less than the time to leave your driver and re-enter it when an interrupt occurs (i.e., less than 200 microseconds on a fast 386). User processes that spin will merely have the CPU taken away from them and given to other processes in turn. The kernel, however, always takes priority over any user process and a driver that is executing a spin loop will prevent the system from doing anything but responding to interrupts.

Summary

As the first figure in this chapter showed, device drivers stand between an operating system and the peripherals it controls. Drivers accept standard requests for I/O services from the operating system and convert them into the hardware-specific commands and operations required to support the peripheral's interface. This not only relieves the operating system of the burden of handling the details of all the different peripherals, it makes it easy to support another peripheral just by adding a driver and without having to modify the operating system itself.

The UNIX operating system supports four different types of drivers (block, character, terminal, and STREAMS) which provide different interfaces between the kernel and the driver. This makes it possible to select the most appropriate driver model and interface for the type of device to be supported.

A driver is implemented as a collection of routines, usually written in the C language, that is linked into the kernel. When the operating system is asked to open or write to a device, it selects the driver's entry point from a table of entry points.

The remainder of this book will be an examination of a selection of drivers including at least one of each of the four types listed earlier.

Chapter 2

Character Driver I: A Test Data Generator

Instead of spending countless chapters droning on about the UNIX operating system and the theory of drivers, let's look at a real driver right now!

The driver we are about to examine is actually a *pseudo-device driver* in that it does not control any hardware. This will allow us to introduce the basic concepts of a UNIX device driver without the complexity of having to deal with a real device.

Read system calls on this pseudo-device will return the "Quick Brown Fox" message repeated infinitely. Writes are just ignored.

This device driver can therefore be used to generate infinite amounts of data for testing without consuming any disk space. For example, to test a terminal, one could type:

```
cat /dev/testdata
```

to test a printer:

```
cat /dev/testdata > /dev/lp
```

or to generate a one-megabyte data file:

```
dd if=/dev/testdata of=bigfile bs=1k count=1024
```

In the first two cases, the test would continue until the process was stopped by typing the interrupt character on your terminal (DEL, ^C, or whatever you have it set to).

Since this driver will handle data byte by byte and reads of arbitrary size, it is best structured as a character driver.

The Design Issues

Since this driver does not control any hardware, we need only concern ourselves with two of the three categories of design issues: the UNIX/driver interface and the internal driver operation. There are no driver/hardware interface issues.

The Operating System/Driver Interface

How does the UNIX kernel tell the driver what it wants it to do?

As we shall see shortly, this is done in two steps. Firstly, the operating system calls one of the device driver's entry points (functions). This causes control to pass to the device driver.

Secondly, the device driver examines the parameters passed and kernel data structures for information on exactly what to do.

Each of the four types of device drivers has its own set of entry points that the operating system expects to find and its own conventions for the exchange of data and commands. A character driver may have any or all of the following entry points:

■   init()

The *init* entry point is called by the kernel immediately after the system is booted. It provides the driver with an opportunity to initialize the driver and the hardware as well as to display messages announcing the presence of the driver and hardware.

- start()

The *start* entry point is called by the kernel late in the bootstrap sequence when more system services are available. It provides the driver with an opportunity to perform initialization that require more system services than are available at the time when *init* is called.

- open(dev, flag, id)

The *open* entry point is called by the kernel whenever a user process performs an open system call on a special file that is related to the driver. It provides the driver with an opportunity to perform initialization that need to occur prior to handling read and write system calls.

- close(dev, flag, id)

The *close* entry point is called by the kernel when the last user process that has the driver open performs a close system call (or exits, causing the operating system to close all open files automatically). Note that the driver's open entry point is called for every user open, while the driver's close entry point is called only for the last user close. It provides the driver with an opportunity to release resources that may be needed only while the device is open and to reset the device or otherwise place it in a quiescent mode.

- halt()

The *halt* entry point is called by the kernel just before the system is shut down. It provides the driver with an opportunity to prepare the hardware for the shutdown and to flush any data that may still be resident in the driver.

■   intr(vector)

The *intr* entry point is called by the kernel whenever an interrupt is received from the hardware. Interrupts are a signal from the hardware that a significant event has occurred (usually the completion of the last I/O operation) which requires the attention of the driver.

■   read(dev)

The *read* entry point is called by the kernel whenever a user process performs a read system call on a special file that is related to the driver. The driver is required to accept the details of the I/O request, perform the necessary operations to obtain the requested data, and arrange for the transfer of the data to the user's process.

■   write(dev)

The *write* entry point is called by the kernel whenever a user process performs a write system call on a special file that is related to the driver. The driver is required to accept the details of the I/O request, arrange for the transfer of the data from the user's process to the driver (or directly to the device), and perform the necessary operations to write the data to the device.

■   poll(pri)

The *poll* entry point is called by the kernel 25 to 100 times a second (depending on the version of UNIX). It provides the driver with an opportunity to perform operations on a periodic basis or to check on the status of the device on a regular basis.

■   ioctl(dev, cmd, arg, mode)

The *ioctl* entry point is called by the kernel whenever a user process performs an ioctl system call on a special file that is related to the driver. The driver is required either to accept the details of the ioctl request and perform the necessary operations, or reject the request with an error. Ioctl calls are used to pass special requests to the driver or to obtain information on the configuration or status of the device and driver.

The actual names of a particular driver's entry points are the name of the entry point (as above) plus a two- to four-letter prefix. For example, the prefix we have chosen for this sample driver is *chr1* (character driver #1). Therefore the *init* entry point is named *chr1init* and the *read* entry point *chr1read*. Each of these entry points will be discussed in detail as we encounter them in the drivers we are about to study.

The Internal Operation of the Driver

The overall purpose of this driver is to transfer data from an internally stored string (the "Quick Brown Fox" message) to a process's buffer (area in memory). When the process issues a read system call, it must specify both the location of the buffer as well as the number of bytes to read. For example, the line of code to perform the read might look something like this:

```
count = read(fildes, buffer, sizeof(buffer));
```

where *fildes* is the file descriptor returned from the *open* system call and *buffer* is a character array. The kernel handles this system call by calling the *read* entry point for our driver and leaving the address of *buffer* as well as the size of the read request (*sizeof(buffer)* in this example) in a location known to the driver. This "known" location is within a data structure called the *user* or *u.* (pronounced *you-dot*) area. The user area contains all of the information about a process that the kernel needs when the process is in memory (i.e., not swapped out to disk for want of memory). As mentioned, this data structure is also used to communicate between the kernel and the driver as will be seen in detail when we consider the *chr1read* entry point below. The contents of the user area are defined by the user structure (see the header file *<sys/user.h>*).

The Driver

What follows is the complete C source for this device driver. This driver, as with all of the others we shall examine, has been divided into sections. The first is the *driver prologue* which contains everything that must precede the first entry point in the source file. The second and subsequent sections are the entry points themselves.

The Driver Prologue

The prologue of a device driver includes all of the definitions and declarations required by the rest of the driver. In particular, most prologues consist of three parts: references to the header files necessary to define various kernel data types and structures; definitions that are local to the driver; and declarations local to the driver.

The prologue for this driver contains the references to the header files and local declarations. It has no local definitions.

```
1    #include <sys/types.h>
2    #include <sys/param.h>
3    #include <sys/dir.h>
4    #include <sys/signal.h>
5    #include <sys/user.h>
6    #include <sys/errno.h>

7    static char foxmessage[] =
         "THE QUICK BROWN FOX JUMPS OVER THE LAZY DOG\n";
```

The first six lines include header files that define various data types and structures that are used within the operating system and/or driver. These header files are found in the directory */usr/include/sys* and ought to be read before writing your first driver. Briefly:

■ *sys/types.h*

contains the definitions of various data types that are used by other include files and by the driver itself (i.e., *dev_t*);

■ *sys/param.h*

contains the definitions of various kernel parameters and macros that are needed by *sys/user.h* to size certain arrays;

■ *sys/dir.h*

contains the definitions of the directory structure needed by *sys/user.h*;

- *sys / signal.h*

contains the definitions related to signals needed by *sys / user.h*;

- *sys / user.h*

contains the definition of the user structure; and

- *sys / errno.h*

contains the definitions of the various error codes that may be returned from a driver.

The last line of our prologue declares the character array that contains our "QUICK BROWN FOX..." message. Note that variables used only within the driver are declared *static* so as not to risk conflict with global variables defined in the kernel.

The remainder of the driver consists of the driver's entry points.

The Init Entry Point

This entry point is called by the operating system shortly after the system is booted. Few system services are available to the driver at this time (i.e., it must not attempt to read a disk file). The primary purpose of calling the *init* routine is for the device driver:

- to check that the device is actually installed on the machine;
- to print a message indicating the presence (or absence) of the device and driver;
- to initialize the device (if necessary) prior to the first open; and
- to initialize the driver and allocate local memory (if necessary) prior to the first open.

Since the system itself is not completely initialized it is important not to use certain system services that are not yet ready. In particular:

- do not call the *sleep*, *delay*, or *wakeup* kernel support routines; and

- do not attempt to reference any members of the user structure (the *u.* area).

Note also that interrupts are not available at *init* time.

The init entry point is optional and need not be included in a driver, although most drivers, even those that do not need to perform any initialization, provide one to announce their presence. Such is the case with the init entry point for this driver.

```
 8   chr1init()
 9   {
10       printf("Test Data Character Device Driver v1.0\n");
11   }
```

Remember that the *printf* called in line 10 is not the standard *printf* available to normal applications C programs. It is a special version that is implemented in the kernel for use by device drivers. It does not support all of the options of the standard C *printf* function. Refer to the device driver reference manual for your version of UNIX to determine exactly what formatting options are available.

Also on most systems the kernel printf routine suspends all system activity while the message is being sent to the console. Use it sparingly. Beware of using it to report errors that may happen frequently if the device malfunctions. Frequent printf messages can so tie up a machine as to make it impossible to log users off and shut down the system properly.

The Read Entry Point

The *read* entry point of a character driver is called when the user's process has requested data from the device using the *read* system call. This routine must coordinate the transfer from the driver to the user's process.

Although the read entry point is optional, it is necessary for any driver that wishes to transfer data from a device (or driver) to a process (i.e., satisfy a read system call). Since our driver's sole purpose is to transfer "QUICK BROWN FOX..." messages from the driver to a process, it has a read entry point.

The pseudo-code for this entry point is below, followed immediately by the actual driver code. This sequence will be used in this book whenever the entry point is sufficiently complex to warrant a pseudo-code overview. In this manner readers wishing an overview of the driver can skim the pseudo-code and avoid the details of the actual driver. Since the line numbers in the pseudo-code listing refer to the lines in the actual driver code, the commentary on the code can be followed by referring to either the pseudo-code or the actual code.

```
12   read entry point:
14       while (the user's read request is not completely satisfied)
15       {
16           copy 1 byte
               from: foxmessage[indexed by u.u_offset]
               to:   the user's buffer addressed by u.u_base

             if (an error occurs)
17-20            set u.u_error and return

21-23        update u.u_offset, u.u_base, and u.u_count
24       }
```

The actual read entry point for this driver follows:

```
12   void chr1read(dev_t dev)
13   {
14       while (u.u_count)
15       {
16           if (copyout(&foxmessage[u.u_offset % sizeof(foxmessage)],
                   u.u_base, 1) == -1)
17           {
18               u.u_error = EFAULT;
19               return;
20           }
21           u.u_base++;
22           u.u_offset++;
23           u.u_count--;
24       }
25   }
```

With the read entry point the information specifying the nature of the transfer is passed to the driver in two ways. Firstly, the device number is passed as a parameter to the *read* routine. Since we are only emulating one (pseudo-)device, we can ignore the device number.

Secondly, the location of the data on the device, the number of bytes to *read*, and the memory location to which the data is to be transferred is stored in the user area.

The User Area   Every process has its own user structure but only the user structure for the currently executing process is accessible directly to the device driver. The kernel sets things up (either by using its memory management unit or by copying the data) so that the kernel variable *u* references the user structure for the currently executing process. Therefore the device driver can reference the (say) *u_base* member of the user structure for the current process by referring to *u.u_base*.

The contents of the user structure are defined by the system header file *<sys/user.h>*. There are a number of interesting members of this structure, but the only ones of use to us are listed below:

Important Members of The User Structure

Member	Description
u_error	error return code
u_uid	user id (UID) of the process
u_gid	group id (GID) of the process
u_base	address in user memory of I/O buffer
u_count	number of bytes to transfer
u_offset	position in file where next I/O is to occur

The *u_offset* value is used for devices that support addressing or direct access (such as disks, etc.) and is the offset in bytes from the beginning of the device to the position where the next read or write operation will occur.

In the case of this driver, we use the *u_offset* value to determine which byte of the message is to be transferred next. For example, if the user first issued a read for five bytes, we would return "The Q". If the user then issued a second *read* for ten bytes, we would want to transfer "UICK BROWN". We keep track of our current position in the message in *u_off-set*. To avoid having to reset *u_offset* to 0 when the last byte of the message is sent, we take the value of *u_offset* modulo the length of the message. In other words, the location of the next byte in the foxmessage string to transfer is *foxmessage[u.u_offset % sizeof(foxmessage)]*. This is the essence of line 26 in the chr1read entry point above.

As an aside, continuous reads of this device can cause *u_offset* to eventually overflow. This is not considered a problem, however, since it will not happen until at least 48 million "QUICK BROWN FOX..." messages have been generated.

Address Spaces   Well, we know what we want to transfer (the message starting at byte *u_offset*), we know how much to transfer (*u_count*), and we know where to put it (*u_base*). So why don't we do something like the following?

```
chr1read(dev_t dev)
{
    while (u.u_count)
    {
        *u.u_base++ = Message[u.u_offset % sizeof(Message)];
        u.u_count--;
    }
}
```

The problem is that *u.u_base* contains an address in the user's address space and the device driver runs in the kernel's address space.

Look at Figure 2-1 on the next page. UNIX is able to run multiple processes at the same time. This means that multiple programs have to be placed into memory at the same time. As a result, programs might be placed anywhere in memory, and the same program run twice in a row might be placed in different locations in memory. (To require otherwise would be to hamstring UNIX.)

Therefore, things must be set up so that a process can run no matter where in memory it resides. The most efficient way to do this is to fiddle with the hardware so that when a process is running, it looks to the process as if it were loaded at address 0.

FIGURE 2-1

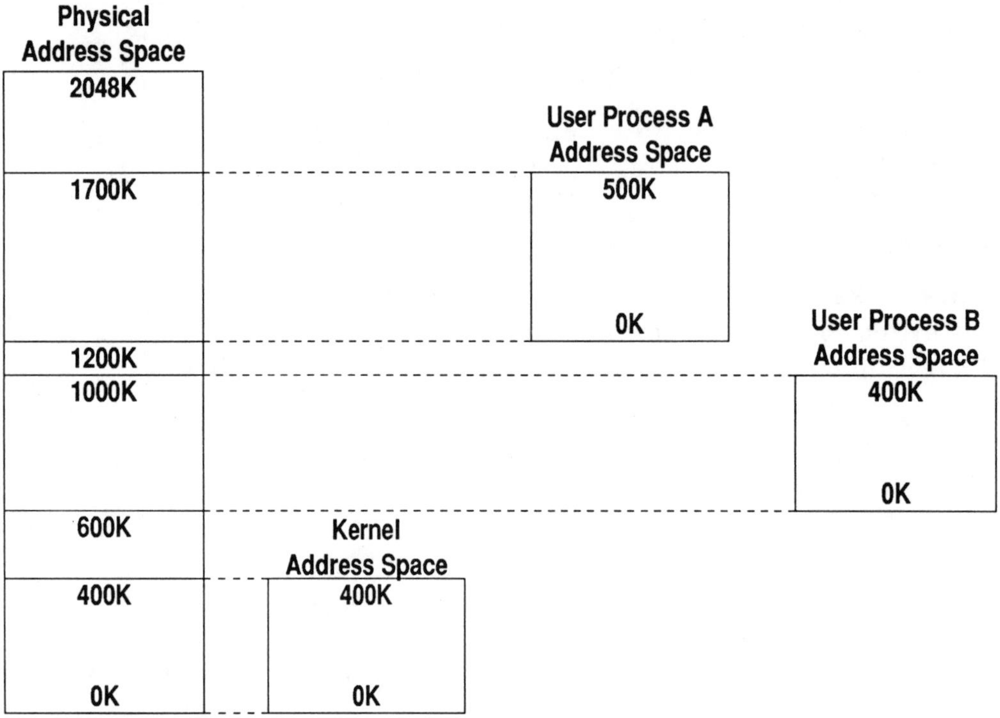

Physical Address Space

2048K	
1700K	
1200K	
1000K	
600K	
400K	
0K	

User Process A Address Space
- 500K
- 0K

User Process B Address Space
- 400K
- 0K

Kernel Address Space
- 400K
- 0K

This is accomplished with the computer's memory management unit (MMU). The MMU can be set up so that every process thinks that it has been loaded at address 0, regardless of the actual location. The operating system itself is also usually loaded so that it appears to start at 0 even though it may not actually start with the first physical memory location on the machine.

The result is that there are many locations with 'address 0'.

Firstly, there is the physical memory itself which will respond when the value 0 is placed on the circuits connecting the memory to the CPU. Addresses that refer to physical memory are called physical addresses or addresses in the physical address space.

Secondly, the kernel's address 0 may or may not refer to physical address 0. Addresses that refer to the kernel's memory are called kernel addresses or addresses in the kernel address space.

Finally, each user process will have an address 0. One process's address 0 might refer to physical address 1,024,000 while another might refer to 3,456,458. There are as many user address spaces as there are processes running on the system.

When a user's process asks for data to be read from a device, it provides an address where that data is to be placed. For example:

```
1   #include <fcntl.h>

2   char buffer[128];

3   main()
4   {
5       int fildes;

6       fildes = open("/dev/testdata", O_RDONLY);
7       read(fildes, &buffer[0], 127);
8       puts(buffer);
9   }
```

In line 7, the address of *buffer* is passed to the operating system as part of the *read* system call. The operating system will take this address and put it into *u.u_base* before calling the device driver's *read* routine.

But this address is still in terms of the current process's address space. It is not directly usable by the device driver. So we have to call on the kernel for help.

The routines *copyin* and *copyout* are provided by the kernel for device drivers in order to handle the transfer of data to and from user address spaces.

Copyout takes: an address in kernel space where the data is to be found; an address in the user space of the current process where the data is to be put; and a count of the number of bytes to transfer. Similarly, *copyin* takes a user address, a kernel address, and a count. Both routines return -1 if they encounter a problem transferring the data.

So if we return to the listing of the *chr1read* routine we can see that the entire routine is one large *while* loop from line 14 to line 24. This loop continues until either: *u.u_count* is zero (i.e. all of the data has been transferred); or an error has occurred (line 18).

Within the loop we call *copyout* (line 16) to copy one byte from the *Foxmessage* string to the user's buffer. If an error occurs (i.e., if *copyout* returns -1), we set *u.u_error* to report an error in the transfer (line 18) and return prematurely (line 19). If *u.u_error* is set, the *read* system call in the user's program will return -1 and the external variable *errno*, which is accessible to the user's program, will be set to the value of *u.u_error* (i.e., *EFAULT*).

If the transfer has succeeded, then we update all of the *u.* variables (lines 21 through 23).

The result is that the data is transferred or an error is reported and the *u.* variables are appropriately adjusted to reflect the data that was transferred.

Other Entry Points

The other entry points that character drivers may support (such as open, close, start, halt, read, write, poll, or ioctl) provide for functions that are not supported by this driver and therefore need not be defined.

For example, there is no need to make any preparations prior to or after reading the data from this driver so there is no need for open or close entry points. Similarly, it does not make sense to write data to this device so there is no write entry point.

The Recapitulation

Now that we have seen and examined all of the parts of this driver, let us tie it together by tracing the detailed flow of control and data as a user process first opens and then reads data from our device driver. The following is a simple program that opens and reads from */dev/testdata*.

```
#include <fcntl.h>

main()
{
    int fildes;
    char buffer[1024];

    fildes = open("/dev/testdata", O_RDONLY);

    read(fildes, buffer, sizeof(buffer));

    write(1, buffer, sizeof(buffer));
}
```

When the operating system receives the *open* call, it sets up a series of data structures that connect the user's process with the driver. The operating system starts by accessing the file referenced in the *open* call (*/dev/testdata*) and determines that it is a special device file. Figure 2-2 shows the output of an *ls -l* on */dev/testdata* and shows that the file type is *c* (for character driver) and that the major and minor device numbers are 23 and 0 respectively.

FIGURE 2-2

```
# ls -l /dev/testdata
crw-rw-rw-   1 root    root    3,   0 Oct 28 06:45 /dev/testdata
```

The operating system uses the major device number to index into the table of character device drivers to obtain a pointer to the driver's open entry point which is called. If the open entry point does not return an error (or if no open entry point exists for this driver), the operating system continues to establish the data structures necessary to connect the process to the driver.

The information that was obtained from the file's inode is placed in a free entry in the inode table. If the file was already open and in use by another process, then the same inode table entry will be shared among all processes that have opened the file.

Next, the system allocates a new entry in the kernel's file table that points to the inode table.

Finally, a free entry in the process's file table is located and set to point to the new entry in the kernel's file table.

The index to this entry in the process's file table is the value return by the open system call. The relationship between these different tables is shown in Figure 2-3.

FIGURE 2-3

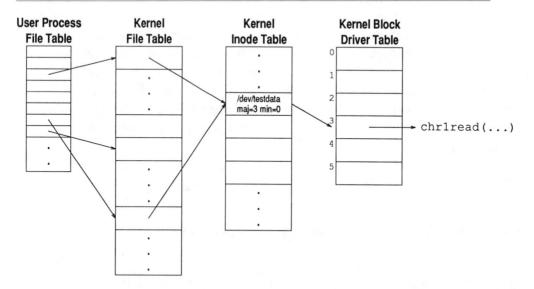

When the user's process executes the *read* system call, the operating system follows this sequence of pointers to obtain a pointer to the driver's *read* entry point. It also takes the pointer to the buffer (the second argument to the *read* system call) and places it in the variable u.u_base. Similarly, the size of the buffer (the third argument) is placed in u.u_count. This is illustrated by Figure 2-4.

The kernel then calls the driver's *read* entry point, passing as parameters to the driver the major and minor device numbers as well as the flags that the user passed during the *open* system call.

FIGURE 2-4

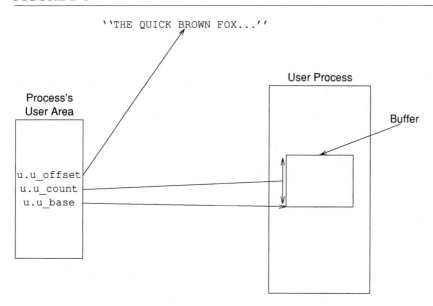

As we have seen, the *chr1read* entry point transfers the data from its internal *foxmessage* string to the user's buffer addressed by u.u_base.

Summary

In this chapter we examined our first real UNIX driver and examined several aspects of device driver design. We examined two of the entry points (init and read) that may be used by character drivers.

We saw examples of the two ways that the operating system kernel can communicate with a device driver: by passing parameters to an entry point or by placing information in a known location (in this case the u. area).

We also learned that memory addresses come in several flavors and that a driver cannot directly reference addresses in user memory. In order to transfer the "QUICK BROWN FOX..." message from the driver to the user's process we had to use the kernel-supplied routine *copyout*.

We learned how a driver indicates to the user's process that an error occurred during the driver's internal operation.

Finally, we tied it all together by tracing the flow of control and data from the user process to the driver.

Exercises

1. Modify this driver to examine the device number and return a different message depending on it. If the minor device number is 0, then return the standard "Quick Brown Fox Message..." with the first letter of each word capitalized. For device 1: return the QBF message all in capitals. For device 2: return the message all in lower case.

2. Modify this driver to transfer as many bytes as possible with each call to *copyout* (instead of one byte per call as in the current driver). For example, if the user asked for 100 bytes, u.u_offset was 10, and the message was 44 bytes long, then the request could be satisfied by (1) transferring 34 bytes starting with *&foxmessage[10]*, then (2) transferring 44 bytes starting with *&foxmessage[0]*, and then (3) transferring 22 bytes starting with *&foxmessage[0]*, leaving u.u_offset set to 22.

3. Modify this driver so that the user can write a message (up to some limit such as 256 bytes) to the device and then read the message back, repeated infinitely. For example:

```
$ echo This is a test. 1234567890 > /dev/testdata
$ cat < /dev/testdata
```

```
This is a test. 1234567890
This is a test. 1234567890
This is a test. 1234567890
This is a test. 1234567890
This is a test. 1234567890
This is a test. 1234567890
This is a test. 1234567890
...
```

Chapter 3

Character Drivers II: An A/D Converter

Having studied our first character driver and learned some basics, let us now turn our attention to a driver that actually controls some hardware. The driver presented in this section controls a simple analog to digital (A/D) converter. This is a device that can measure analog signals such as the temperature in a room by determining the voltage generated by a sensor that converts temperature to voltage.

The device we are using is the PC-LPM-16 board from National Instruments. The board supports sixteen channels of analog input as well as eight channels of digital output and eight channels of digital input. Figure 3-1 illustrates the general architecture of the LPM-16 board. Our device driver will allow a user's process to read the values of any of these input channels or to set any of the output signals. For example, a program to display the room temperature (assuming the appropriate sensor is attached to channel 1) could be written as follows.

```
#include <fcntl.h>

main()
```

```
{
    int sensor;
    int fildes;
    short temp_voltage;

    extern double convert_temp(short voltage);

    fildes = open("/dev/adc01", O_RDONLY);

    read(fildes, (char *)temp_voltage, sizeof(temp_voltage));

    printf("Room Temp: %f\n", convert_temp(temp_voltage));

    close(fildes);
}
```

FIGURE 3-1

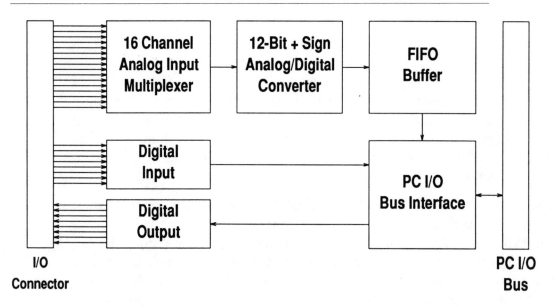

The routine convert_temp is used to convert between the voltage reading and the temperature (in Fahrenheit or whatever).

Considering that this driver will handle data which is not in block-sized units, it is best structured as a character device.

The Design Issues

Since this driver controls actual hardware we will have to consider all three categories of design issues: the kernel/driver interface; the internal operation of the driver; and the driver/hardware interface.

The kernel/driver interface is very similar to that illustrated in the previous driver. The significant changes here include: (a) handling of multiple "devices" (we consider each analog channel a separate "device"); (b) support of both read and write system calls; and (c) actual hardware to identify and initialize.

The internal operation of the driver is much more complicated than in the previous driver since we now must manage an actual I/O device. In particular, we will have to consider how to synchronize the driver with the hardware (i.e., how to cope with the fact that the driver can execute faster than the A/D converter can convert).

The driver/hardware interface was entirely missing in the previous driver since it did not control any hardware (recall it was a pseudo-driver). In this driver we must 'talk' to the hardware and we will have to consider how software communicates with hardware.

All in all, this relatively simple hardware device provides an excellent introduction to many of the issues that arise with drivers which control hardware (as opposed to pseudo-drivers that do not interface to a hardware device).

The Driver

Recall from Figure 3-1 that this device supports sixteen analog input channels, eight digital input channels, and eight digital output channels. A simple and obvious way to structure the device would be to assign a different minor device number to each analog channel, and one minor device number to the two digital channels (they can share the same minor device number without ambiguity since reads are always and only associated with the input channel and writes with the output channel). With this structure, the entries in the /*dev* directory for this driver might look like those listed in Figure 3-2.

FIGURE 3-2

```
# ls -l /dev/adc?? /dev/dio
cr--r--r--   1 root      root       17,   0 Oct 04 23:14 /dev/adc00
cr--r--r--   1 root      root       17,   1 Oct 04 23:14 /dev/adc01
cr--r--r--   1 root      root       17,   2 Oct 04 23:14 /dev/adc02
cr--r--r--   1 root      root       17,   3 Oct 04 23:14 /dev/adc03
cr--r--r--   1 root      root       17,   4 Oct 04 23:14 /dev/adc04
cr--r--r--   1 root      root       17,   5 Oct 04 23:14 /dev/adc05
cr--r--r--   1 root      root       17,   6 Oct 04 23:14 /dev/adc06
cr--r--r--   1 root      root       17,   7 Oct 04 23:14 /dev/adc07
cr--r--r--   1 root      root       17,   8 Oct 04 23:14 /dev/adc08
cr--r--r--   1 root      root       17,   9 Oct 04 23:14 /dev/adc09
cr--r--r--   1 root      root       17,  10 Oct 04 23:14 /dev/adc10
cr--r--r--   1 root      root       17,  11 Oct 04 23:14 /dev/adc11
cr--r--r--   1 root      root       17,  12 Oct 04 23:14 /dev/adc12
cr--r--r--   1 root      root       17,  13 Oct 04 23:14 /dev/adc13
cr--r--r--   1 root      root       17,  14 Oct 04 23:14 /dev/adc14
cr--r--r--   1 root      root       17,  15 Oct 04 23:14 /dev/adc15
crw-rw-rw-   1 root      root       17,  16 Oct 04 23:14 /dev/dio
```

The A/D converter converts voltages into 16-bit binary numbers. Reads on one of the analog channels will therefore return a short (16-bit) integer. The eight digital I/O channels can each be represented as a single bit, therefore reads and writes on the digital device can be handled as a single byte that represents all eight channels.

This driver supports the following entry points:

- init
- open
- read
- write

In addition to these, there is one internal routine (*adcreset*) that is used within the driver. As with the previous driver, the other entry points that are available to character drivers are not required or supported.

The Prologue

The prologue to this driver is similar to that seen in the previous character driver with the addition of the definitions describing the hardware.

```
1    #include <sys/types.h>
2    #include <sys/param.h>
3    #include <sys/dir.h>
4    #include <sys/signal.h>
5    #include <sys/user.h>
6    #include <sys/errno.h>
7    #include <sys/sysmacros.h>

8    #define BASE          0x260

9    #define CR1_W         (BASE)          /*  Command Register 1  */
10   #define SR_R          (BASE)          /*   Status Register  */
11   #define CR2_RW        (BASE + 0x07)   /*  Command Register 2  */

12   #define FIFO_LSB_R    (BASE + 0x02)   /* FIFO Low Byte */
13   #define FIFO_MSB_R    (BASE + 0x03)   /* FIFO High Byte */
14   #define AD_CLR_W      (BASE + 0x01)   /* A/D Clear */

15   #define DO_W          (BASE + 0x04)   /* Digital Output */
16   #define DI_R          (BASE + 0x05)   /* Digital Input */

17   #define CNTR_CR_W     (BASE + 0x0B)   /* Counter Control */

18   #define CR1_NOSCAN    0x80    /* Disable scanning */

19   #define SR_REVID      0x80    /* Rev Level */
20   #define SR_BUSY       0x10    /* A/D Converter Busy */
```

```
21   #define SR_OVFLW       0x02    /* FIFO Overflow */
22   #define SR_DREADY      0x01    /* FIFO Data Ready */

23   #define CR2_CLBRT      0x01    /* Enable Auto-Calibration */

24   #define CCR_0_LOW      0x30    /* set counter 0 output low */
25   #define CCR_0_HIGH     0x34    /* set counter 0 output high */

26   #define DIO_DEV        16
27   #define TIMEOUT_COUNT  1000

28   static short present;
29   static int adreset(void);
```

All of the header files were described in the previous chapter with the exception of *<sys/sysmacros.h>*. This file contains various macros that are useful within drivers. In our case, the macro of interest is *minor()* which takes a device number and returns the minor device number component.

As we shall discuss shortly, the driver communicates with the hardware through a set of registers. These registers are similar in many ways to memory locations except that when data is written into a register it frequently causes the device to perform some operation. Similarly, if the device wishes to communicate some information to the driver, it will set certain bits in a register (or indeed the entire register) which can then be read by the driver.

Figure 3-3, shown on the next page, shows the layout of the registers for this A/D converter. The addresses used to access these registers is defined on lines 8-17. The registers and register bits that are not shown in the figure or defined in the prologue are for features that this driver does not support.

The defines on lines 17 through 25 provide descriptive names for the various register bits or significant values written to various registers.

Line 26 defines the minor device number that represents the digital I/O device, while line 27 defines a timeout value that limits the time we shall wait for the A/D converter to convert a single channel.

FIGURE 3-3

CR1 (W) (0x260)	Scan Disable				Analog Channel Number (0..15)			

SR (R) (0x260)	Revision ID			Converter Busy			Overflow	Data Available

A/D Clear (W) (0x261)	All Data Ignored (Write Clears Converter)

FIFO LSB (R) (0x262)	Least Significant Byte of Conversion

FIFO MSB (R) (0x263)	Most Significant Byte of Conversion

DO (W) (0x264)	Digital Output Channel 7	Digital Output Channel 6	Digital Output Channel 5	Digital Output Channel 4	Digital Output Channel 3	Digital Output Channel 2	Digital Output Channel 1	Digital Output Channel 0

DI (R) (0x265)	Digital Input Channel 7	Digital Input Channel 6	Digital Input Channel 5	Digital Input Channel 4	Digital Input Channel 3	Digital Input Channel 2	Digital Input Channel 1	Digital Input Channel 0

CR2 (W) (0x267)								Auto-Calibrate Enable

CCR (W) (0x26B)	Counter Select		Read/Write Select		Mode Select		BCD Select

Line 28 declares a variable that we shall use to record the presence (or absence) of the hardware. Note that as with the driver in the previous chapter, this variable is declared static to avoid possible name conflicts with other variables in the kernel.

Finally, line 29 is a forward declaration of a routine used only within this driver and defined after it is first used (see line 32 and lines 40-58).

The Init Entry Point

As discussed earlier, the init routine is responsible for performing those operations required when the system is booted. The pseudo code for this entry point, is:

```
30   init entry point:
32       if (the device cannot be reset or is not present)
33           print: device not found
34       else
36           print: device and driver installed
37           present = TRUE
```

The actual entry point:

```
30   void adcinit()
31   {
32       if (adcreset())
33           printf("A/D Device NOT FOUND!\n");
34       else
35       {
36           printf("A/D Device and Driver installed (v1.0).\n");
37           present++;
38       }
39   }
```

The *init* entry point is called during system startup and provides the driver the opportunity to prepare the device and driver. The archetypal *init* routine ought to: (a) check that the device is indeed present (line 32); (b) initialize the device (line 32); (c) initialize internal driver data structures (line 37); and (d) display a message to that effect (line 36).

In this driver we have taken the code that initializes the device (and verifies that it is indeed present) and put it into a separate routine (*adcreset*). This routine attempts to initialize the device and if it is unable to do so or believes that the device is not installed, it returns a non-zero (i.e., true) value. This causes line 33 to execute. Otherwise, lines 36 and 37 are executed.

This code has been placed into a separate routine because there is another place in the driver where we need to initialize the hardware. But before we examine the code for *adcreset* we need to answer a key question about the driver/hardware interface. *How does a device driver talk to the device it controls?*

Hardware Device Registers   All devices contain internal registers that control the operation of the device. These registers function like memory locations in that they can be read and written. The difference is that the contents of each register either affect the operation of the device or indicate the status of the device.

For example, with our A/D converter there is a register called "Command Register 1" which controls several aspects of the conversion process. In particular, the lower four bits of this register contain the number of the channel to measure (convert). In addition, there is the "Status Register" which provides information on the operation of the device. Bit 4 of this register goes on (1) when a conversion is in progress and goes off when the conversion has been completed. And finally, there is a register (actually two, one to hold the most significant byte and the other for the low byte) to contain the result of the voltage measurement. Figure 3-3 illustrated the layout of the I/O registers for this device (some of the other bits in these registers will be explained later).

But how do we actually read and write these registers? On some machines, such as the M680x0, and the DEC PDP and VAX computers, the device registers appear as fixed memory locations that are directly addressable. For example, on a given computer the status register might be located at FFFFCD02. We could then use code similar to the following to access this register:

```
char *status = (char *)0xFFFFCD02;

...
if (*status & 0x04)
{
    /* conversion is complete */
    ...
}
...
```

On other machines such as the Intel 386 or 486, the registers are accessed using special instructions that use addresses allocated to I/O devices only. On UNIX systems these special instructions are invoked by calling the kernel support routines in and out (or inb and outb for byte access).

If our status register had an I/O address of FC2, then we would use the following code to access it:

```
#define    STATUS    0xFC2

...
if (inb(STATUS) & 0x04)
{
    /* conversion is complete */
    ...
}
...
```

Since the driver we are examining is for UNIX on an Intel 386, it uses the in/out instructions.

The addresses to which a device responds can usually be selected by setting switches on the controller board itself. On the A/D converter used for our example, we have set the first register at *260*. The other registers appear immediately after.

Note that some registers are read-only or write-only. Also, sometimes two registers (one read-only and one write-only) will share the same address. A read to the address will access the read-only register while a write will access the write-only register.

Detecting the Presence of Hardware   Now that we better understand how software talks to hardware, we are ready to consider the problem of detecting if our device has been installed again. In general, this is accomplished by writing to certain registers and then reading certain registers looking for certain values. If the values are found, we assume the hardware is present. Note that there is always the possibility that another device might behave in the same manner and thereby be mistaken for the device of interest. In order to prevent that occurrence, the init routine ought to exercise some limited functionality in the device in order to reduce the chance that another device would return the same value if probed in the same manner.

So we read certain registers and check for known results. But what happens if the device is not installed? This depends on the design of the system. On some computers, this is an error. On these computers, UNIX may have to be set up to handle the possibility of this error when probing for hardware that may not exist (refer to the reference manual for your computer). On machines with an IBM PC bus, the result is usually 0xff. For this reason, we ought to arrange the hardware present test to return a value other than 0xff from a certain register.

Let us return to our driver to see how this theory is put into practice.

The Adcreset Routine

The *adcreset* routine is internal to this driver and is responsible for resetting the A/D converter as well as verifying its presence. Again we present the pseudo-code first followed by the actual code.

```
40      driver internal routine adcreset:
43-46       reset various device registers
47-48       read (and ignore) various device registers

49          set the calibrate command bit
50          start calibration by reading the command register
51          if (status register bits != expected pattern)
52              return true  (i.e. error indication)

53-55       spin until device is not busy or we get impatient
56          reset device (i.e. disable calibration mode)
```

```
57              return false (i.e. device good) only if status looks o.k.

40  static int adcreset()
41  {
42      int timeout;

43      outb(CR1_W, CR1_NOSCAN);
44      outb(CR2_RW, 0);
45      outb(CNTR_CR_W, CCR_0_LOW);
46      outb(AD_CLR_W, 0);

47      (void) inb(FIFO_LSB_R);
48      (void) inb(FIFO_MSB_R);

49      outb(CR2_RW, CR2_CLBRT);
50      (void) inb(CR2_RW);

51      if ((inb(SR_R) & (SR_REVID | SR_BUSY | SR_OVFLW)) !=
            (SR_REVID | SR_BUSY ))
52              return (1);

53      timeout = TIMEOUT_COUNT;
54      while ((inb(SR_R) & SR_BUSY ) && timeout--)
55          ;

56      outb(CR2_RW, 0);

57      return ((inb(SR_R) & (SR_BUSY | SR_OVFLW)));
58  }
```

This routine starts by writing a series of values into four registers (lines 43-46) and then reading two registers and discarding the results (lines 47 and 48). This sequence is taken directly from the manual for the PC-LPM-16 A/D converter as the recommended sequence for initializing the device.

Next we set the calibrate bit in command register 2 (line 49) and read the command register (line 50) to start the self-calibration cycle. We then check the status register immediately (line 51) to see if the 'Revision ID' bit and the 'Device Busy' bit are set and the 'Overflow' bit is clear. If not, we assume either than the device is not present or is malfunctioning. In either case, we return 1 (true) which will cause the init routine (line 33) to declare the device as not present.

If the device passes this test we then loop (lines 54 and 55) until the device is no longer busy. Since the device may malfunction and continuously report that it is busy, we set a limit (line 53) on the number of times we will loop for the A/D converter to complete calibration.

Although spin loops are usually to be avoided in drivers, this one is acceptable since it usually (a) occurs only during init time when the machine is being bootstrapped and (b) executes for only a short time (100-200 loops on a 20MHz 386).

After calibration, we clear 'Command Register 2' (line 56) thus enabling normal conversion mode (and disabling calibration mode). We then return a value that is based on the status register (line 57). If either the 'Busy' or 'Overflow' bit is set, we return true indicating a malfunctioning device. Otherwise we return false indicating the device is present and has been successfully initialized. This will cause the init routine to announce the presence of the device (line 36) and set the *present* variable (line 37). This variable is checked by the open entry point to make sure that the open be permitted to succeed.

The Open Entry Point

The *open* entry point is invoked when the user's process executes an *open* system call naming the device driver's special file. (See the *open* call in the program on the second page of this chapter.) If the device is opened by more than one process (or by the same process more than once) the *open* entry point will be called each time. It is the driver's responsibility to handle multiple opens.

The *open* entry point is responsible for, among other things, validating the device number (if used) and initializing the device and internal driver data structures.

```
59  open entry point:
61      if (minor device number not in valid range)
62          set ENXIO error code
```

```
63        if (device present flag not set earlier by init entry point)
64            set ENODEV error code
```

```
59  void adcopen(dev_t dev, int flag, int id)
60  {
61      if (minor(dev) > DIO_DEV)
62          u.u_error = ENXIO;
63      else if (!present)
64          u.u_error = ENODEV;
65  }
```

In this driver we verify that the minor device number is valid (line 42) and that the device is actually present and functioning (line 44). Recall that the variable *present* was set by the init entry point if the device was found and successfully initialized by the adcreset routine.

If either of these tests fail, we set the appropriate error code into u.u_error and return. This error code will cause the open system call issued by the user process to fail and return an error indication.

The Read Entry Point

The *read* entry point is responsible for obtaining from the device the data requested and transferring it to the user process.

In this driver the read entry point consists of two parts, the first handles reads of the digital input channels and the second handles reads of an analog input channel. We shall examine each part separately below.

```
66  read entry point:
71      if (minor device number == digital I/O device)
73          if (read count > 0)
75              read digital input register and store in di
76              copy contents of di to user process
            if (an error occurred)
78-79               set error code and return
81              update u.u_count to reflect successful transfer
```

```
66  void adcread(dev_t dev)
67  {
68      int timeout;
```

```
69        short value;
70        unsigned char di;

71        if (minor(dev) == DIO_DEV)
72        {
73            if (u.u_count)
74            {
75                di = inb(DI_R);
76                if (copyout(&di, u.u_base, 1) == -1)
77                {
78                    u.u_error = EFAULT;
79                    return;
80                }
81                u.u_count--;
82            }
83        }
```

We first check the minor device number (line 71) to see if this is a read of the digital input channels. If so, we check to see if any data has been requested (line 73). Since it is valid (although pointless) to issue a read for 0 bytes, this test is necessary.

Assuming all is well, we obtain the values for the eight digital input channels by reading the 'Digital Input' register (line 75). We then use the kernel supplied routine *copyout* to transfer this byte of data to the user process. (Recall that the operation of copyout was discussed at length in Chapter 2.)

If copyout fails, we set an error code and return (lines 78 and 79). Otherwise we decrement u.u_count to indicate that one byte was successfully transferred (line 81).

The remainder of the read entry point handles the case of a read of an analog input channel.

```
84      else (i.e. minor device number specifies analog input channel)
            if (count > size of a short integer (i.e. 2 bytes))
86              set analog channel number = minor device number
87-88           trigger immediate conversion of specified channel
89-91           spin until device conversion done or we get impatient
92              if (conversion in error or not completed)
```

```
94                    reset A/D converter
95-96                 set error code and return
98            else
100-101               read low and high byte and assemble 16-bit value
102                   transfer value to user process
                      if (an error in the transfer)
104-105                   set error code and return
107                   update u.u_count to reflect successful transfer
```

```
84      else if (u.u_count >= sizeof(short))
85      {
86          outb(CR1_W, CR1_NOSCAN | minor(dev));
87          outb(CNTR_CR_W, CCR_0_LOW);
88          outb(CNTR_CR_W, CCR_0_HIGH);
89          timeout = TIMEOUT_COUNT;
90          while (((inb(SR_R) & (SR_OVFLW | SR_DREADY)) == 0) &&
                       timeout--)
91                  ;

92          if ((timeout == 0) || (inb(SR_R) & SR_OVFLW))
93          {
94              (void) adcreset();
95              u.u_error = EIO;
96              return;
97          }
98          else
99          {
100             value = (inb(FIFO_LSB_R) & 0xff);
101             value |= ((inb(FIFO_MSB_R) & 0xff) << 8);

102             if (copyout(&value, u.u_base, sizeof(short)) == -1)
103             {
104                 u.u_error = EFAULT;
105                 return;
106             }
107             u.u_count -= sizeof(short);
108         }
109     }
110 }
```

We first check (line 84) to see if the read is for at least two bytes (to handle the case where the user mistakenly issues a read for zero or one

bytes). If there is enough room to put the result of the conversion we select the desired analog channel by writing the minor device number into 'Command Register 1' (line 86). The 'No Scan' flag (CR1_NOSCAN) tells the A/D converter that we wish to convert only one channel rather than scanning multiple channels. We start the conversion by setting certain bits in the 'Counter Control Register' (lines 87 and 88). As its name implies, the Counter Control Register is used to control counters internal to the A/D converter. These counters can be used in advanced applications to trigger conversions at fixed intervals. In our case, we only wish to perform single conversions on demand so we set the counter to trigger a single, immediate conversion.

We then loop (lines 90-91) until the device is no longer busy. Again we set a counter (line 89) to ensure that the loop always terminates, even if the device malfunctions and never stops being 'busy'.

As mentioned, spin loops are usually avoided in drivers. So why have we one here? Well, in an early version of this driver we placed a printf statement immediately after the loop to determine how many times it looped and found on a 20MHz 386 that the loop iterated between one and ten times. Since the UNIX kernel cannot exit a driver read entry point, field an interrupt, and reschedule the read in the time it takes to execute such a simple loop ten times, we are far better off looping than using interrupts to signal the completion of the conversion.

In the next chapter we shall examine a driver that can take a long time to complete an I/O request and therefore requires the use of interrupts. But here using a spin loop is actually more efficient than using interrupts.

A related issue is determining an appropriate value for TIMEOUT_COUNT, the value used to limit the maximum number of iterations while waiting for the device to complete an operation. As described, we used printf statements to print the value of the *timeout* variable after every loop (here and on lines 54-55) and determined that the longest loop was the calibration loop (lnes 54-55) which normally took between 100 and 200 iterations. Setting TIMEOUT_COUNT to 1000 provided more than enough headroom for this loop. Although the conversion loop (lines 90-91) usually finished within ten iterations, it is not really necessary to specify a different (lower) TIMEOUT_COUNT for this loop since its purpose is only to handle the exceptional failure of the hardware.

Once the loop completes we check to see if the iteration limit was reached or if the 'Overflow' flag is set (line 92). If either case is true, we attempt to reset the device (line 94) and return an error indication (line 95).

Otherwise, the conversion was successful and we obtain the 16-bit value by reading the 'Least Significant Byte' (LSB) and 'Most Significant Byte' (MSB) registers and assembling the value (lines 100 and 101).

As an aside, it is important to read the documentation for the device and determine if the registers need to be read in a specific order. In the case of this device, reading the MSB causes both the LSB and MSB register to be cleared. Needless to say, reading these in the wrong order would result in the LSB always appearing to be 0.

A related trap for the unwary is trying to read these two registers in a single statement similar to

```
value = (inb(FIFO_LSB_R) & 0xff) |
        ((inb(FIFO_MSB_R) & 0xff) << 8);
```

Although this code looks correct, the ANSI C standard warns us that we may not assume any particular sequence of operations within a single expression such as this. The compiler is free to issue the second *inb* before the first, thus reading the MSB first and causing the LSB to be cleared before it is read.

Back in our driver we take the 16-bit value and pass it to the user process using copyout (line 102). Errors are handled as before (lines 104-105). On line 107 we update the u.u_count variable to reflect the two bytes that were successfully transferred.

The Write Entry Point

The *write* entry point's responsibilities in a driver are in some ways the opposite of those for a read entry point. The write entry point must: obtain the information to be written from the user process; instruct the device to accept the data; and finally manage the transfer of data to the device. The entry point must also take care of housekeeping such as validating the minor device number.

```
111   write entry point:
114        if (minor device number == digital I/O device)
116            if (write count > 0)
118                obtain from user process data to be written
                   if (an error occurred)
120-121                set error code and return
123                update u.u_count to reflect successful transfer
124                write data to digital output register
127        else
128            set error code
```

```
111   void adcwrite(dev_t dev)
112   {
113        unsigned char data;

114        if (minor(dev) == DIO_DEV)
115        {
116            if (u.u_count)
117            {
118                if (copying(u.u_base, &data, 1) == -1)
119                {
120                    u.u_error = EFAULT;
121                    return;
122                }
123                u.u_count--;

124                outb(DO_W, data);
125            }
126        }
127        else
128            u.u_error = ENXID;
129   }
```

We check (line 114) to see if the minor device number is that associated with the digital I/O device. If not, we report an error (line 128).

Otherwise we check that there is at least one byte to be written (line 116) and we copy the byte from the user process to the driver's *data* variable using copying (line 118). *Copyin* is the opposite of *copyout* and transfers data from a user process to the driver. Errors are handled in the usual manner (lines 120-121).

If the byte was successfully obtained, we update the u.u_count variable (line 123) to reflect that fact and then write the byte to the 'Digital Output' register (line 124). This will cause the eight digital output lines to take on the value associated with each bit of the written byte.

Exercises

1. This driver assigns a channel to each "device" (minor device number). This means that a program that wishes to read all sixteen analog input channels would have to open sixteen files. Modify the driver to provide yet another "device" that permits any or all channel to be read through a single special file. (Hint: use the u.u_offset value to specify the first channel to convert and u.u_count to specify the number of channels to convert.)

2. This driver requires the user process to write all eight digital output lines at once. Modify the driver so that eight separate minor device numbers are allocated, one for each digital output channel, so that a user process can open and write a single digital output channel without affecting any other channels.

Chapter 4

Character Drivers III: A Line Printer

Our study of character drivers has included a simple pseudo-device driver that generated test data and a slightly more interesting driver for an analog to digital converter. Although the A/D converter driver controlled actual hardware, the device was relatively simple.

In this chapter we shall consider a driver for a line printer controller. We shall encounter a number of design issues in this driver for the first time. The primary problem is that a user's process can almost always generate data faster than a printer can print it. It will therefore be necessary to suspend the program while the printer is busy. In addition, we shall have to store a certain amount of data within the driver so that we do not incur the overhead of suspending and resuming the program every time the printer is ready for another byte of data. Also, we will encounter interrupts that can arrive at any time as well as interrupts that do not arrive at all.

In other words, this driver is an excellent example of how to talk to a real world device, warts and all.

The Device

The registers for this device are illustrated by Figure 4-1. The data register contains the byte of data to be transferred to the printer. The status register indicates whether the printer is ready for more data and if any problems have been detected. The control register enables interrupts and automatic line feeds as well as signals to the printer that the data in the data register is valid. We shall see how these registers are used when we examine the device driver.

FIGURE 4-1

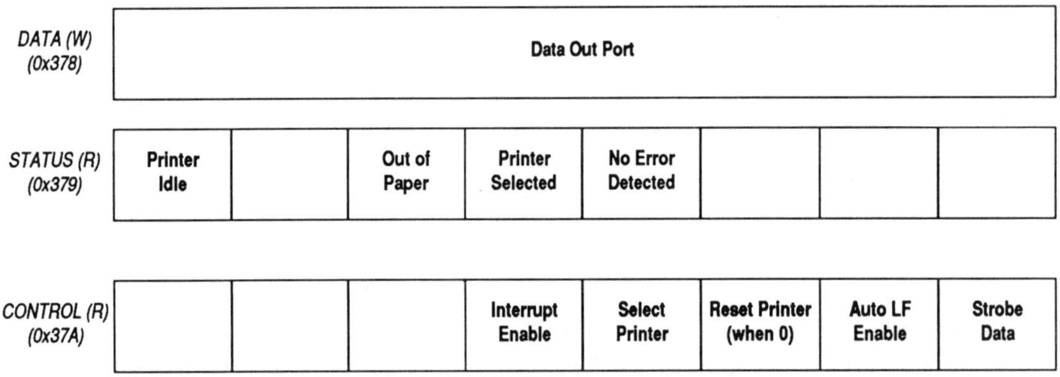

DATA (W) (0x378)	Data Out Port						
STATUS (R) (0x379)	Printer Idle		Out of Paper	Printer Selected	No Error Detected		
CONTROL (R) (0x37A)				Interrupt Enable	Select Printer	Reset Printer (when 0)	Auto LF Enable	Strobe Data

The Driver

The device driver supports a single line printer. Data written to the driver is buffered within the driver and fed to the line printer as fast as it will accept it.

The Prologue

This prologue, as with those examined earlier, consists of the include directives (lines 1-8), the definitions of useful constants (mostly related to the register layout, lines 9-31), and the declaration of some local variables (lines 32 and 33).

```
1     #include <sys/param.h>
2     #include <sys/errno.h>
```

```
3      #include <sys/types.h>
4      #include <sys/signal.h>
5      #include <sys/dir.h>
6      #include <sys/user.h>
7      #include <sys/tty.h>
8      #include <sys/sysmacros.h>

9      #define LPPRI     PZERO+5
10     #define LOWAT     50
11     #define HIWAT     250
12     #define TOINT     HZ/10

13     #define LPBASE    0x378
14     #define LPDATA    (LPBASE + 0)
15     #define LPSTAT    (LPBASE + 1)
16     #define LPCTRL    (LPBASE + 2)

17     #define LPNERR    0x08
18     #define LPON      0x10
19     #define LPRDY     0x80

20     #define LPSTRB    0x01
21     #define LPLF      0x02
22     #define LPINIT    0x04
23     #define LPSEL     0x08
24     #define LPIENB    0x10

25     #define LPEXIST   0x01
26     #define SLEEP     0x02
27     #define LPBUSY    0x04
28     #define TOPEND    0x08
29     #define WAIT      0x10
30     #define EXCLOPEN  0x20
31     #define OPEN      0x40

32     static unsigned short Lpflags = 0;
33     static struct clist Lpqueue;
```

This prologue references a header file we have not encountered before. The <sys/tty.h> header provides the definitions for the clist structure that we shall be using to buffer data.

The defines on lines 9 through 12 provide self-documenting names for some constants that we shall need within the driver. The addresses of the various line printer controller registers are the subject of lines 13 through 16, while the individual bits of these registers are given names in lines 17 through 24. Lines 25-31 define flags that may be set in the lpflags variable declared on line 32. The clist structure declared on line 33 will be discussed when we start using it later in the driver.

The Init Entry Point

This *init* function is very similar to the previous one we studied. It performs all of the standard functions of a driver *init* entry point. It checks that the hardware is present, initializes the hardware, prints a message announcing the presence of the driver (and hardware), and initializes data structures internal to the driver. The pseudo-code below outlines the structure of the routine while the detailed code follows.

```
34   init entry point:
36       clear control register
37-38    if (control register != expected value) then return
39       write special value to control register
40-41    if (control register != expected value) then return
42       disable device by clearing control register
43       print: line printer exists message
44       set device exists flag

34   lpinit()
35   {
36       outb(LPCTRL, 0);
37       if (inb(LPCTRL) != 0xe0)
38           return;

39       outb(LPCTRL, 0xfe);
40       if (inb(LPCTRL) != 0xfe)
41           return;

42       outb(LPCTRL, 0);

43       printf("Line printer at address %x\n", LPBASE);
```

```
44          Lpflags = LPEXIST;
45      }
```

In this driver we take a slightly more involved approach to verify that the hardware is present. Firstly (line 34), we zero the control register and then check for the expected result. Then we set a specific value and make sure that the result is as expected. Only then are we willing to declare the hardware as present.

As an aside we ought to discuss how the 'expected' results were determined. Briefly, an earlier version of the driver wrote several values to the control register and printed the results. After running the driver on several different systems (with different brands of line printer interface boards) the above algorithm was obtained. Sometimes one can determine a reasonable sequence to test for the presence of the hardware just by examining the documentation for the device. In most cases, however, judicious experimentation is required.

Back in the driver, we again zero the control register (line 40). This has the effect of disabling the device totally until we need it.

Line 41 announces the presence of the device and driver and the next line initializes the lpflags variable (and marks the device as "present").

The Open Entry Point

The *open* entry point for this driver is very similar to the example in Chapter 3. We check to see if the device has been detected and if so, initialize it. Otherwise we return an error.

An additional feature supported by this driver is the exclusive-open flag. When the user opens the device, the open call can include the O_EXCL flag indicating that no other open of the same device is to be permitted while this process has the device open (for example, *open("/dev/lp",* *O_WRONLY | O_EXCL);*).

```
46  open entry point:
50      if (device exists flag is not set)
51          set error code
52      else if (device has already be opened exclusively)
```

```
53              set error code
54        else if (device has already been opened)
56              if (this open is for exclusive use)
57                   set error code
59        else
61              clear lp data register
62              set line feed, init, and select bits in control register
64              set lp open flag
65              if (this open is for exclusive use)
66                   set exclusive open flag
```

```
46     lpopen(dev, flags, otyp)
47     dev_t dev;
48     int flags, otyp;
49     {
50         if ((Lpflags & LPEXIST) == 0)
51             u.u_error = ENODEV;
52         else if (Lpflags & EXCLOPEN)
53             u.u_error = EBUSY;
54         else if (Lpflags & OPEN)
55         {
56             if (flags & FEXCL)
57                 u.u_error = EBUSY;
58         }
59         else
60         {
61             outb(LPDATA, 0);
62             outb(LPCTRL, LPLF | LPINIT | LPSEL);
63
64             Lpflags |= OPEN;
65             if (flags & FEXCL)
66                 Lpflags |= EXCLOPEN;
67         }
68     }
```

We start with a series of checks to see whether the device exists (line 50), is already open for exclusive use (line 52), or is already open and this open is for exclusive use (lines 54 and 56). In all cases, the appropriate error code is returned by setting u.u_error.

If no errors are detected (and the device is not already open), we initialize the printer (lines 61 and 62), mark the device as open (line 64), and check to see if this open is for exclusive use (line 65) and if so, set a flag to remember that fact.

The Close Entry Point

The *close* entry point for this driver has a problem none of our previous drivers have had to cope with. It is possible for the driver still to be busy processing previous output requests when the applications program issues the *close*. Therefore, we must wait until the printer has printed everything before we complete the close operation and shut down the printer.

```
69   close entry point:
74       raise processor priority in order to disable interrupts
75       while (lp busy flag is set)
77           set flag indicating we are waiting to close
78           put the user process to sleep until awakened

80       clear all flags except the lp exists flag
81       clear lp control register thus disabling the device
82       restore processor priority
```

```
69   lpclose(dev, flags, otyp)
70   dev_t dev;
71   int flags, otyp;
72   {
73       int x;

74       x = spl5();
75       while (Lpflags & LPBUSY)
76       {
77           Lpflags |= WAIT;
78           sleep(&Lpflags, LPPRI);
79       }

80       Lpflags = LPEXIST;
81       outb(LPCTRL, 0);
82       splx(x);
83   }
```

In line 75 we check to see if the device is still busy. If so, we set a flag telling the rest of the driver that we are waiting for the printer to complete printing and then we go to sleep. As we shall see later, when the printer is finished, the driver will check for the WAIT flag and if set, will issue a wake up which will cause our call to sleep to return.

By line 80 we know that the printer is quiet so we clear all of the flags except LPEXIST (line 80) and disable the printer (line 81).

We shall talk more about the call to sleep, as well as the spl5 and splx routines later.

The Write Entry Point

The *write* entry point is the opposite of the *read* entry point seen in earlier drivers. The write entry point is invoked whenever the user's process issues a write system call and is responsible for transferring the data to be written from the user's process to the driver.

The special problem this device presents is that printers are slow devices. The user's process can usually generate data faster than the printer can print it. This means that we shall have to suspend the user's process when the printer is busy printing the data already passed to it.

The overhead of suspending a user's process and later resuming it is significant, so we shall want to reduce the number of times this is done. In other words, we want to maximize the amount of data that the user's process can transfer to the driver between suspensions. To accomplish this we shall store data within the driver, filling the buffer as quickly as possible before suspending the user's process and then passing the data along to the printer.

```
 84   write entry point:
 90       while (still data to be obtained from the user process)
 92           copy one byte from the user process to the driver
              if (an error occurred during copy)
 94-95           set error code and return
 97-98       update u. variables to reflect successful transfer
 99          while (more than HIWAT bytes in the clist buffer)
101             raise the process priority thus disabling interrupts
```

```
102                 call lpwork to try to print some data
103                 if (more than HIWAT bytes in clist buffer)
105                     set flag indicating we are waiting for more
                                        room in the buffer
106                 put user process to sleep
108             restore processor priority
110         place byte just copied from user process on clist

112     raise processor priority
113     call lpwork to try to print some data
114     restore processor priority


 84    lpwrite(dev)
 85    dev_t dev;
 86    {
 87        char c;
 88        int x;
 89        extern void lpwork();

 90        while (u.u_count)
 91        {
 92            if (copyin(u.u_base, &c, 1) == -1)
 93            {
 94                u.u_error = EFAULT;
 95                return;
 96            }
 97            u.u_base++;
 98            u.u_count--;

 99            while (Lpqueue.c_cc > HIWAT)
100            {
101                x = spl5();
102                lpwork();
103                if (Lpqueue.c_cc > HIWAT)
104                {
105                    Lpflags |= SLEEP;
106                    sleep(&Lpqueue, LPPRI);
107                }
108                splx(x);
109            }
110            putc(c, &Lpqueue);
111        }
```

```
112          x = spl5();
113          lpwork();
114          splx(x);
115     }
```

Most of this routine is a while loop that starts at line 90 and ends at line 111 and continues as long as there is data to be transferred from the user's process to the device.

The first part of this entry point (lines 92-98) is relatively straightforward. In line 92 we use the kernel-supplied routine *copyin* to obtain the next byte of data the user's process is writing to the printer. If *copyin* reports an error, then we return an error indication (lines 94-95) to the user. Otherwise, we merely update the user area variables that specify where and how much data to transfer (lines 97-98).

The next part of this routine (lines 99-110) is concerned with taking the data we have just obtained from the user's process and storing it in our internal buffer. But before we study this part of the driver, let us consider the subject of clists.

Clist Buffers   Frequently within a device driver we have to store small amounts (50-500 bytes) of data. While it is possible for each driver that needs such buffering to declare its own local storage, it is more efficient for the kernel to provide such buffering for all drivers. In this manner the same space can be shared between all drivers and only those drivers that are active and have to store data need consume space in the shared buffers.

In UNIX, the kernel provides a mechanism for storing smaller amounts of data within drivers called clists. The definition of a clist header is contained in <sys/tty.h> (see lines 7 and 33). The kernel provides a number of routines for storing a byte on a clist and for retrieving the next byte from the clist. Clists function as a first in, first out (FIFO) data structure.

While the actual structure of the clist is of no concern to the device driver writer (since all of the details are handled by the kernel-supplied routines), Figure 4-2 shown on the next page provides a schematic of the clist organization.

FIGURE 4-2

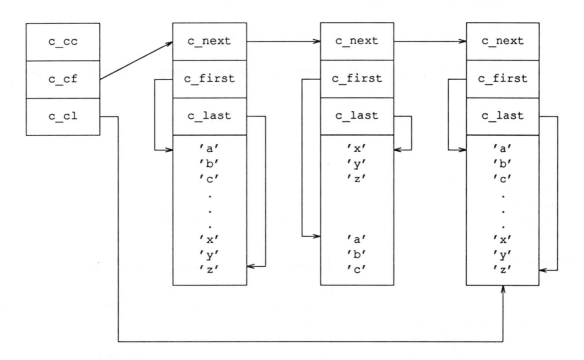

Using Clists   In line 99 we check to see if the clist is full. Obviously we do not wish to use all of the memory available for clists—otherwise no other device driver would be able to store data in a clist. So we establish an arbitrary limit (called a *high water mark*, see line 11) to the amount of data we will store in the clist.

If we have reached this limit we do two things. Firstly (line 102), we start the printer. The lpwork routine will attempt to transfer some of the data from the clist to the printer and may relieve the congestion. Secondly (lines 103-107), we check if the clist is still full (i.e., lpwork was unable to do anything) and if so, we suspend the user's process. We shall talk shortly about the sleep call (line 106) as well as the spl5 and splx functions (lines 101 and 108).

If we reach line 110, then we know that there are fewer than HIWAT characters in the clist and so we add the character we have just copied from the user's process in line 92.

The loop (lines 90 to 111) continues until either there is no more data to transfer (i.e., u.u_count is 0) or the clist is full and the user's process is suspended.

When the loop terminates, we call lpwork to make sure the printer is started.

The Lpwork Routine

The *lpwork* routine is not a true entry point (i.e., it is not called by the operating system). It is a routine local to the driver that is called by other parts of the driver to start activity on the device.

The lpwork routine is where the real work is done. As we have seen, the lpwrite routine is responsible for copying the data to be printed from the user's process to the clist. Lpwork is responsible for copying the data from the clist to the printer itself.

Why do we do things in two steps? Why not copy the data from the user's process directly to the printer? The reason is that the printer cannot accept data as fast as we can copy it from the user's process and furthermore, by copying the data to a buffer we can reduce the number of times we have to suspend the user's process.

The first half of this routine (lines 122-135) is concerned with transferring data from the clist to the printer. The remainder of the routine handles cases such as the clist being empty.

Before we consider this routine in detail it would be useful to know when this routine is called. The first case we have already seen: within the lpwrite routine when the data has been put on the clist and the printer ought to be started to print some of this data (see lines 102 and 113).

The other case (which we have not yet seen) occurs when an interrupt arrives. The interrupt handler will call lpwork if the printer has finished printing and there is still data in the clist to be printed.

So remember that lpwork may be called from the interrupt handler as well as from lpwrite.

Our discussion of this routine is divided into two sections to make the commentary appear closer to the code which it describes.

```
116   lpwork routine:
121       set flag indicating device is busy
122       while (true i.e. forever)
124-127       spin until device is ready for data or we lose patience
128           if we lost patience,
129               break out of loop
130           try to obtain byte from clist buffer
              if (no more data in clist buffer)
131               break out of loop
132           write byte to lp data register
133-134       tell printer to accept data
```

```
116     static void lpwork()
117     {
118         int ch;
119         short spinloop;
120         extern void lprestart();

121         Lpflags |= LPBUSY;

122         while (1)
123         {
124             spinloop = 100;
125             while (((inb(LPSTAT) & (LPNERR|LPON|LPRDY))
!=
126                 (LPNERR|LPON|LPRDY)) && --spinloop)
127                 ;

128             if (spinloop == 0)
129                 break;

130             if ((ch = getc(&Lpqueue)) < 0)
131                 break;

132             outb(LPDATA, ch);
```

```
133                outb(LPCTRL, LPSTRB | LPLF | LPINIT | LPSEL);
134                outb(LPCTRL,         LPLF | LPINIT | LPSEL);
135          }
```

Now let us look at what lpwork does in detail.

To start, we set the LPBUSY flag (line 121). This is checked by the lpclose routine to see if the printer is still printing and by the lpintr routine to see if the interrupt came from a busy printer (spurious interrupts from idle devices are not unheard of).

The loop from line 122 to 135 attempts to transfer as much data to the printer as possible. Most printers print a line at a time and have a small amount of memory in which to store the contents of the line before it is actually printed. When we transfer data to the printer we find that while we are filling that memory the printer can accept data very quickly. But when the memory is full, the printer starts to print and refuses to accept any more data until the line has been printed.

In order to take advantage of this behavior, we keep on sending data to the printer as long as it is accepting it relatively quickly (i.e., filling up its memory). When it pauses to print a line, we leave the driver since printing the line can take many tenths of a second and waiting in the driver will prevent other processes from running.

The variable *spinloop* (line 124) is used to limit the time we shall wait for the printer to accept more data. We shall loop up to 100 times, waiting for the printer. Although spin loops within device drivers are normally frowned upon, the one in this driver actually improves system through-put.

If we were to feed one byte to the printer and wait for an interrupt, the operating system would have to incur the overhead of fielding an interrupt and executing the interrupt handler (which would call lpwork to feed another byte). It turns out that when the printer is accepting data it will usually accept the next byte well within 100 loops, and furthermore, the overhead of leaving the driver and fielding the interrupt is far greater than 100 simple loops. Therefore, we spin on lines 125-127, waiting for the printer to become ready to accept another byte.

If the loop exits because we spun 100 times without the device becoming ready (i.e., line 128, spinloop is zero), then we stop trying to transfer data from the clist to the printer (line 129). The limit of 100 was chosen after some experimentation and may not be appropriate for all computers or printers.

On the other hand, if spinloop is greater than zero, then the device must be ready since we leave the loop only if the device is ready *or* spinloop is zero.

We then try to fetch a character from the clist (line 130). If there are no more characters in the clist, then we also stop trying to transfer data from the clist to the printer (line 131).

By line 132 we know the printer is ready to accept data and we have data to print. In line 132 we put the character in the data register and then raise and lower the strobe line (lines 133 and 134). This signals to the printer that there is data in the data register to be transferred to the printer's memory.

This loop (122-135) continues until either the printer takes longer than 100 loops to become ready to accept more data or there is more data in the clist to print.

```
136         if (room in clist and process is sleeping waiting for room)
138             clear flag indicating user process is sleeping
139             wake up sleeping process

141         if (clist is empty)
143             clear device busy flag
144             if (someone is sleeping waiting to close)
145                 wake up process
147         else if (timeout pending flag is clear)
149             request that lprestart be called in a tenth of a second
150             set timeout pending flag
152         enable device interrupts
```

```
136         if ((Lpqueue.c_cc < LOWAT) && (Lpflags & SLEEP))
137         {
138             Lpflags &= ~SLEEP;
```

```
139                   wakeup(&Lpqueue);
140              }

141              if (Lpqueue.c_cc <= 0)
142              {
143                   Lpflags &= ~LPBUSY;
144                   if (Lpflags & WAIT)
145                        wakeup(&Lpflags);
146              }
147              else if ((Lpflags & TOPEND) == 0)
148              {
149                   timeout(lprestart, 0, TOINT);
150                   Lpflags |= TOPEND;
151              }
152              outb(LPCTRL, LPLF | LPINIT | LPSEL | LPIENB);
153         }
```

When we have transferred as much data to the printer as possible, we then check (line 136) to see if we have taken enough data from the clist that we ought to wakeup the process waiting for more space in the clist (lines 138, 139).

We also check (line 141) to see if there is any more data in the clist to print. If not, then we mark the device as not busy (line 143) and check to see if anyone is in the lpclose entry point waiting for us to become idle (line 144). If so, we wake them up (line 145).

Lines 147 to 151 will be discussed later.

Finally, we enable interrupts (line 152).

Process Scheduling

We have now examined the two halves of the driver. The top end (the lpwrite routine) takes data from the user's process and stores it in the clist. The bottom end (the lpwork routine) takes data from the clist and sends it to the printer.

Since there is not an infinite amount of storage available in the clist, we have to limit the amount of data we store in the clist. What we need to do is to suspend the user's process until lpwork can catch up.

We can suspend the user's process by calling the kernel's sleep function from within the lpwrite entry point. Go back and look at the lpwrite entry point and read the description about lines 99 through 109. As discussed, if we have more than HIWAT characters in the clist and have just called lpwork (so we know the printer is busy and has taken as much data as it can for now), then we have to suspend the user's process. We do this by calling sleep in line 106.

This causes the user's process to be suspended until further notice. The state of the user's process (and the driver) is stored at that point and the kernel removes the user's process from the list of processes ready to run. It then selects the process on the ready-to-run list that has the highest priority. The sleep call will not return until a wakeup call is made from elsewhere in the driver.

But how do we wake the process once the clist has drained and there is room for more data? Eventually the printer will finish printing and signal an interrupt. The interrupt handler calls lpwork to send more data to the printer. If we look back at the lpwork routine (line 136) we check to see whether there are fewer than LOWAT (low water mark) characters in the clist and if we have suspended the user's process (i.e., the SLEEP flag, set in line 105, is present). If so, then we use the kernel's *wakeup* routine to unsuspend the user's process (line 139). The kernel will then take the previously suspended process (still in the driver's lpwork routine) and put it on the ready-to-run list.

Note that the current execution of lpwork will continue immediately after making the *wakeup* call. The woken process will not resume (i.e., return from the sleep call) until the current execution of lpwork leaves the driver and no other process has a priority higher than the woken process.

The first argument to sleep is an arbitrary number that is used to connect the wakeup call with the sleep call. The trick is to select the same unique number to use in the two calls. One could choose an integer at random, but would still run the risk that another driver writer might choose the same number. A more reliable technique is to take the address of a variable that is local to the driver. The data structure chosen is unimportant;

the only thing that is important is that both the *sleep* and *wakeup* calls use the same address.

The second argument to sleep is the priority that the user's process will run at when it is resumed. With UNIX, the lower the priority number the higher the scheduling priority. The actual number is relatively unimportant—except that if a process is put to sleep with a priority lower than or equal to PZERO (see the file /usr/include/sys/param.h as well as line 9), then it will be immune to signals (i.e., it will not be possible to kill it). Conversely, sleeping at a priority above PZERO means that signals will cause the system call to be interrupted and the signal handled in the normal manner.

Obviously, if you put a process to sleep at a priority lower than PZERO, you must be absolutely positive that your driver will shortly wakeup the process. If there is any possibility that the wakeup will never occur (i.e., the printer is turned off), then you must sleep above PZERO or risk creating a process that hangs and can never be killed. In this driver, we sleep at a priority above PZERO (line 9).

Another example of process scheduling occurs when the user's process is finished with the printer and wants to close the device. Because of the clist, it is possible that up to HIWAT characters are still waiting to be printed when the user's process invokes the close entry point.

In line 75 we check to see if the printer is still busy, and if so, we set the WAIT flag (line 77) and then suspend the user's process. In lpwork, we check to see if the WAIT flag is set (line 144) when we have finished printing everything that is in the clist. And if it is, it means that a user's process was suspended in the close routine so we wake it up (line 145).

The Lpintr Entry Point

When the printer is finished printing and is ready for more data it will signal the computer by raising an interrupt. Unless the interrupt has been disabled, this will cause the CPU to stop whatever it is doing and execute the interrupt handler for the printer (lpintr). It is important to remember that when the interrupt arrives, the CPU could be executing any process, not necessarily the process that originally sent the data to the printer. Because of this the interrupt handler (and any routine such as lpwork called by the interrupt handler) must not touch the contents of the current user area (the u. area).

Note that while the interrupt handler is executing, the system automatically raises the CPU priority to disable further interrupts from this device and coincidentally, all other devices of the same or lower priority. This means that while the system is executing the interrupt handler (and any routines called from the handler), other devices may be prevented from interrupting the system. If interrupts are blocked for too long the performance of the system will be adversely affected and in some situations, such as data being received on a serial port, data may be lost. For this reason it is imperative to minimize the time spent within the interrupt handler.

```
154 intr entry point:
157     if (device busy flag is clear)
158         return (i.e. interrupt is spurious)

159     if (there is at least one byte in the clist buffer)
160         call lpwork to try to print it

154     lpintr(dev)
155     dev_t dev;
156     {
157         if ((Lpflags & LPBUSY) == 0)
158             return;

159         if (Lpqueue.c_cc > 0)
160             lpwork();
161     }
```

Handling interrupts is simple.

If the device is not busy, we ignore the interrupt (lines 157 and 158).

Otherwise, if there is still work to do (i.e., data in the clist, line 159), then we call lpwork to move more data from the clist to the printer (line 160).

Deferring Interrupts

Although handling the interrupt is simple, there are some very subtle problems that can arise in drivers that use interrupts.

These problems all arise from the fact that unless precautions are taken, interrupts can arrive at any time.

Let us consider an example of what can go wrong when interrupts arrive at the wrong time. Look back at lines 103-107. At line 103, we determine that there is no more room in the clist. We must therefore suspend the user's process until there is room. In line 105 we set the SLEEP flag indicating that we are waiting to add more data to the clist, and in line 106 we go to sleep.

But imagine that an interrupt arrives after we have executed line 105 but before we execute line 106. We have set the SLEEP flag but have not actually gone to sleep.

The interrupt routine calls the lpwork routine (line 160). The lpwork routine manages to transfer all of the data from the clist to the printer (lines 122-135 and then checks to see if anyone was sleeping (line 136).

The SLEEP flag was set so we clear it (line 138) and call wakeup (line 139). But remember that the interrupt arrived just before we executed the sleep call in line 106. So the call to *wakeup* has no effect.

The lpwork routine finishes and the lpintr exits. The CPU then picks up where it was interrupted and executes the call to sleep (line 106). Remember, however, that when the interrupt came in it called lpwork which cleared the SLEEP flag. So we have gone to sleep but without the SLEEP flag set.

When the next interrupt comes in, the test at line 136 will always fail because the SLEEP flag is not set, hence the wakeup in line 139 will never execute. We have effectively gone to sleep forever.

This problem arises because we have two routines (lpwork and lpwrite) that access the same variable and which can be executed at the same time. A section of code that can be adversely affected by the untimely execution of another part of the code is called a critical section. Lines 103 through 107 comprise such a critical section. We must prevent an interrupt from arriving during this critical section.

Process Priority

Each device that can interrupt the CPU is assigned a priority (more than one device can share the same priority). The CPU keeps track of the current processor priority and will only service interrupts that are higher in priority than the current processor priority. Note that processor priority is totally unrelated to the concept of scheduling priority discussed in the previous section.

When we want to prevent interrupts from our device, we raise the processor priority to a level equal to the level of the interrupt our device generates. The kernel provides a series of routines (i.e., spl4, spl5, ..., spl7) to set the processor priority. When they are called, they will change the processor priority to the specified level and return the priority level to the level prior to the change.

Since running with interrupts disabled can delay the system, the driver must restore the priority level to the previous level as soon as possible after the critical section. Restoring the processor priority is done by calling the splx routine and passing it the desired processor level (i.e., the value returned by the previous *spl_* call).

In this driver there are a number of critical sections protected using calls to spl_. Examine lines 74 through 82 and 101 through 108. In fact, most of the lpwork routine is a critical section so we must make sure we disable interrupts whenever we call it. The calls to lpwork (lines 102 and 113) are all made after calls to spl5.

The call to lpwork from lpintr (line 160) is automatically protected because the CPU sets the processor priority equal to the level of the interrupt before calling the interrupt handler. Note that the driver may only raise the processor priority and restore it to the original level. Never use an spl routine to lower the current priority (except when restoring the previous processor priority).

Dropped Interrupts

One last problem exists with this device. This driver depends on the line printer's interrupting the CPU when it is ready for more data. The lpwork routine merely exits after sending as much data to the printer as possible. It does not wait for the printer to finish, rather it depends on the interrupt causing lpintr to call lpwork to send more data to the printer.

But what if the expected interrupt never arrives? The user's process will sleep forever (at line 106) waiting for more room in the clist.

Most devices are quite reliable and always generate an interrupt when they become ready for more data. The line printer controller on most PC-bus computers is an exception, however. Frequently, the line printer controller will drop interrupts (i.e., the interrupt will either not be generated or not be detected by the computer).

So what is a poor device driver writer to do?

Simple. Fake it.

When we are about to leave the lpwork routine expecting an interrupt to come later, we ask the kernel to call us at some point in the future (say a tenth of second later). If no interrupt arrives, the kernel will call us after a tenth of a second and we shall check if the device is ready for more data. In this manner we are protected from dropped interrupts.

Look back at line 149 in lpwork. The kernel-supplied routine *timeout* is called with three parameters: the name of the routine to call later, the single argument to pass that routine, and the delay before calling the routine. The delay (defined in line 12) is measured in clock ticks. The frequency of the system clock is defined by HZ so that HZ/10 is one-tenth of a second (regardless of the actual clock rate).

Note that interrupts do not always fail. Normally, an interrupt will arrive well within the tenth of a second and lpwork will be called. The kernel can only keep track of a limited number of timeout requests so we cannot just ask for another timeout. Also, why incur the overhead of cancelling the previous timeout request and issuing another? We just check to see if there is a timeout pending (line 147) and call timeout only if there is not.

The Lprestart Routine

What happens when the timeout finally occurs? This will happen one-tenth of a second after the call to timeout regardless of whether the printer is busy or not, regardless of whether an interrupt has been dropped or not. When the time delay specified in the call to timeout expires, the kernel will call the specified routine (in this case lprestart).

```
162   lprestart routine:
165       clear the timeout pending flag
166       raise processor priority (disable interrupts)
167       call lpwork
168       restore processor priority
```

```
162   static void lprestart()
163   {
164        int x;

165        Lpflags &= ~TOPEND;

166        x = spl5();
167        lpwork();
168        splx(x);
169   }
```

Lprestart first clears the timeout-pending flag (line 165) so that lpwork knows (in line 147) that no timeout is pending. It then raises the process priority and calls lpwork. This simulates a real interrupt. Compare this with the lpintr routine.

If an interrupt has been dropped, then lpwork will start things going again. If an interrupt has not been dropped, then lpwork will find the printer still busy and will do nothing (other than posting another timeout request).

In this manner we use the timeout kernel routine to protect against dropped interrupts. Lpwork will handle the situation should a timeout occur when an interrupt has not been dropped and the printer is busy printing.

Summary

With this driver we start to see some of the complex design issues that confront device driver writers. The slow speed of the printer (relative to the computer) required us to schedule the user's process and slow it down to the speed of the printer. We also used the clist buffering mechanism provided by the kernel to store data in order to reduce the number of times we had to wakeup the user's process to obtain more data.

The driver also had to cope with interrupts arriving at inopportune times. We saw how critical sections of code can malfunction and how deferring interrupts by raising the processor priority can prevent these problems.

Finally, we considered the problem of dropped interrupts and saw how we could make sure that the driver continued to function even if the device did not interrupt as it ought to.

If you have reached this point and feel that you understand even a part of this driver, then congratulations. We have covered a lot of ground in this one chapter. Take a rest and return to this chapter later. You will find that this driver makes more sense the second time through. The first time we had to postpone the discussion of various parts of the code until we had seen more of the driver. Now that you have seen the entire driver, these earlier parts will be easier to understand.

Exercises

1. Recall that this driver takes special precautions to prevent the loss of an interrupt from disrupting things. In particular, the driver posts timeouts that call the routine lprestart. This routine merely calls lpwork to start the device again. Although this will work, if interrupts are not often dropped, it can be very inefficient. Modify lprestart to check if the printer is busy (use a test similar to line 125), and if so, merely post another timeout. If a timeout arrives when the device is not busy, then call lpwork.

2. This driver takes one character at a time from the user's process and puts it on the clist. While this works well, it is somewhat inefficient. A

more efficient approach would be to transfer larger blocks of data from the user's process. Similarly, one can transfer multiple bytes to the clist at once using the kernel routine *putcbp*. This routine takes three arguments: (1) the address of the clist structure, (2) the address of the buffer, and (3) the number of bytes to transfer. Putcbp returns the number of bytes successfully transferred.

Modify the driver to copy more than one byte at a time from the user process to the clist.

Chapter 5

Block Drivers I: A Test Data Generator

After examining three character drivers of increasing complexity it is time to turn our attention to block drivers.

The main difference between block drivers and character drivers is that character drivers transfer data directly to and from the user's process, while block drivers transfer data to and from the kernel's buffer cache. This difference is illustrated in Figure 5-1 on the next page.

The purpose of this buffer cache is to optimize I/O to devices that (a) handle data in fixed blocks, and (b) can store a UNIX file system. Block drivers are ideally suited to support disk drives. Block drivers are inappropriate for devices that typically perform I/O in variably-sized blocks, possibly as small as a single byte. In contrast, while character drivers are ideally suited to such devices, they cannot be used to support a device that must contain a UNIX file system.

As we might expect, the different architecture for block drivers results in a different kernel/driver interface. As compared with a character driver, the entry points that a block driver must supply are different and the

method of communicating information between the driver and the kernel
and user process is different.

FIGURE 5-1

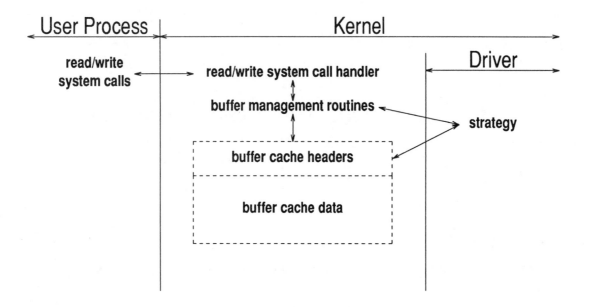

The first driver we shall examine is a test data generator. Reads to this
device return blocks of data that contain every possible eight-bit data pattern repeated infinitely. Writes are ignored.

This driver could be used, for example, to generate data to test a tape
drive using the following UNIX command:

```
dd if=/dev/blktest of=/dev/tape bs=10k count=1000
tape rewind
dd if=/dev/tape bs=10k | cmp - /dev/blktest
```

Since this driver is the block driver equivalent of the character test data generator discussed in Chapter 2, it might be helpful to reread that chapter quickly and to compare that driver with the one presented in this chapter.

The Design Issues

In general, the design issues are the same as for the character version of the test data generator discussed in Chapter 2. What we shall concentrate on here are the issues that are different for a block driver.

The Operating System/Driver Interface

Block drivers may provide all of the entry points that are available to character drivers with the exception of read and write. With block drivers, the function of these entry points is handled by a single *strategy* entry point that is responsible for processing both read and write requests. The strategy entry point is mandatory for all block drivers.

In addition, block drivers must supply a *print* entry point that may be used by the kernel to report errors related to the device driver.

All other entry points are optional (except that some UNIX implementations require open and close entry points, which may be empty).

The Internal Operation of the Driver

The different architecture of block drivers leads to a different mechanism for transferring data to and from the driver and the rest of the UNIX system.

Recall that the read and write entry points of character drivers obtained the details of the I/O request from variables in the u. structure. With block drivers all I/O requests come from the kernel in the form of requests to fill or empty block buffers in the cache (as illustrated earlier in Figure 5-1). As we shall see shortly, the strategy routine is passed a pointer to a buffer header which contains all of the information describing the I/O request.

Another difference is that the buffer pointed to by the buffer header is within the kernel address space. This means that special routines like copyin or copyout are not necessary, and no tests are needed to handle errors that might occur during the transfer.

Let us now examine the driver itself to see how the different kernel/driver interface affects the structure of the driver.

The Driver

The Driver Prologue

The prologue of a device driver includes all of the definitions and declarations required by the rest of the driver.

```
1   #include <sys/types.h>
2   #include <sys/buf.h>
3   #include <sys/cmn_err.h>

4   static char testpattern[1024] =
5   {
6        0x00, 0x01, 0x02, 0x03, 0x04, 0x05, 0x06, 0x07,
..       ...
133      0xf8, 0xf9, 0xfa, 0xfb, 0xfc, 0xfd, 0xfe, 0xff
134  };
```

The include files *<sys/buf.h>* and *<sys/cmn_err.h>* are new to us with this driver. Buf.h contains the definition of the buffer headers that are used to coordinate the transfer of data to and from block drivers. Cmn_err.h contains definitions used by the error reporting routine that appears later in this driver.

The missing lines (7..132) merely contain the remainder of the initialization for the array *testpattern*.

The Init Entry Point

```
135  blk1init()
136  {
137      printf("Test Data Block Driver v1.0\n");
138  }
```

As a pseudo-driver that has no data structures needing to be initialized at boot time, the init routine merely announces the presence of the driver.

The Open and Close Entry Points

Although this driver does not require an open or close entry point, some UNIX systems (including the one used to test this driver) require all block drivers to provide them even if they are empty.

```
139   blk1open(dev_t dev, int flag, int id)
140   {
141   }

142   blk1close(dev_t dev, int flagm, int id)
143   {
144   }
```

The Strategy Entry Point

The strategy entry point is one of the two entry points that exist in block drivers but not in character drivers. The other is the print entry point discussed later. It is responsible for handling requests for data (in or out) and replaces both the read and write entry points found in character drivers.

Unlike character drivers which look in the user (u.) area to determine the details of the I/O request, block drivers are given a pointer to a buffer header that contains all of the necessary information describing the I/O operation (including whether it is a read or a write).

This pointer is passed to the strategy routine when the kernel wishes to fill or empty a buffer in the buffer cache. Unlike character drivers, the block driver does not have to concern itself with process scheduling. If the strategy routine cannot complete the I/O immediately, it merely returns. When the I/O operation completes, the block driver notifies the kernel by calling *iodone(bp)*, passing it a pointer to the buffer that has been processed. If a user process is waiting for the I/O to complete, the kernel will handle the process scheduling issues.

The strategy routine for this driver is even simpler than the read entry point for the character test data driver we examined in Chapter 2.

```
145  strategy entry point:
148      if (read request)
149          copy data from testpattern to buffer
150      set residual count to 0 (indicating a successful transfer)
151      report that the I/O request has been completed
```

```
145  blk1strategy(bp)
146  struct buf *bp;
147  {
148      if (bp->b_flags & B_READ)
149          bcopy(testpattern,
                       paddr(bp),
                       bp->b_bcount);
150      bp->b_resid = 0;
151      iodone(bp);
152  }
```

The single parameter is the pointer to the entry in the buffer cache that is
to be read or written. The driver checks (line 148) to see if it is a read
request, and if so, calls bcopy to copy the contents of the *testpattern* to the
buffer. The driver then indicates to the driver that the I/O has completed
successfully (lines 150-151).

Since both the source of the data (testpattern) and the destination (the
buffer cache) are in the kernel address space, we could copy the data ourselves using a simple loop with two character pointers. We use bcopy
instead because it is optimized to transfer data quickly and will use special machine instructions where possible to copy the data faster than we
could ourselves. Unlike copyin or copyout which have to perform special
functions to transfer data to and from user address space (and which can
return errors if the user-supplied buffer address is invalid), bcopy does
nothing special other than copying data. Unlike copyin/copyout, bcopy
always succeeds and therefore has no return value.

Before we consider this code in greater detail, let us examine the nature
of the buffer cache more fully.

The Buffer Cache   The buffer cache is used by the UNIX kernel to store
data that has come from a block device, is going to a block device, or both
(has been read and changed, and will soon be written back). The buffer

cache provides two advantages: it allows user processes to perform I/O without regard to the fundamental block structure of the device and it significantly improves the performance of the system.

Think a moment about how a user process accesses a disk and how a disk operates. User processes usually access disk files using I/O requests of differing sizes. For example, the record size for a particular file might be 105 bytes, and the user process wishes to read record 1097. Then the process might change the record and write it back out. Or it might want to replace record 4032 with another.

While these are entirely reasonable things for a user process to do, they cause operating systems no end of trouble. Almost all disk drives are structured as fixed-block devices. This means that the data on the disk is stored in blocks of a fixed size (usually 512 or 1024 bytes). If the user process wants to reach record 1097, the operating system will have to read the 224th block of the file and return the last 15 bytes, and then read the 225th block and return the first 90 bytes of that block. This is illustrated in Figure 5-2 on the next page.

If the user process wants to write out a record, the work is even more involved. Since the record does not span an entire block, the operating system must first read in the block (or blocks) affected, change the appropriate bytes, and then write the block back out to the disk.

Also, after reading a record, user processes frequently rewrite the same record, or read the next record. So after reading record 1097 the process is quite likely to want to change it or read record 1098. If the disk block(s) containing these records is (are) still in memory, then these operations can happen instantly without requiring any actual disk I/O operation. The more disk blocks that are kept in the buffer cache, the greater the probability that a read or write request from a user process will be able to be satisfied from data already in the buffer cache. Obviously this can substantially improve the performance of the system.

So we see the two purposes of the buffer cache: (a) to permit user processes to remain ignorant of the block structure of the underlying disk hardware; and (b) to provide higher average disk throughput by keeping frequently used data in memory.

FIGURE 5-2

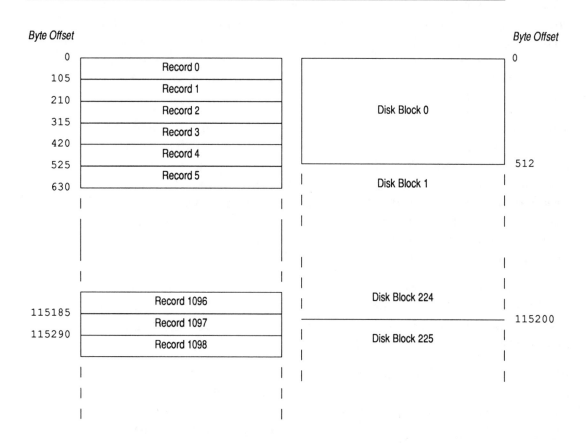

All of the management of the buffer cache is handled within the kernel. The device driver merely has to fill or empty buffers as requested. The rest is handled automatically.

Each buffer in the buffer cache is represented by a buffer header. This data structure is defined in the include file /usr/include/sys/buf.h and contains information about the contents of the actual buffer. The table below defines the important members of this structure.

Important Members of the Buf Structure

Member	Description
b_flags	flags
b_forw	pointer used by kernel to associate block with device
b_back	pointer used by kernel to associate block with device
av_forw	available list pointer
av_back	available list pointer
b_dev	major and minor device numbers
b_bcount	block count
b_blkno	block number
b_sector	sector number
b_resid	bytes not transferred
b_error	error flags
paddr(bp)	kernel virtual address of buffer contents

The b_flags member contains information about the status of the buffer. There are only two flags that drivers need be concerned about: B_READ (which marks a buffer that is to be filled) and B_ERROR (which the driver sets if the I/O fails). Note that the driver must take pains not to disturb any other flags that may be set. Set a flag by using the OR operator, not straight assignment. For example:

```
bp->b_flags |= B_ERROR;
```

The b_forw and b_back pointers are used by the kernel to keep the buffer on a doubly linked list of all buffers associated with a single device. The driver never need access these members.

When the buffer is not busy (in the process of being read or written) it is kept on a list of buffers available for re-use. The more recently used buffers are nearer the end of the list. When the kernel needs a buffer, it takes the first buffer off the front of the available list. The av_forw and av_back are used to maintain this list.

When the buffer is busy (as it always is when the driver is dealing with it), then these members are not used by the kernel and are free for the driver to use as desired. Drivers that cannot perform I/O immediately (i.e., drivers for real disk drives) usually use the av_forw member to maintain a list of outstanding I/O requests (buffers waiting for the disk).

We shall see how this is done in a later chapter when we study the driver for a SCSI disk drive.

The b_dev member identifies the device (major and minor device number) associated with this block. To access the minor device number, use code similar to the following:

```
if (minor(bp->b_device) == 0)
    ...
```

(The minor macro is defined in the header <sys/sysmacros.h>.)

The b_bcount member specifies the number of bytes to be transferred. In almost all block drivers this will be equal to the size of the buffers in the cache as defined by BSIZE (from the header <sys/param.h>), usually 1024 bytes. The two exceptions are block drivers with raw interfaces (described in Chapter 8) and on some systems, block drivers used to contain the system swap area.

The location on the disk that is to be read or written is specified by b_blkno (which is in units of 512 bytes). The b_sector field is available for use by the driver and will be explained in our SCSI disk driver.

If the driver encounters an error and is unable to complete the I/O request it must put the number of bytes not transferred in b_resid, set the B_ERROR flag in b_flags, and put the error code from the header file <sys/errno.h> in b_error.

Remember that the buffer structure we have been studying is the buffer header, not the buffer itself. The data associated with the buffer header is stored in a separate area referenced by paddr(bp). The member of the buffer structure that contains the address of the data has changed from release to release of the UNIX kernel, so the macro paddr() has been defined to provide a more portable way of accessing the buffer's data area. (The argument to paddr is a pointer to a buffer structure.)

With UNIX System V Release 3.2 and Release 4.0, the value of paddr(bp) is a kernel address (recall the discussions on address spaces in Chapter 2). On some other versions of the UNIX kernel paddr is a physical address. Refer to the documentation that came with your system to determine the type of address returned by paddr.

The Strategy Entry Point (Revisited)   If we return to our driver, we see how (in line 148) it checks to see if the request is a read or a write. The presence of the B_READ flags in the b_flags member of the buffer header indicates the request is a read. The absence of the B_READ flag indicates a write. Although B_WRITE exists, it is defined as 0 and is intended to be used in code such as the following:

```
if ((bp->b_flags & B_READ) == B_WRITE)
    . . .
```

If the request is a read, we call on the kernel routine bcopy to transfer the data from the testpattern array (declared and initialized in the driver prologue) to the buffer referenced by the buffer header.

Bcopy copies data which is given source and destination addresses that are both in the kernel address space. The third argument is the number of bytes to transfer. In this driver, the number would always be equal to one block (i.e., B_SIZE blocks). Recall that paddr is a kernel macro that returns the virtual (not physical as the name implies) address of the actual memory used to store the contents of the buffer.

In line 150 we set the residual count to zero indicating the entire transfer was successful (regardless of whether it was a read or a write), and then we call the kernel routine iodone (line 151) to inform the kernel that we are finished with the buffer.

The kernel will handle the transfer of the data in the buffer into the user's address space as well as the scheduling of any processes waiting for the I/O to complete.

The Print Entry Point

Every block driver must provide a print entry point that may be used by the kernel to report problems related to the driver. The entry point only needs to print the error message on the console and usually calls upon the kernel routine cmn_err (an extended version of printf) to display the message.

```
153   blk1print(dev, message)
154   dev_t dev;
155   char *message;
156   {
157         cmn_err(CE_WARN, "blk1 driver error: %s\n", message);
158   }
```

Summary

In this chapter we examined our first block driver. We saw how the interface between the driver and the kernel differed from the drivers we studied earlier. We also examined the structure of the buffer cache and learned how the kernel passes I/O requests to a block driver.

Exercises

1. One of the problems with using test data that is the same, block after block, is that the loss of an entire block cannot be detected. Modify this driver to mark each block of data returned with a unique block number (i.e., the b_blkno value).

2. Modify this driver to examine the device number and return different test data based on its value. If the minor device number is 0, then return blocks that contain only the value 0. If the minor device number is 1, then return blocks that contain the value 0xff only.

3. Modify this driver so that the user can write a single block of data that replaces the contents of the testpattern array and that is returned when the device is read.

Chapter 6

Block Drivers III: A RAM Disk Driver

Recall that one of the main differences between character drivers and block drivers is that block drivers can support UNIX file systems. This means that the device can be mounted and accessed as an extension of the root file system for storing and retrieving data organized as files (within directories).

This chapter will explore a simple driver that uses memory to emulate a disk drive. This driver will help illustrate the key aspects of all block drivers that support storage devices which can contain file systems.

The Design Issues

There are no driver/hardware interface issues to consider since this driver, like the previous one, does not control any hardware. The kernel/driver interface issues related to block drivers were discussed at length in Chapter 5 and this driver does not introduce anything new in this area. Where this driver differs significantly from the previous one is in its internal operation.

In particular, we have two major concerns:

- how to allocate the memory used for the RAM disk; and
- how to handle I/O requests that start or extend beyond the last block of the RAM disk.

We shall see in the open and close entry points for this driver how a driver may request memory from the kernel. And in the strategy routine we shall examine how to validate I/O requests.

The Driver

Since this driver does not control actual hardware, it is properly referred to as a *pseudo-device driver*. As a RAM disk driver, this device driver will allocate a part of the system's main (RAM) memory and use it to store data that is written to the device. Requests to read data will be satisfied by accessing the data previously stored in the RAM memory. In this way the device will appear to the operating system and applications programs just like a disk storage device with an extremely fast access time.

This driver determines the size of the RAM disk to create by taking the minor device number, adding one, and multiplying by 128K. Therefore, if this driver were accessed using a special file with a minor device number of 15, the driver would create a RAM disk two megabytes in size. Note that this driver de-allocates the memory upon the last close of the device, so maintaining the contents of the RAM disk requires the device remain open.

For example, the following commands would first open the device (and keep it open) while an *mkfs* command creates a file system on the RAM disk and the *mount* command makes it accessible. The *sleep* command is merely to keep the RAM disk open for the few seconds between the end of the mkfs command and the issuing of the mount command.

```
sleep 60 < /dev/ramdisk
/etc/mkfs /dev/ramdisk 4096
/etc/mount /dev/ramdisk /mnt
```

The mkfs and mount commands may only be issued by the system administrator (i.e., root). The size of the file system (4096 in this example) is specified in units of 512-byte blocks and must not be greater than the size of the RAM disk.

The Driver Prologue

The prologue contains some of the header files we used in the previous block driver as well as some from previous character drivers.

```
 1   #include <sys/types.h>
 2   #include <sys/param.h>
 3   #include <sys/immu.h>
 4   #include <sys/buf.h>
 5   #include <sys/dir.h>
 6   #include <sys/user.h>
 7   #include <sys/errno.h>
 8   #include <sys/cmn_err.h>
 9   #include <sys/sysmacros.h>
10   #include <sys/open.h>

11   #define SIZE_UNIT    128*1024

12   #define btoblkno(b)    (((b) + 511) >> 9)
13   #define blknotob(b)    ((b) << 9)

14   static long sizebyte;
15   static int sizeblock;
16   static caddr_t ramptr;
17   static int multiopens;
18   static int matchedopens;

19   static char SCCSid[] = "@(#)RAM Disk Driver v1.0\n";
```

The header *<sys/immu.h>* (line 3) contains definitions used when requesting memory from the operating system. The header *<sys/open.h>* (line 10) contains the definitions of the values that may be passed as the third argument (the id parameter) to the open entry point. We shall discuss this further when we consider the open entry point.

The other header files we have seen from previous drivers. The only reason we bring in the user structure (line 6) is so that we can report errors during the opening of the device.

SIZE_UNIT (line 11) is used to determine the size of the RAM disk. We calculate the size of the disk by adding one to the minor device number and multiplying by SIZE_UNIT. For example, minor device number 7 specifies a RAM disk of 1Mb in size; 23 = 3Mb; 127 = 16Mb; and so on. If this define is changed, then the size of the RAM disks will change.

The UNIX kernel specifies the offset (address) of the disk block to be read or written as a block number calculated in 512-byte units regardless of the actual block size used by the kernel (i.e., *BSIZE*) or the block size of the device. The two macros defined on lines 12 and 13 provide conversions between addresses (offsets) in block numbers and in bytes.

The variable *sizebyte* (line 14) will be used to store the size of the RAM disk in bytes while *sizeblock* (line 15) will store the size of the RAM disk in 512-byte blocks. If sizebyte is 0, then no RAM disk exists. If sizebyte is not zero, then memory has been allocated and is pointed to by *ramptr* (line 16).

The variables *multiopens* and *matchedopens* on lines 17 and 18 are used to determine when the last close occurred and hence when the memory allocated for the RAM disk may be freed. This will be discussed in detail when we consider the open entry point.

Finally, line 19 contains the SCCS identification string for the driver. SCCS (Source Code Control System) is a set of UNIX utilities for managing source files. The *what* utility examines binary or executable files for strings that start with the string '@(#)' and prints them out. If we were to install this driver on a UNIX system we could run *what* on the /unix file and obtain the SCCS id strings for all of the drivers and kernel modules that defined one. For example:

```
# what /unix
/unix:
    RAM Disk Driver v1.0
    cfax.c    2.9 - 91/3/16
```

```
weitek.h 22.1 90/01/15
stream.h 22.3 90/02/15
...
```

The Init Entry Point

```
20   int ramdinit()
21   {
22       printf(&SCCSid[4]);
23   }
```

This init entry point need only announce our presence to the world. Instead of declaring a separate string, we print the SCCS id string (declared on line 19). By giving *printf* the address of byte number 4 (the fifth byte), we skip the SCCS id prefix '@(#)'.

The Open Entry Point

The open entry point performs several functions.

- It keeps track of the number of opens so that the driver can determine when the final close occurs.
- It allocates memory for the RAM disk if not already done.
- Otherwise (if memory has already been allocated) it checks that the amount previously allocated matches the amount required by this open.

```
24   open entry point:
28       if (a layered open OR a mount open)
29           increment matchedopens
30       else
31           multiopens = 1

32       request = RAM disk size in bytes
                   (calculated from minor device number)

33       if (no memory allocated yet)
35           allocate kernel memory
36           if (no memory available to allocate)
37               set error code
38           else
```

```
40-41              remember size of RAM disk in bytes and blocks
44        else if (memory previously allocated != request size)
45             set error code

24  int ramdopen(dev_t dev, int flag, int id)
25  {
26      long request;
27      extern caddr_t sptalloc(int, int, int, int);

28      if ((id == OTYP_LYR) || (id == OTYP_MNT))
29          matchedopens++;
30      else
31          multiopens = 1;

32      request = (minor(dev) + 1) * SIZE_UNIT;

33      if (sizebyte == 0)
34      {
35          ramptr = sptalloc(btoc(request), PG_P, 0, 1);
36          if (ramptr == NULL)
37              u.u_error = ENOSPC;
38          else
39          {
40              sizebyte = request;
41              sizeblock = btoblkno(sizebyte);
42          }
43      }
44      else if (sizebyte != request)
45          u.u_error = EEXIST;
46  }
```

The variable *request* (declared on line 26) will be used during the calculations of the RAM disk size while line 27 declares the kernel routine that we shall be calling to obtain the necessary memory for the RAM disk.

Back in Chapter 2 when we first started talking about driver entry points, we mentioned that a driver's close entry point was only called when the last user process that had opened the device issued a close system call. While this is true for MOST drivers, it is not true for ALL drivers. In particular, block device drivers that contain file systems may have their close entry point called while other processes still have the device open.

This is of some concern to us since we wish to de-allocate the RAM disk's memory when the last user process is finished with it. But if we de-allocate the memory while other processes still have the device open, we run the risk of losing data or corrupting main memory. So we need to be able to tell when we have received the last close.

A detail that has been omitted from our discussions to date is that there are different types of opens. The third argument (*id*, see line 24) contains a flag indicating the type of open. The possible values are listed in the header <sys/open.h>. Using this argument we can determine how many times our close entry point will be called: there will be one close for each open of type OTYP_LYR or OTYP_MNT; and there will be one close for all other opens.

On lines 28-29 we keep track of the number of closes that we can expect from layered opens (of type OTYP_LYR) and from the opens related to file system mounts (type OTYP_MNT). On line 31 we keep track of the number of closes that we can expect from all other types of opens. As we will see in a moment, the close routine decrements each of these counts when appropriate so that when the total of multiopens and matchedopens is zero we know we have received our last close.

We then (line 32) calculate the size of the desired RAM disk by multiplying the minor device number (plus one) by SIZE_UNIT (128K, see line 11).

If *sizebyte* is 0 (line 33) then no space has been allocated for this RAM disk. The kernel routine *sptalloc* is the kernel routine that will allocate the requested amount of memory. The first argument is the size (in pages) of the memory required. The actual size of the memory pages is immaterial since the macro *btoc* (from the header <sys/sysmacros.h>) will convert from bytes to memory pages for us.

The second argument specifies the page descriptor table entry field mask and must always be *PG_P* (page present bit), which is defined in the header <sys/immu.h>.

The third argument to sptalloc is the base address which must be set to 0 if we are requesting kernel memory allocation. Finally, the fourth argument indicates whether we wish to wait if insufficient memory is free to satisfy our request or if we wish an immediate return. A value of 1 indicates that sptalloc ought to return with a NULL pointer if the request cannot be satisfied. Be warned that it is possible to go to sleep forever if the request is so large that it can never be satisfied.

We then check to see if the memory was allocated (line 36). If not (line 37) we report an error. The exact error code to return is up to the driver writer and in this case we have chosen *ENOSPC* (not enough space) as a reasonably descriptive error to return if insufficient memory exists to permit the RAM disk to be created.

If the RAM disk has been created we store the size of the RAM disk in bytes (line 40) and in blocks (line 41).

If the original test (line 33) determined that the RAM disk had already been allocated (by a previous open), then we check (line 44) if the size of the existing RAM disk is the same as the one requested by this open. If not, we return an error indicating that a RAM disk already exists (our driver only supports the creation of one RAM disk at a time).

The Close Entry Point

Our close routine is responsible for determining when the last close has occurred and de-allocating the memory that was used for the RAM disk.

```
47   close entry point:
48       if (a layered open OR a mount open)
49           decrement matchedopens
50       else
51           clear multiopens
53       if (matchedopens + multiopens == 0 (i.e. last close))
55-56        release memory allocated to RAM disk
```

```
47   int ramdclose(dev_t dev, int flag, int id)
48   {
49       if ((id == OTYP_LYR) || (id == OTYP_MNT))
50           matchedopens--;
51       else
52           multiopens = 0;

53       if ((matchedopens + multiopens) == 0)
```

```
54        {
55              sptfree(ramptr, btoc(sizebyte), 1);
56              sizebyte = 0;
57        }
58   }
```

We first adjust the counters that tell us when the last close has occurred (lines 49-52). If this is a close that corresponds to a single open (line 49) then we decrement the matchedopens counter (line 50). Otherwise, we clear the multiopens counter (line 52).

If the total of these two counters is zero (line 53) then this is the last close and it is time to de-allocate the memory used for the RAM disk.

In line 55 we call the kernel routine *sptfree* to free the allocated memory. Remember that *ramptr* was used to store a pointer to the block of memory allocated and that sizebyte contains the size in bytes of the RAM disk. The final argument specifies that actual memory (as opposed to merely memory-mapped address space) is to be freed.

We then zero sizebyte to indicate that no memory is currently allocated to a RAM disk (line 33).

The Strategy Entry Point

The strategy routine is responsible for taking requests to read or write data from or to the (RAM) disk, verifying that they are valid, and performing the necessary I/O. In our case, no actual I/O occurs. Rather, the strategy routine will merely copy the data between the kernel buffer and the memory allocated for the RAM disk.

The trick here is to handle properly requests that extend (or even start) beyond the end of the RAM disk. The rules for handling such requests are:

- any request that starts more than one block beyond the end of the disk is in error;
- write requests that extend beyond the last block of the disk are in error; and

■ read requests that extend beyond the last block are adjusted to end
with the last block of the disk.

This is illustrated in Figure 6-1.

FIGURE 6-1

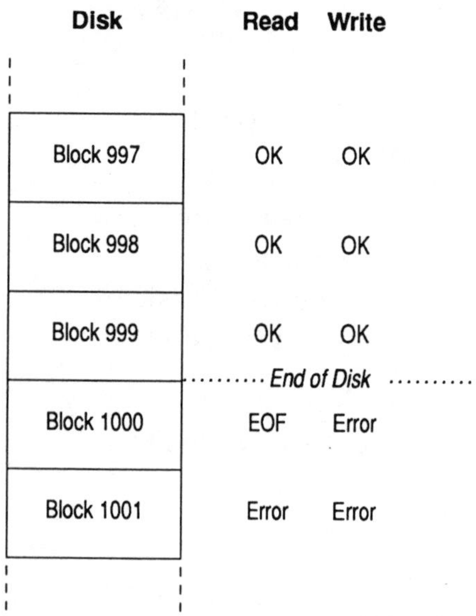

Disk	Read	Write
Block 997	OK	OK
Block 998	OK	OK
Block 999	OK	OK
·········· *End of Disk* ··········		
Block 1000	EOF	Error
Block 1001	Error	Error

One side-effect of the last rule is that a request to read the first block
beyond the end of the disk will be adjusted to read 0 bytes. A read that
returns 0 bytes is the standard EOF indication in UNIX. This is exactly
what should to happen when an attempt is made to read the first block
beyond the end of the disk.

Because of the length of this entry point we shall consider it in two sections, the first validates the request and the second copies the data.

```
59   strategy entry point:

62       blkcount = number of (512 byte) blocks to transfer
```

```
63      if ((request starts at or before the end of the RAM disk) AND
64          ((the request ends at or before the end of the disk) OR
65          (the request is a read)))

67          if (the request extends beyond the end of the disk)
69              calculate number of bytes before end of disk
70              residual count = number of bytes beyond the end of
                                the disk (i.e. that could not be
                                transferred)
71              trim request to fit
73          else
74              residual count = 0 (i.e. transfer successful)
76      else
78-80       mark request as invalid
81          report that the I/O request has been completed
82          return
```

```
59   ramdstrategy(struct buf *bp)
60   {
61       int blkcount;

62       blkcount = btoblkno(bp->b_bcount);

63       if ((bp->b_blkno <= sizeblock) &&
64           ((bp->b_blkno + blkcount <= sizeblock) ||
65           (bp->b_flags & B_READ)))
66       {
67           if (bp->b_blkno + blkcount > sizeblock)
68           {
69               blkcount = sizeblock - bp->b_blkno;
70               bp->b_resid = bp->b_bcount - blknotob(blkcount);
71               bp->b_bcount = blknotob(blkcount);
72           }
73           else
74               bp->b_resid = 0;
75       }
76       else
77       {
78           bp->b_flags |= B_ERROR;
79           bp->b_error = ENXIO;
80           bp->b_resid = bp->b_bcount;
81           iodone(bp);
```

```
82              return;
83         }
```

This entry point starts by (line 62) calculating the number of (512-byte) blocks of data this request is for. This will help us determine if the request attempts to access data beyond the end of the (RAM) disk. Note that most block drivers will only see requests of *BSIZE* (usually 1024) bytes, but for reasons we shall explore further in a later chapter, it is always best to write our driver to accept requests of any size. It is permissible, however, to round requests up to a multiple of the block size.

The test that starts on line 63 consists of several parts. First (line 63) it tests if the request starts before the end of the disk or starts with the first block beyond the end. Next (line 64) it checks if the request does not extend beyond the end of the disk. Last (line 65) it checks to see if the request is a read request.

If the request starts before or at the end of the RAM disk *and either* does not extend beyond the end of the disk *or* is a read request, then line 67 is executed.

If the request starts beyond the end of the RAM disk, or extends beyond the end of the disk and is not a read request, then it is an error and lines 78 through 82 are executed.

Line 67 checks to see if the request extends beyond the end of the disk, and if so, adjusts the read to end with the last block of the (RAM) disk. (We know that this is a read because if it had been a write request that extended beyond the end of the disk we would not have got past lines 64 and 65.)

Line 69 computes the number of blocks until the end of the disk, line 70 determines how many bytes that were requested are beyond the end of the disk and therefore cannot be read, and line 71 sets b_count to the number of bytes that can actually be read.

Line 74 is executed if the request—read or write—does not extend beyond the end of the disk. This clears *b_resid* to indicate a successful transfer.

If the tests on lines 63-65 fail, we mark the request as being in error (lines 78-80), indicate to the kernel that the request is complete (line 81), and return (line 82).

We now know the request is valid and that the request has been modified if necessary to ensure that it does not extend beyond the end of the RAM disk.

```
84      if (a read request)
85          copy data from RAM disk to buffer cache
86      else
87          copy data from buffer cache to RAM disk
88      report that the I/O request has been completed
```

```
84      if (bp->b_flags & B_READ)
85          bcopy(ramptr + blknotob(bp->b_blkno), paddr(bp),
                bp->b_bcount);
86      else
87          bcopy(paddr(bp), ramptr + blknotob(bp->b_blkno),
                bp->b_bcount);
88      iodone(bp);
89  }
```

If the request is a read (tested in line 84), then we call the kernel routine *bcopy* (line 85) to copy the data from the RAM disk to the buffer. The address of the first byte to copy from the RAM disk is obtained by taking the pointer to the memory allocated and adding the offset to the first byte of the desired block (obtained by converting b_blkno into bytes using the macro defined in line 13).

The address of the kernel buffer is obtained by using the *paddr* macro defined in the header <sys/buffer.h>. Note that in spite of its name, paddr does not return a physical address but rather the kernel (virtual) address of the data area associated with the buffer header pointed to by *bp*.

On the other hand, if the request is a write, then the routine bcopy is called (line 87) to copy data from the buffer to the RAM disk. The arguments to bcopy are the same as in the previous call (just in a different order reflecting the different direction of the data transfer).

The Print Entry Point

The print entry point is called by the kernel whenever it detects a problem related to the driver. The driver merely has to report on the error passed it by the kernel.

```
90   ramdprint(dev_t dev, char *string)
91   {
92       cmn_err(CE_WARN, "Ramdisk error (dev %x): %s\n",
                 dev, string);
93   }
```

This print entry point uses the kernel-supplied routine *cmn_err* (a glorified *printf*) to report a warning message. The first argument to cmn_err is the severity of the warning while the remaining arguments are those expected by printf.

Summary

In this driver we saw for the first time the structure of a relatively complete block driver. This driver managed memory and emulated the functionality of a fixed disk drive. The result was a simple driver that exhibited many of the important functions of a disk device driver which could be used to store a UNIX file system.

We learned how to allocate and free memory, a technique that is frequently useful in drivers that wish to allocate buffers dynamically. By using sptalloc, drivers can allocate memory only when they need it, rather than statically declaring the space in the prologue and consuming memory even when the driver is not in use.

This driver also showed us how to handle I/O requests that attempt to access data beyond the end of the storage media. All disk drivers use code to validate and adjust requests that is similar to the code we studied in the strategy entry point to this driver.

As we continue examining block drivers in the next chapter , we shall see that a real hard-disk device driver which is several times the size of this driver, shares the same essential structure.

Exercises

1. One of the problems with this RAM disk driver is that the memory allocated is freed immediately after the device is closed. Modify the driver (a) to use the lower seven bits of the minor device number to specify the size and (b) to allocate the memory permanently if the most significant bit of the minor device is set. For example, minor device 7 would specify a temporary RAM disk 1Mb in size while minor device 143 would specify a permanent RAM disk 2Mb in size.

2. Modify this driver to permit up to eight RAM disks of varying sizes to be created and accessed at the same time.

Chapter 7

Block Drivers III: A SCSI Disk Driver

The time has come to examine a driver for a real block device. In this chapter we shall consider the driver for a SCSI fixed disk that is connected to the computer using an Adaptec 1542 Host Adapter.

SCSI disks are a nice example to use since they are relatively straightforward to control. Much of the low-level work is done by the disk controller, yet this driver illustrates all of the important aspects of disk drivers. The Adaptec is also a good adapter for this example since it hides many of the details of the SCSI bus protocol that are not germane to our discussion about UNIX device drivers. But even with these simplifications, this SCSI disk driver is four times the size of the previous RAM disk driver.

The Design Issues

The kernel/driver interface issues for this driver are no different from those encountered in the previous driver.

Although the internal operation of this driver is broadly similar to the RAM disk driver, it differs in the details because of the complexity of managing the host adapter and the SCSI disk.

The big difference between this and the RAM disk driver is the presence of an actual device. This driver has to concern itself with the driver/hardware interface. Recall that in Chapter 3 we discussed device registers at length. In this driver we will communicate with the host adapter using device registers in much the same manner as the previous drivers that controlled hardware.

In addition, however, this driver introduces the concept of *direct memory access* (DMA). DMA is the ability of the device to transfer data directly to and from main memory without the intervention of the CPU. In previous drivers we always copied data ourselves using routines like *copyout* or *bcopy*. In this chapter we shall see that with devices like the host adapter the driver can supply the address in memory and the device will transfer the data itself.

Although many devices support DMA transfer of data to and from main memory and disks, the unusual aspect of the Adaptec host adapter is that is also uses DMA to obtain control information describing the I/O requests.

The Device

The device this driver controls is an Adaptec 1542 Host Adapter. This controller card provides the interface between the computer and a SCSI bus. Up to seven devices can be attached to the SCSI bus. We shall assume that the only device on the SCSI bus is a disk drive that responds as logical unit 0.

The Adaptec controller is somewhat unusual in that it communicates with the driver through two mechanisms. Firstly, it provides a set of five registers (called "ports" in the Adaptec documentation) that are accessed using three different I/O addresses (see Figure 7-1 on the next page). Secondly, it has the ability to read and write main memory directly. During the initialization of the board, the driver sets aside memory to contain 'mailboxes' that are used to send messages to and from the host adapter.

FIGURE 7-1

CSP (R) (0x330)	Hard Reset	Soft Reset	Interrupt Reset	SCSI Bus Reset				
CSP (W) (0x330)	Self Test in Progress	Diagnostic Failure	Mailbox Initialisation	SCSI Adapter Idle	Cmd/Data Out Port Full	Data In Port Full		Invalid Command
CDATAIO (R) (0x331)	Command and Data Out Port							
CDATAIO (W) (0x331)	Data In Port							
INTR (0x332)	Any Interrupt				SCSI Reset Interrupt	Host Adapter Cmd Complete	MBO Empty Interrupt	MBI Full Interrupt

For example, when the driver wants to send a certain SCSI command to a device on the bus, it sets the appropriate values in a CCB (command and control block) to describe the command. See Figure 7-2 on the next page. It then writes the address of the CCB in the mailbox and sets a flag on the mailbox. Finally, it sends a command to the host adapter by writing to the command port telling it to check the mailbox(es).

The Adaptec reads the mailbox, copies the address of the CCB, clears the flag, and reads the CCB to determine the SCSI command to process.

Conversely, when the Adaptec host adapter has completed the SCSI command, it chooses an empty 'in' mailbox, stores the address of the CCB that contains the SCSI command that has just been completed, sets a flag in the mailbox, and sends an interrupt to the driver.

FIGURE 7-2

CCB Operation Code			
Target ID	Data Out	Data In	LUN
SCSI Command Length			
Reserved			
Data Length (MSB)			
Data Length (MID)			
Data Length (LSB)			
Data Pointer (MSB)			
Data Pointer (MID)			
Data Pointer (LSB)			
Link Pointer (MSB)			
Link Pointer (MID)			
Link Pointer (LSB)			
Command Length ID			
Host Status			
Target Status			
Reserved			
Reserved			
SCSI Command and Sense Data			

The driver then examines all of the 'in' mailboxes for ones with flags set and then examines the CCB to determine the status (success or failure) of the SCSI command.

To make things simpler in our example driver we only define one 'out' mailbox and one 'in' mailbox.

SCSI Devices

Although the primary concern of our driver is communicating with the host adapter, we also have to concern ourselves with the device(s) on the

SCSI bus, in our case a disk drive. In order to determine the SCSI commands that the disk will accept, we need to refer to the programmer's manual that applies to the disk. In order to determine the exact format of each SCSI command we must refer to the ANSI specification for the SCSI bus (ANSI specification X3.131). This document is available directly from the American National Standards Institute in New York and is essential reading for a programmer working with SCSI devices.

Although the SCSI specification defines many possible commands for disk devices, we only need to use three of them: *read*, *write*, and *get disk size*.

The Driver Prologue

The prologue for this driver is massive, over a third of the driver. This is not uncommon for drivers that control actual devices. The number of options, commands, and miscellaneous defines that are needed to control the hardware can be truly amazing.

In previous chapters we have presented the entire prologue prior to discussing it. In this case we shall break the prologue up into related sections and follow each with a short commentary. We have also kept the comments in the code both to clarify the code and to demonstrate the appropriate level of internal documentation for driver prologues.

```
 1   #include <sys/types.h>
 2   #include <sys/param.h>
 3   #include <sys/buf.h>
 4   #include <sys/iobuf.h>
 5   #include <sys/dir.h>
 7   #include <sys/user.h>
 8   #include <sys/errno.h>
 9   #include <sys/sysmacros.h>
10   #include <sys/cmn_err.h>

11   static char SCCSid[] = "@(#) SCSI Device Driver 1.00\n";

12   typedef unsigned char uchar_t;

13   #define spldev()        spl3()
```

```
14   #define IOBASE        0x330        /* adapter I/O addr */
15   #define CSP           (IOBASE)     /* cntrl/status port */
16   #define CDATAIO       (IOBASE+1)   /* cmd and data I/O */
17   #define INTR          (IOBASE+2)   /* intr flags (RO) */
```

The include files are the same as for the previous block driver. The *typedef* on line 12 gives us a shorter name to use when declaring variables and structure members of type *unsigned char*.

Line 13 assumes that this device will interrupt at level 3 and defines the processor level to use to protect critical sections (see Chapter 4 for a complete discussion of critical sections).

Lines 14 through 17 define the I/O addresses used to communicate with the Adaptec SCSI host adapter. Figure 7-1 graphically illustrates the device registers and the definitions of the individual bits in those registers.

```
18   #define CSPWHRST      0x80   /* hard reset */
19   #define CSPWSRST      0x40   /* soft reset */
20   #define CSPWIRST      0x20   /* interrupt reset */
21   #define CSPWSCRST     0x10   /* scsi bus reset */

22   #define CSPRSTST      0x80   /* self testing in progress */
23   #define CSPRDIAGF     0x40   /* internal diag failure */
24   #define CSPRINIT      0x20   /* mailbox init required */
25   #define CSPRIDLE      0x10   /* scsi adapter idle */
26   #define CSPRCDF       0x08   /* command/data (out) full */
27   #define CSPRDF        0x04   /* data (in) port full */
28   #define CSPRINVDCMD   0x01   /* invalid adapter command */

29   #define CMDNOP        0x00   /* No Operation */
30   #define CMDMBOXINIT   0x01   /* Mailbox initialisation */
31   #define CMDSTARTSCSI  0x02   /* Start SCSI Command */
32   #define CMDSTARTBIOS  0x03   /* Start PC/AT Bios Command */
33   #define CMDINQ        0x04   /* Adapter Inquiry */
34   #define CMDMBOXINTR   0x05   /* Enable MBO Avail Intr */
35   #define CMDSETSELTO   0x06   /* Set Selection Timeout */
36   #define CMDSETBUSON   0x07   /* Set Bus-On Time */
37   #define CMDSETBUSOFF  0x08   /* Set Bus-Off Time */
38   #define CMDSETXFERRT  0x09   /* Set Transfer Speed */
39   #define CMDRTNDEVS    0x0a   /* Return Installed Devices */
40   #define CMDRTNCONFIG  0x0b   /* Return Config Data */
```

```
41  #define CMDWRTFIFO   0x1c  /* Write Adapter FIFO */
42  #define CMDREADFIFO  0x1d  /* Read Adapter FIFO */
43  #define CMDECHO      0x1f  /* ECHO Command Data */

44  #define INTANY       0x80  /* any interrupt */
45  #define INTSCRD      0x08  /* SCSI Reset detected */
46  #define INTHACC      0x04  /* Adapter command complete */
47  #define INTMBOE      0x02  /* MBO empty */
48  #define INTMBIF      0x01  /* MBI full */
```

These defines (lines 18-48) provide somewhat self-documenting names for
each of the bits or commands that can be written (or read) from the
Adaptec's registers. The values (and in many cases the names) are
obtained from the hardware reference manual for the Adaptec controller.
Although many of these values are not used in the driver, it is common
practice to define all of the values during the initial design of the driver
just in case they might be used later.

The meaning of the four bits that can be written to the control port are
defined in lines 18-21. The seven different status bits that can be read
from the status port are defined in lines 22-28. The fifteen different commands that can be sent to the command port are defined in lines 29-43.
The five bits in the interrupt register are defined in lines 44-48.

```
49  #define SCSIDONE     1     /* MBI successful status */

50  #define G0READ       0x08  /* SCSI Group 0 Read Cmd */
51  #define G0WRITE      0x0a  /* SCSI Group 0 Write Cmd */
52  #define G1GETSZ      0x25  /* SCSI Group 1 GetSize Cmd */

53  #define DATAOUT      0x10  /* Data out on SCSI bus */
54  #define DATAIN       0x08  /* Data in on SCSI bus */

55  #define DMA2WSMR     0xd4  /* write single mask reg bit*/
56  #define DMA2WMR      0xd6  /* write mode register */
57  #define DMACLRMSK    0x00  /* clear mask bit */
58  #define DMACH5       0x01  /* DMA chan 5 (CH 1 chip 2) */
59  #define DMACASCADE   0xc0  /* DMA cascade mode */
```

SCSIDONE is the value that the Adaptec controller writes in the mailbox (to be discussed) when a SCSI command has completed. Lines 50-52 define the three different SCSI commands that this driver issues.

DATAOUT and DATAIN define the bits that are set in the CCB (see Figure 7-2) to indicate to the host adapter the anticipated direction of the data flow as a result of the SCSI command.

The DMA defines (lines 55-59) are used to initialize the DMA controller on the computer and will be discussed further when they are used in the driver.

```
60   struct mailbox
61   {
62     uchar_t  command;    /* adapter command or status */
63     uchar_t  ptr_msb;    /* CCB pointer, MSB */
64     uchar_t  ptr_mid;    /* CCB pointer, middle */
65     uchar_t  ptr_lsb;    /* CCB pointer, LSB */
66   };

67   struct capacity
68   {
69     uchar_t  lba_msb;    /* logical block address - MSB */
70     uchar_t  lba_nmsb;   /* lba - next most sig. byte */
71     uchar_t  lba_lmsb;   /* lba - least MSB */
72     uchar_t  lba_lsb;    /* lba - least significant byte */
73     uchar_t  bsz_msb;    /* block size - MSB */
74     uchar_t  bsz_nmsb;   /* block size - next MSB */
75     uchar_t  bsz_lmsb;   /* block size - least MSB */
76     uchar_t  bsz_lsb;    /* block size - LSB */
77   };
```

The mailbox structure (lines 60-66) defines the format of the four-byte mailbox used to communicate between the driver and the host adapter.

With SCSI disks it is possible to ask the driver itself how large the drive is (in blocks) and the size of each block (in bytes). The command used to obtain this information is the SCSI 'get size' command (see line 52). The *capacity* structure defines the format of the data that is returned from the disk drive when it receives this 'get size' command.

Note that the result is actually two four-byte (i.e., long) values. The values are stored from most-to-least-significant byte. If the C compiler used for this driver stored long values in the same most-to-least-significant byte order, then we could just declare the structure as shown below:

```
struct capacity
{
    long lba;
    long bsz;
};
```

There are two problems with this. Firstly, most compilers on 386 machines (the system used to test these examples) do not store data in the correct order. Secondly, writing code that depends on the byte order used by the system is not portable and less reliable than explicitly processing each byte in turn.

Therefore, we declare each byte of the two four-byte values explicitly (see lines 67-77). When we want to access the *lba* or *bsz* value, we have to put the bytes together in the appropriate order. The following code illustrates the technique:

```
lba = (diskinfo.lba_msb  << 24L) |
      (diskinfo.lba_nmsb << 16L) |
      (diskinfo.lba_lmsb <<  8L) |
       diskinfo.lba_lsb;

bsz = (diskinfo.bsz_msb  << 24L) |
      (diskinfo.bsz_nmsb << 16L) |
      (diskinfo.bsz_lmsb <<  8L) |
       diskinfo.bsz_lsb;
```

Each byte of the four-byte value is shifted to its appropriate position and *or*ed in with the other bytes to produce a 32-bit value.

```
78   struct group0
79   {
80     uchar_t  opcode;    /* SCSI operation code */
```

```
 81    uchar_t  lun_lba;   /* LUN + LBA */
 82    uchar_t  lba_mid;   /* more logical block address */
 83    uchar_t  lba_lsb;   /* more logical block address */
 84    uchar_t  length;    /* transfer length */
 85    uchar_t  misc;      /* miscellaneous bit fields */
 86    uchar_t  sense[14]; /* sense data from adapter */
 87  };

 88  struct group1
 89  {
 90    uchar_t  opcode;    /* SCSI operation code */
 91    uchar_t  lun;       /* logical unit number */
 92    uchar_t  lba_msb;   /* logical block address - MSB */
 93    uchar_t  lba_nmsb;  /* lba - next most sig. byte */
 94    uchar_t  lba_lmsb;  /* lba - least MSB */
 95    uchar_t  lba_lsb;   /* lba - least significant byte */
 96    uchar_t  pad;       /* reserved */
 97    uchar_t  len_msb;   /* transfer length (for I/O cmds) */
 98    uchar_t  len_lsb;   /* transfer length - LSB */
 99    uchar_t  misc;      /* miscellaneous bit fields */
100    uchar_t  sense[14]; /* sense data from adapter */
101  };

102  union scsi
103  {
104    struct group0 group0;
105    struct group1 group1;
106  };
```

Let us examine these declarations in reverse order. On lines 102-106 we
declare that a SCSI command is either a group 0 command or a group 1.
The structure of a group 0 command is defined on lines 78-86 and a group
1 command on lines 88-101. The primary differences between group 0 and
group 1 commands are the lengths of the logical block field and the transfer length field. With group 1 commands, a larger logical block and larger
transfer length may be referenced. Figure 7-3 illustrates the two forms of
the SCSI command.

FIGURE 7-3

SCSI Group 0 Command Descriptor Block	
Operation Code	
Logical Unit Number	Logical Block Address (MSB)
Logical Block Address	
Logical Block Address (LSB)	
Transfer Length	
Control Byte	

SCSI Group 1 Command Descriptor Block		
Operation Code		
Logical Unit Number	Reserved	RelAdr
Logical Block Address (MSB)		
Logical Block Address		
Logical Block Address		
Logical Block Address (LSB)		
Reserved		
Transfer Length (MSB)		
Transfer Length (LSB)		
Control Byte		

Many commands (such as read and write) have both group 0 and group 1 forms. Since our driver will never have to process requests for more than 256 blocks in a single request and, to make it simple, will never handle a disk with more than two million blocks (one gigabyte), we shall only issue group 0 read and write commands.

Some commands only have a group 1 form. The 'get size' command is such a command. Since we need to obtain the size of the disk in order to validate the I/O requests the driver will be handed, we must issue a 'get size' group 1 command during initialization. Hence we define the structure of a group 1 command.

```
107  struct ccb
108  {
```

```
109    uchar_t  opcode;      /* CCB Operation Code */
110    uchar_t  target;      /* target ID, Out/In, LUN */
111    uchar_t  scsi_length;  /* SCSI Command Length  */
112    uchar_t  pad1;        /* reserved byte */
113    uchar_t  dlen_msb;  /* data length */
114    uchar_t  dlen_mid;
115    uchar_t  dlen_lsb;
116    uchar_t  dptr_msb;  /* data pointer */
117    uchar_t  dptr_mid;
118    uchar_t  dptr_lsb;
119    uchar_t  lptr_msb;  /* link pointer */
120    uchar_t  lptr_mid;
121    uchar_t  lptr_lsb;
122    uchar_t  linkid;     /* command link ID */
123    uchar_t  hastat;     /* host status */
124    uchar_t  tarstat;    /* target status */
125    uchar_t  pad2;       /* reserved byte */
126    uchar_t  pad3;       /* reserved byte */
127    union  scsi scsi;   /* SCSI cmd block and sense bytes */
128    };
```

The command and control buffer is used to communicate most of the
information to and from the Adaptec controller. Figure 7-4 illustrates this
data structure.

As we shall see in the driver, commands are sent to SCSI devices by filling in the fields of the CCB structure and then handing the CCB to the
Adaptec host adapter. The documentation for the Adaptec controller
describes the contents of the various CCB fields in detail.

```
129    #define MBO  0      /* outgoing mailbox */
130    #define MBI  1      /* incoming mailbox */

131    static struct ccb ccbbuffer;        /* Cmd Control Blk */
132    static struct mailbox mbox[2];      /* mboxes (in+out) */
133    static long disksize;               /* Store disk size */

134    struct iobuf scsi_tab;              /* Buf list header */
135    static int present;

136    #define TRUE   1
137    #define FALSE  0
```

```
138   #define btoblkno(b)     (((b) + 511) >> 9)
139   #define blknotob(b)     ((b) << 9)
```

FIGURE 7-4

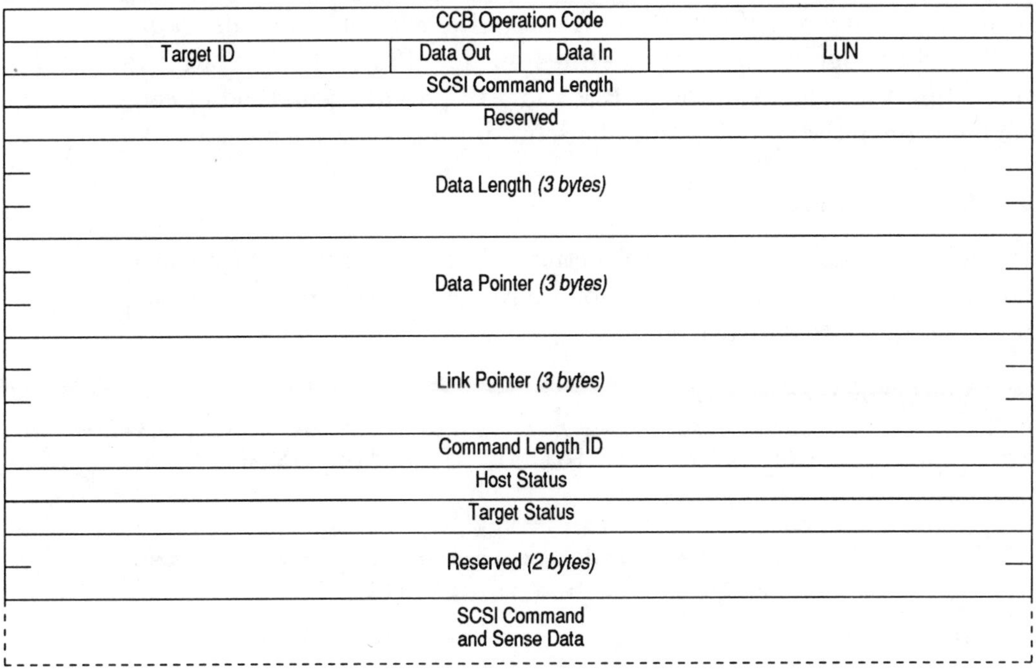

CCB Operation Code			
Target ID	Data Out	Data In	LUN
SCSI Command Length			
Reserved			
Data Length *(3 bytes)*			
Data Pointer *(3 bytes)*			
Link Pointer *(3 bytes)*			
Command Length ID			
Host Status			
Target Status			
Reserved *(2 bytes)*			
SCSI Command and Sense Data			

The method used to hand a CCB over to the Adaptec (and receive it when the Adaptec has finished with it) is to place the address of the CCB into an outgoing mailbox and set a flag indicating the mailbox is full. Similarly, when the Adaptec host adapter has completed processing a CCB, it will place the address of the CCB into an incoming mailbox and set a flag.

A driver may have many CCB structures and many mailboxes so that multiple requests may be passed to the Adaptec at one time. To simplify our driver, we have chosen to declare only one CCB structure and one pair of mailboxes (one incoming, one outgoing).

The defines on lines 129 and 130 indicate which mailbox is which. The single CCB structure is declared on line 131 and the pair of mailboxes on line 132. The variable *disksize* (line 133) will be used to store the size of the disk. The *iobuf* structure *scsi_tab* (line 134) will be used to maintain the queue of outstanding disk requests. The variable *present* (line 135) will be used to remember if a working Adaptec host adapter and disk were detected during boot. Finally, the defines on line 136 and 137 state the obvious, while the macros on lines 138 and 139 provide a method of converting between bytes and block numbers (assuming 512-byte blocks).

The Waitfor... Routines

The two *waitfor* routines are short functions that loop waiting for a specified bit in one of the Adaptec host adapter's registers to change from 0 to 1 (waitfor1) or from 1 to 0 (waitfor0).

```
140       waitfor0 routine:
142-144       spin until specified bit is clear or we lose patience
145           return TRUE only if bit is (finally) clear

147       waitfor1 routine:
149-151       spin until specified bit is set or we lose patience
152           return TRUE only if bit is (finally) clear
```

```
140   static int waitfor0(int ioaddr, int bit)
141   {
142     long i = 1000000;

143     while ((inb(ioaddr) & bit) && --i)
144         ;

145     return (i == 0);
146   }

147   static int waitfor1(int ioaddr, int bit)
148   {
149     long i = 1000000;

150     while (((inb(ioaddr) & bit) == 0) && --i)
151         ;
```

```
152     return (i == 0);
153  }
```

The code for these two routines is essentially the same so only the first will be discussed.

The loop on lines 143 and 144 is relatively straightforward. We merely spin until the value of the register at address *addr*, when masked with the bit pattern in *bit*, is not zero. To make sure we do not loop forever, we keep a counter that runs from 1,000,000 down to 0. The value must be this large so it will never reach 0 during the normal operation of the Adaptec controller. In this driver the value was chosen after using *printf*s in a test version of the driver to prove that the counter never normally dropped below 900,000 (on a 20MHz 386).

Be careful, however, when running this driver on a much faster CPU. In that situation the loop may execute so much faster that the counter reaches zero while the Adaptec is still functioning normally.

If the counter should reach 0, it is an indication that the hardware has malfunctioned and in this case the routine returns a non-zero value (indicating an error).

The Putbyte Routine

When writing commands or data to the host adapter's data port (register), it is first necessary to check the Command Data Full bit (see Figure 7-2) to see that it is clear (i.e., the data port is not full). If the bit is set, it indicates that the microprocessor on the host adapter has not yet had the opportunity to read the previously written byte.

This routine checks the bit, waits (if necessary) for it to clear, and writes a byte to the data port.

```
154  putbyte routine:
157      wait for 'data register full' flag to clear
         if (it never clears)
158          return error indication
159      put byte in data register
```

```
160     return indication of success
```

```
154  static int putbyte(byte)
155  uchar_t byte;
156  {
157    if (waitfor0(CSP, CSPRCDF))
158        return (TRUE);

159    outb(CDATAIO, byte);

160    return (FALSE);
161  }
```

Since the flag usually clears within a fraction of a millisecond, it is acceptable to loop waiting for the bit to clear. So in line 157 we call waitfor0 to check the appropriate bit in the CSP register. If waitfor0 spins one million times without the bit clearing, it returns a true (i.e., non-zero) value which is our signal to exit with an error (i.e., true) return value (line 158).

Otherwise everything is fine and we write out the byte (line 159) and return a false (i.e., success) value (line 160).

The Waitforhacc Routine

When the host adapter has finished processing a command that was sent to it (as opposed to a command sent to a device on the SCSI bus) it sets the 'host adapter command complete' bit in the interrupt register. If there is an error it also sets bits in the status port.

During the initialisation of the host adapter there are times when we want to wait for a command to complete rather than leaving the driver and waiting for an interrupt. To simplify this process we have written a routine *waitforhacc* (wait for host adapter command complete).

```
162  waitforhacc routine:
164      wait for host adapter command complete flag
166      if (error or other unexpected status)
168          print: error message on console
169          return error indication
171      return indication of success

162  static int waitforhacc()
```

```
163  {
164    if (waitfor1(INTR, INTHACC))
165        return (TRUE);

166    if ((inb(CSP) & (CSPRIDLE | CSPRINIT | CSPRINVDCMD)) !=
         CSPRIDLE)
167    {
168        printf("SCSI Adapter Command Failure\n");
169        return (TRUE);
170    }
171    return (FALSE);
172  }
```

The routine starts (line 164) by waiting for the host adapter command complete bit (INTHACC, see line 46 and Figure 7-1) to be set. It then checks (line 166) that of the three status bits idle, initialize, and invalid command, only idle is set. If initialize or invalid command is set, or if idle is not set, we have an error. This is reported on line 168 and we return with an error indication (line 169).

Otherwise, everything is fine and we return a value indicating success.

The Reporterr Routine

If an error occurs during the processing of a SCSI command, the host adapter will automatically query the device for details of the problem and place the response from the device in the sense array at the end of the CCB. The routine *reporterr* is used to display: the important registers from the host adapter; the status bytes from the mailboxes and CCB; and the sense bytes. This information can be used to diagnose the problem.

```
173  reporterr routine:
178      print: contents of key variables and registers
179-182  print: entire 14-byte sense array

173  static void reporterr(routine, sense)
174  char *routine;
175  uchar_t sense[];
176  {
177    int i;
```

```
178     printf("SCSI error(%s): %x %x %x %x %x %x\n", routine,
            inb(CSP), mbox[MBI].command, mbox[MBO].command,
            ccbbuffer.hastat, ccbbuffer.tarstat, inb(INTR));

179     printf("SENSE: ");
180     for (i = 0; i < 14; i ++)
181         printf("%x ", sense[i]);
182     printf("\n");
183   }
```

The Init Entry Point

The init routine is responsible for performing any device and driver initializations required when the system is first started (i.e., bootstrapped). In this case, we need to initialize the host adapter and verify that it passes its own self-diagnostic checks. That done, we then query the disk to determine its capacity. This not only allows us to verify that the disk is present and responding, it also provides us with information needed to validate future requests passed to this driver by the kernel.

```
184   scsiinit entry point:
189       raise processor priority thus disabling interrupts
190       issue a 'hardware reset command' to host adapter
191       wait for host adapter to reset
          if (host adapter does not reset within a reasonable time)
193-194       print an error message and return
196       if (host adapter self-diagnostic tests have failed)
198-199       print an error message and return
201       if (host adapter 'initialised' flag is not set)
203-204       print an error message and return

184   scsiinit()
185   {
186     paddr_t mboxaddr, ccbaddr;
187     int target, lun, data, error;
188     extern int getcapacity();

189     spldev();

190     outb(CSP, CSPWHRST);
```

```
191    if (waitfor0(CSP, CSPRSTST))
192    {
193        printf("SCSI Adapter Reset Timeout\n");
194        return;
195    }

196    if (inb(CSP) & CSPRDIAGF)
197    {
198        printf("SCSI Adapter Diagnostic Failure\n");
199        return;
200    }

201    if ((inb(CSP) & CSPRINIT) == 0)
202    {
203        printf("SCSI Adapter Initialisation Failure\n");
204        return;
205    }
```

To initialize the host adapter we send a "hard reset command" (lines 190 and 18) which will cause the adapter to initialize itself and all devices on the SCSI bus. It will also cause the adapter to perform a number of tests on itself.

On line 191 we loop waiting for the "self-test in progress" bit in the host adapter's status register to clear. The waitfor0 routine will loop until either the specified bit becomes 0 or a certain time has elapsed. If the time-out occurs waitfor0 will return a TRUE value. We then assume that the device has failed, report same, and leave the init entry point (lines 193 and 194).

When the self-test has completed, we check the "diagnostic failure" bit (line 196). If set, this indicates that the host adapter has detected a problem with itself. Again we report an error and exit the init entry point (lines 198-199).

Next we check the "mailbox initialization required" bit. This is an indication that the host adapter has successfully completed all of its initialization tasks and is ready to receive the physical address of the mailboxes that will be used to communicate between the driver and the host adapter. If this bit is not set then something has gone wrong with the adapter. Again we report an error and exit the init entry point (lines 203-204).

```
206        mboxaddr = physical address of mbox array
208        send 'mail box initialise' command to the host adapter
209        send the number of mailboxes available to the adapter
210-212    send the physical address of the mailboxes to the adapter
213        if (any error sending info OR
               host adapter command complete not detected)
215-216        print error message and return
```

```
206    mboxaddr = ktop(&mbox[0]);

207    error = 0;
208    error |= putbyte(CMDMBOXINIT);
209    error |= putbyte(1);
210    error |= putbyte((uchar_t)((mboxaddr >> 16) & 0xff));
211    error |= putbyte((uchar_t)((mboxaddr >> 8) & 0xff));
212    error |= putbyte((uchar_t)(mboxaddr & 0xff));

213    if (error || waitforhacc())
214    {
215        printf("SCSI Adapter Mailbox Init Failure\n");
216        return;
217    }
```

The manner in which the mailboxes are used to communicate between the driver and the adapter was discussed earlier when we examined the declaration of the mailboxes in the prologue. What we are concerned about here is the method of telling the host adapter where in memory the mailboxes are located so the adapter can read and write them directly.

The first step is to obtain the physical address of the mailbox array. We must pass the physical address to the adapter because when the adapter makes memory references it does so directly rather than through the memory management unit (MMU). Remember (see the discussion in Chapter 2) that all addresses from the CPU pass through the MMU which converts virtual addresses into physical addresses. Addresses of data structures within the kernel are called kernel addresses. The address of the mailbox array (*&mbox[0]*) is a kernel address. To convert this logical address into a physical address we use the kernel-supplied routine *ktop* (line 206).

The next step is to feed this physical address to the host adapter. We do this by sending a five-byte sequence to the adapter's data-in port. The first byte is the "mailbox initialization" command byte (lines 208 and 30). The second byte is the number of mailboxes available in each direction (line 209). In this driver we have simplified things somewhat by only having one mailbox in each direction. The final three bytes are the low 24-bits of the physical address of the mailbox array (lines 210-212), most-significant byte first.

Note that we use the putbyte routine to feed this data to the adapter. This routine, as previously discussed, handles the necessary handshaking to ensure that the data is not fed to the adapter faster than it can accept it. If the adapter refuses to accept the data, the putbyte routine will timeout and return a TRUE (i.e., error) value. Note that in lines 208 through 212 we *or* the return value with the variable *error*. As a result, if any putbyte returned TRUE, *error* will be true.

In line 213 we check to see if the *error* is true and if so, we report the error and exit the init entry point (lines 215 and 216). We also check to see if the "host adapter command complete" bit has been set by the adapter indicating the mailbox initialisation is complete. If not, the waitforhacc routine will return TRUE and we will also report an error and return.

```
218       send interrupt reset command to host adapter
219       obtain physical address of ccb buffer
220-222   write physical address in outgoing mailbox
223-225   initialise pointers used to maintain list of I/O requests
226-227   initialise computer's DMA controller chip on motherboard
228       call getcapacity to determine size of disk
          if (any problem reported by getcapacity)
229           return
230       flag the device as being present
```

```
218   outb(CSP, CSPWIRST);
```

```
219     ccbaddr = ktop(&ccbbuffer);
220     mbox[MBO].ptr_msb = ccbaddr >> 16;
221     mbox[MBO].ptr_mid = ccbaddr >> 8;
222     mbox[MBO].ptr_lsb = ccbaddr;

223     scsi_tab.b_actf = NULL;
224     scsi_tab.b_actl = NULL;
225     scsi_tab.b_active = 0;

226     outb(DMA2WMR, DMACASCADE | DMACH5);
227     outb(DMA2WSMR, DMACLRMSK | DMACH5);

228     if (getcapacity())
229         return;

230     present = TRUE;
231 }
```

Every time the host adapter completes a command, it generates a command complete interrupt. Although we are running with the processor priority raised, the adapter still attempts to signal the interrupt and we must clear the interrupt before proceeding (line 218).

We now initialize some of the data structures used in the driver. As discussed earlier, the mailboxes are used to communicate between the driver and the adapter. Each mailbox contains four bytes; the first is a flag indicating the mailbox is full; the remaining three bytes are the physical address of the command and control buffer (CCB) being transferred between the driver and the adapter.

Since our driver only uses one mailbox and one CCB, we can initialize the CCB address part of the outgoing (i.e., to the adapter) mailbox once during init time rather than every time when we use the mailbox (as would be required if we had more than one mailbox and/or CCB).

We use the *ktop* routine (line 219) to convert the kernel address of the CCB into a physical address. We then chop the address up into three bytes and place them in the appropriate parts of the mailbox (lines 220-222).

We set the pointers to the queue of outstanding requests to NULL indicating that the queue is empty (lines 223 and 224) and we zero the device active flag indicating that the device is currently idle (line 225).

Channel five (CH 5) of the second DMA controller should be set to cascade mode and the request mask cleared (lines 226 and 227). This initialises the controller to accept requests for bus-master DMA transfers from the host adapter on channel five. When we install the host adapter we must make sure that the jumpers on the board are also set to use channel five. The values used here were provided in the documentation supplied with the host adapter.

Finally, we call the *getcapacity* routine (line 229) to verify that there is a disk drive connected to the SCSI bus and to obtain the size of the drive (which will be used later to verify that I/O requests are valid). If the call to getcapacity returns without error, we set the present flag (line 230) to indicate that everything is working properly and that processes are to be permitted to open this device.

The Getcapacity Routine

The *getcapacity* routine is called once at boot time to determine the size of the disk that is attached to the SCSI bus. Since this routine is executed at boot time we can loop waiting for the disk to respond (instead of using interrupts).

Because of this, this routine makes a good example of how to send a simple SCSI command to the host adapter and on to the disk.

```
232  getcapacity routine:
239      raise processor priority thus disabling interrupts
240-264  build a ccb buffer that contains the SCSI 'get size' command

232  static int getcapacity()
233  {
234    long i;
235    paddr_t physaddr;
236    int x;
237    long blocksize;
238    struct capacity diskinfo;
```

```
239    x = spldev();
240    ccbbuffer.opcode = 0;
241    ccbbuffer.target = DATAIN;
242    ccbbuffer.scsi_length = 10;
243    ccbbuffer.dlen_msb = 0;
244    ccbbuffer.dlen_mid = 0;
245    ccbbuffer.dlen_lsb = 8;

246    physaddr = ktop(&diskinfo);
247    ccbbuffer.dptr_msb = (physaddr >> 16) & 0xff;
248    ccbbuffer.dptr_mid = (physaddr >> 8) & 0xff;
249    ccbbuffer.dptr_lsb = physaddr & 0xff;
250    ccbbuffer.lptr_msb = 0;
251    ccbbuffer.lptr_mid = 0;
252    ccbbuffer.lptr_lsb = 0;
253    ccbbuffer.linkid = 0;
254    ccbbuffer.hastat = 0;
255    ccbbuffer.tarstat = 0;

256    ccbbuffer.scsi.group1.opcode = G1GETSZ;
257    ccbbuffer.scsi.group1.lun = 0;
258    ccbbuffer.scsi.group1.lba_msb = 0;
259    ccbbuffer.scsi.group1.lba_nmsb = 0;
260    ccbbuffer.scsi.group1.lba_lmsb = 0;
261    ccbbuffer.scsi.group1.lba_lsb = 0;
262    ccbbuffer.scsi.group1.len_msb = 0;
263    ccbbuffer.scsi.group1.len_lsb = 0;
264    ccbbuffer.scsi.group1.misc = 0;
```

Firstly (line 239), we raise the processor priority so that any interrupts generated by the host adapter are ignored. Then we set the appropriate fields in the command and control block (CCB) (lines 240-263). The *opcode* is set to 0 indicating a SCSI command to be passed to a device on the bus. The *target* field is set to indicate the device we wish to reach is target id 0, logical unit 0; and the direction of data transfer will be from the device to the host adapter (i.e., 'in' as opposed to 'out'). The *scsi_length* field is set to 10 indicating a Group 1 SCSI command (a ten-byte command). The three bytes of the *dlen* field are set to 8 indicating that we are expecting eight bytes of data from the disk (i.e., the contents of the capacity structure).

In line 246 we obtain the physical address of the capacity structure (see line 67) by converting the kernel address (*&diskinfo*) to a physical address. This is necessary because we must tell the Adaptec the actual location in memory of the data structure that is to contain the data received from the disk driver. When the host adapter receives the data, it will transfer it directly to the diskinfo data structure using a mechanism known as bus-master direct memory access (DMA).

With DMA, data is transferred directly between memory and the device without the intervention of the CPU. With PC architecture machines there are two types of DMA. One uses the DMA controller that is present on the motherboard of every PC-type machine. The other relies on the intelligence within the controller board to perform the transfer. This latter method is referred to as bus-master DMA because the controller board takes control of the bus.

Since the host adapter is going to transfer data directly to memory, it needs to know the physical address of the memory that is to receive the data. (See the discussion on address spaces in Chapter 2.)

In lines 247-249 we chop the physical address up into three bytes and load them into the appropriate fields in the CCB. We then zero the link pointer (lines 250-252), the link id (line 253), the host adapter status (line 254), and the target status (line 255).

The remaining initializations involve setting up the SCSI command block itself (see Figure 7-3). The SCSI operation code for the *get size* operation (hex 25, see line 52) is placed in the first byte of the SCSI block. The remaining bytes are cleared. The *lun* field specifies the logical unit number (assuming our disk is LUN 0). The remaining fields are not used for a get size operation.

```
265-266    initialise computer's DMA controller chip on motherboard
267        raise flag on outgoing mailbox
268        send 'start SCSI' command to host adapter
273-275    spin until SCSI command is done or we lose patience
276        if (SCSI command not done)
278            call reporterr to report error
279            return error indication
```

```
281       clear incoming mailbox
282-283   assemble disk size and block size information
284       print disk size and block size information
285       if (block size is not 512)
287-288       print message and give up
290       reset interrupts on host adapter
291       restore processor priority
292       return with indication of success
```

```
265   outb(DMA2WMR, DMACASCADE | DMACH5);
266   outb(DMA2WSMR, DMACLRMSK | DMACH5);
```

```
267   mbox[MBO].command = 1;
268   if (putbyte(CMDSTARTSCSI))
269   {
270       printf("SCSI Adapter Command Start Failure\n");
271       return (TRUE);
272   }
```

```
273   i = 2000000;
274   while ((mbox[MBI].command == 0) && --i)
275       ;
```

```
276   if (mbox[MBI].command != SCSIDONE)
277   {
278       reporterr("getcapacity", ccbbuffer.scsi.group1.sense);
279       return (TRUE);
280   }
```

```
282   disksize = (diskinfo.lba_msb  << 24L) |
                 (diskinfo.lba_nmsb << 16L) |
                 (diskinfo.lba_lmsb <<  8L) |
                 diskinfo.lba_lsb;
```

```
283   blocksize = (diskinfo.bsz_msb  << 24L) |
                  (diskinfo.bsz_nmsb << 16L) |
                  (diskinfo.bsz_lmsb <<  8L) |
                  diskinfo.bsz_lsb;
```

```
284   printf("SCSI Disk size %ld blks, blk size %ld b.\n",
              disksize, blocksize);
```

```
285    if (blocksize != 512)
286    {
287        printf("ERROR! SCSI disk block size not 512.\n");
288        return (TRUE);
289    }

290    outb(CSP, CSPWIRST);
291    splx(x);
292    return (FALSE);
293  }
```

On lines 265 and 266 we initialize one of the DMA controller chips located on the motherboard. Although this host adapter uses bus-master DMA (i.e., the host adapter manages the transfer of data itself), it must request control of the bus (the connection between the host adapter and the main memory) from the DMA controller. This arbitration of possibly competing requests for control of the bus is done by the DMA controller chips. These two lines set up the DMA controller chip so that the host adapter may request (and obtain) control of the bus by asserting a request for DMA channel five. When this happens, the DMA controller chip will take the necessary steps to make sure no one else (including the CPU) can use the bus and then it will tell the host adapter to proceed with its DMA activity.

The actual values used here were provided by the Adaptec documentation.

In line 267 we set the flag on the mailbox indicating that a CCB is ready to be sent to the host adapter, and then signal (line 268) the host adapter to read all of its mailboxes—in this case one—looking for flags.

On lines 273 to 275 we loop waiting for the host adapter to raise a flag in the 'in' mailbox indicating that the command we have just sent has been processed.

On line 276 we check that the command completed successfully. If not, we call reporterr to dump diagnostic information on the console and report failure.

On lines 282 and 283 we take the eight bytes of data received from the disk in response to the get size command and convert them into two long-integers representing the number of blocks on the disk and the size of each block. This information is displayed on the console (line 284) and checked to ensure that the drive has been formatted with 512-byte blocks (lines 285-289) since our driver cannot handle blocks of any other size.

On line 290 any interrupts that may have been signalled are cleared. Remember we increased the processor priority on line 239 to ensure that we were not disturbed by any interrupts. Although we could not have been interrupted during this routine, we must clear any pending interrupts so that they do not occur when we lower the processor priority. We then lower the processor priority (line 291) and return a value indicating success (line 292).

The Open Entry Point

Our open entry point is very simple. We merely check to see if the host adapter and disk were detected during boot time and if not, return an error indicating that no device exists to open.

```
294   scsiopen(dev_t dev, int flags, int id)
295   {
296     if (!present)
297         u.u_error = ENXIO;
298   }
```

The present flag is set at the end of the init entry point (line 230) only if no problems were encountered during the initialization of the host adapter and the sizing of the disk. The ENXIO error is defined as "No such device or address" and is the standard error to return if the device does not exist (i.e., was not detected or successfully initialized at boot time).

The Strategy Entry Point

The strategy entry point is called by the kernel whenever it wishes to fill or empty a buffer. The entry point must check that the request is valid; place it in the queue of pending requests; and, if necessary send the next request to the device.

```
299   scsistrategy(struct buf *bp)
300   {
301      int minordev;
302      long lba;
303      long blkcnt;
304      short x;

305      if (minor(bp->b_dev) != 0)
306      {
307         u.u_error = ENXIO;
308         return;
309      }

310      blkcnt = btoblkno(bp->b_bcount);

311      if ((bp->b_blkno <= disksize) &&
312          ((bp->b_blkno + blkcnt <= disksize) ||
313           (bp->b_flags & B_READ)))
314      {
315         if (bp->b_blkno + blkcnt > disksize)
316         {
317            blkcnt = disksize - bp->b_blkno;
318            bp->b_resid = bp->b_bcount - blknotob(blkcnt);
319            bp->b_bcount = blknotob(blkcnt);
320         }
321      }
322      else
323      {
324         bp->b_flags |= B_ERROR;
325         bp->b_resid = bp->b_bcount;
326         iodone(bp);
327         return;
328      }
```

The first part of the strategy routine validates the request. Since code is exactly the same as that discussed at length in Chapter 6 the explanation is not repeated here.

```
329      raise processor priority thus disabling interrupts
330      set this request's 'next pointer' to null
         (preparing it to be the last of a linked list)
331      if (no requests on linked list)
```

333-334   set the pointers to the first and last item on list
               to point to this request
336   else
338   add this request to end of the linked list
339   set the pointer to the last item to point to this item
341   call scsiwork (to process the next request on the list)
342   restore the processor priority

```
329    x = spldev();
330    bp->av_forw = NULL;
331    if (scsi_tab.b_actf == NULL)
332    {
333        scsi_tab.b_actf = bp;
334        scsi_tab.b_actl = bp;
335    }
336    else
337    {
338        scsi_tab.b_actl->av_forw = bp;
339        scsi_tab.b_actl = bp;
340    }
341    scsiwork();
342    splx(x);
343    }
```

By line 329 we know the request is valid and we elevate the processor priority to prevent interrupts from the device from interfering with our manipulation of the request queue.

We now must add the request to the queue of outstanding requests. In our driver we take the simple approach of 'first-come, first-served' and add new requests to the end of the queue.

First set the 'next' pointer in the buffer header to NULL, indicating that this request is the last in the queue. Then check to see if the queue is empty (line 331). If so, add the request to the queue as the only request (lines 333 and 334). If not, add the request to the end of the queue. Note that *scsi_tab.b_actl* always points to the request at the end of the queue so that adding a new request is easy. Figure 7-5 illustrates these queue manipulations.

FIGURE 7-5

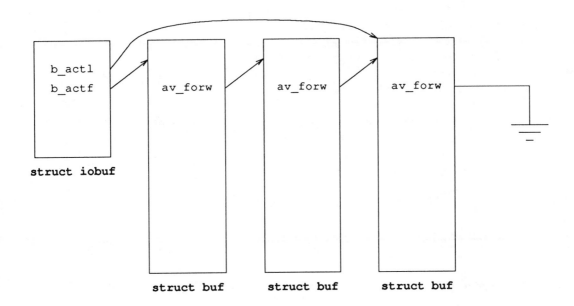

With the request added to the queue, we call *scsiwork* (line 344) to start the device on this request (if it is not already busy). Finally, we reset the processor priority (line 342) and exit.

The Scsiwork Routine

The *scsiwork* routine is called to make sure the device is busy. If it is not, then scsiwork takes the next request from the queue, converts it into a form that can be handled by the host adapter and disk, and passes it to the adapter.

This routine is called from two places within the driver: from the strategy entry point when a new request has been added to the queue and from the

interrupt handler when a request has been completed and the device is
idle.

```
344   scsiwork routine:
348       if (no I/O requests on linked list)
349           return
350       if (device is currently busy with another request)
351           return
352       if (outgoing mailbox is full)
353           return
```

```
344   static scsiwork()
345   {
346     register struct buf *bp;
347     paddr_t physaddr;

348     if ((bp = scsi_tab.b_actf) == NULL)
349         return;

350     if (scsi_tab.b_active)
351         return;

352     if (mbox[MBO].command != 0)
353         return;
```

The first check determines if there are any requests on the queue and if
not, exits immediately (lines 348-349). The next check sees if the device is
already busy with a request (line 350) and if so, exits (line 351). The last
check makes sure the outgoing mailbox is free (line 352-353).

The largest part of this routine analyzes the request at the head of the
queue (now pointed to by *bp*) and fills in the appropriate values in the
CCB.

```
354       if (request is a read)
356-357       set ccb buffer to perform a read
359       else
361-362       set ccb buffer to perform a write
```

```
354     if (bp->b_flags & B_READ)
355     {
```

```
356            ccbbuffer.target = DATAIN;
357            ccbbuffer.scsi.group0.opcode = G0READ;
358    }
359    else
360    {
361            ccbbuffer.target = DATAOUT;
362            ccbbuffer.scsi.group0.opcode = G0WRITE;
363    }
```

If the request is a read we set the data direction to 'IN' (line 356) and the
SCSI command to 'READ' (line 357). Otherwise we set the data direction
to 'OUT' (line 361) and the command to 'WRITE' (line 362).

364-365 set ccb buffer opcode and SCSI command length
366-368 set ccb buffer data transfer length
369-372 obtain physical address of data buffer and put in ccb buffer

```
364    ccbbuffer.opcode = 0;
365    ccbbuffer.scsi_length = 6;

366    ccbbuffer.dlen_msb = (bp->b_bcount >> 16) & 0xff;
367    ccbbuffer.dlen_mid = (bp->b_bcount >> 8) & 0xff;
368    ccbbuffer.dlen_lsb = bp->b_bcount & 0xff;

369    physaddr = vtop(paddr(bp), bp->b_proc);
370    ccbbuffer.dptr_msb = (physaddr >> 16) & 0xff;
371    ccbbuffer.dptr_mid = (physaddr >> 8) & 0xff;
372    ccbbuffer.dptr_lsb = physaddr & 0xff;
```

The adapter opcode is always 0 indicating a SCSI command to be sent to
the specified device (line 364). The command length is always six bytes
(all group 0 commands are six bytes in length—line 365). The length of
the data transfer is taken directly from the byte count field in the
request's buffer header (lines 366-368). The physical address of the data
buffer is obtained by converting the buffer's virtual address (obtained
using *paddr*) into a physical address using *vtop* (line 369). This is then
divided into three bytes and placed in the appropriate locations in the
CCB (lines 370-372).

In certain circumstances (discussed in the next chapter) the address of
the buffer (paddr(bp)) can be a user address rather than a kernel address.

Unlike ktop, which is restricted to kernel addresses only, vtop can handle user as well as kernel addresses.

```
373-378   complete initialisation of ccb buffer
379-381   place block number from request into SCSI command block
382       place size of request into SCSI command block
383       complete initialisation of ccb buffer.
```

```
373       ccbbuffer.lptr_msb = 0;
374       ccbbuffer.lptr_mid = 0;
375       ccbbuffer.lptr_lsb = 0;

376       ccbbuffer.linkid = 0;
377       ccbbuffer.hastat = 0;
378       ccbbuffer.tarstat = 0;

379       ccbbuffer.scsi.group0.lun_lba = (bp->b_blkno >> 16) & 0x1f;
380       ccbbuffer.scsi.group0.lba_mid = (bp->b_blkno >> 8) & 0xff;
381       ccbbuffer.scsi.group0.lba_lsb = bp->b_blkno & 0xff;

382       ccbbuffer.scsi.group0.length = blknotob(bp->b_bcount);
383       ccbbuffer.scsi.group0.misc = 0;
```

The link pointer and link id are not used and are always cleared (lines 373-376). The host adapter and target status flags are cleared so that any errors can be detected (lines 377-378). Finally, the remaining parts of the SCSI command itself are set up. The address of the start of the transfer is loaded in to the proper fields (lines 379-381) as is the length of the transfer in bytes (line 382). An unused field in the SCSI command block is then cleared (line 383).

```
384-385   initialise computer's DMA controller chip on motherboard
386       raise flag on outgoing mailbox
387       mark device as busy
388       send 'start SCSI' command to host adapter
```

```
384       outb(DMA2WMR, DMACASCADE | DMACH5);
385       outb(DMA2WSMR, DMACLRMSK | DMACH5);

386       mbox[MBO].command = 1;
387       scsi_tab.b_active++;
```

```
388    (void)putbyte(CMDSTARTSCSI);
389  }
```

The DMA controller is initialised to permit the host adapter to perform bus-master DMA transfers (lines 384 and 385). The mailbox flag is raised to indicate that it contains the (physical) address of a CCB that is to be read and processes by the adapter (line 386). The 'device active' flag is set (line 387) and the 'start SCSI' command is sent to the host adapter (line 388).

The adapter is now responsible for handling the request and will interrupt the CPU when it has finished with it. The driver exits the scsiwork routine at this point. When the interrupt occurs, the kernel will cause the *scsiintr* entry point to be executed.

The Intr Entry Point

The intr entry point is called by the system whenever the host adapter generates a hardware interrupt. This indicates that the adapter has completed a request. We need to check to: see if any errors occurred; remove the request from the queue of requests; mark the request as complete; and send the next request in the queue to the host adapter.

In our somewhat simplified driver, there can only be one request outstanding at a time so we know immediately which request has completed. In a production driver we might have dispatched more than one request to the host adapter and would have to check the mailbox to determine which request caused the interrupt.

```
390  intr entry point:
393      if (device was not active (i.e. interrupt not expected))
395-396      print message and return
398      clear flag marking device as busy
399      obtain pointer to current request
400      if (request not completed successfully)
402-404      mark request as failed
406      else
407          mark request as succeeded
408      take request off of the linked list of pending requests
409      notify kernel that request has been completed
```

```
410        clear incoming mailbox
411        call scsiwork (to process the next request on the list)
412        reset device interrupts
```

```
390  scsiintr(dev_t dev)
391  {
392    register struct buf *bp;

393    if (scsi_tab.b_active == 0)
394    {
395        printf("Spurious SCSI interrupt.\n");
396        return;
397    }
398    scsi_tab.b_active = 0;
399    bp = scsi_tab.b_actf;

400    if (mbox[MBI].command != SCSIDONE)
401    {
402        reporterr("scsiintr", ccbbuffer.scsi.group0.sense);
403        bp->b_error = B_ERROR;
404        bp->b_resid = bp->b_bcount;
405    }
406    else
407        bp->b_resid = 0;

408    scsi_tab.b_actf = bp->av_forw;
409    iodone(bp);
410    mbox[MBI].command = 0;

411    outb(CSP, CSPWIRST);
412    scsiwork();
413  }
```

We first check to see if the driver had marked the device as active (line 393). If not, then the interrupt cannot be related to this driver so we report an error and ignore it.

Otherwise, we clear the active flag (line 398) and obtain a pointer to the request that has just been completed (i.e., the request that caused the interrupt) (line 399).

We then check the incoming (from the adapter) mailbox to see if the command completed successfully (line 400). If not, we report the error by printing a message on the console (line 402) and set the appropriate fields in the buffer header to indicate an error (lines 403 and 404). Otherwise we clear the residual byte count to indicate that the entire transfer was completed without error (line 407).

The next step is to remove the completed request from the queue (line 408) and indicate to the kernel that the request has been completed (line 409). We clear the incoming mailbox flag (line 349) to indicate to the host adapter that it may be used again. Finally, we call scsiwork to handle the next request in the queue if any (line 411) and reset the interrupt (line 412).

Summary

Although this driver is roughly three times the size of any driver seen up until now, most of it is concerned with the details of managing the host adapter. The overall architecture is the same as for the RAM disk seen previously.

The design issues that were introduced in this chapter were related to the driver/hardware interface. In particular, we learned how DMA operates and saw how it can be used to transfer command information as well as data to and from memory and the device. Since DMA operates with physical addresses, we had to recall the discussions on memory spaces from Chapter 2. And we saw how we can use the *ktop* and *vtop* routines to convert from virtual addresses to physical addresses.

This chapter brings us to the end of our consideration of block drivers. Our study of block drivers from the simple test data generator in Chapter 5 to the full-blown disk driver presented in this chapter has covered all of the essentials of block drivers.

Special Note

On many systems the C compiler will introduce padding with the ccb structure that the adapter does not expect. Tp avoid this problem, compiler directives such as *#pragma pack (2)* may need to be added before the structure declarations.

Exercises

1. This driver assumes that the disk drive contains fewer than two million blocks. With the increasing availability of drives over one gigabyte in capacity, this is no longer a reasonable assumption. Rewrite the driver to use group 1 read and write commands whenever a request is received for a block beyond the limit of a group 0 command (i.e., with bp->b_blkno >= 2097152). The group 1 read command is 0x28 and the group 1 write command is 0x2a (c.f., lines 50 and 51 of the example driver).

2. As discussed in the introduction to this driver, the Adaptec host adapter can support multiple mailboxes. Modify this driver to declare eight 'in' mailboxes and eight 'out' mailboxes (and eight CCBs) and to be able to track up to eight simultaneous requests that have been passed to the host adapter.

Chapter 8

Character Drivers IV: The Raw Disk Driver

In the past few chapters we studied how the kernel passes requests to block drivers. As we saw, block drivers are normally used with storage devices (i.e., disk drives) that contain UNIX file systems. The block interface has been developed to work with the buffer cache, which in turn is used to support file systems.

Although the buffer cache and the block driver model is a particularly efficient method for managing file systems and handling the usual file I/O performed by applications programs, it can be less than optimal when one wishes to read or write many blocks of data sequentially on a disk. Instead of optimising I/O activity, the buffer cache merely forces an additional, unnecessary copy of the data.

Recall that one of the primary differences between character drivers and block drivers is that character drivers transfer data directly between the user's process and the device, while block drivers always transfer data between the buffer cache and the device. The kernel is responsible for the transfers between the user's process and the buffer cache.

What if we were to develop a character driver for a disk drive? Although we could not use the driver to mount the disk as a file system, we could use it to access the device directly. And for bulk data transfers (transfers of multiple blocks) this would be much faster than going through the buffer cache.

This is indeed what is frequently done with UNIX systems. A character driver is developed in addition to the block driver for disk devices. The character driver permits direct access to the device for bulk data transfers, while the block driver permits access by way of the buffer cache (thereby supporting file systems). Because the character driver bypasses the cache and permits the user's process to control the disk directly, the disk when accessed through the character driver is frequently referred to as the 'raw' device.

As we shall see in this chapter, developing a character driver for a device that has an existing block mode driver is trivial. The kernel provides routines to perform most of the tricky work, and the rest is done using the existing strategy routine from the block driver.

DMA and Character Drivers

There are a couple of complications that arise when we start considering DMA access directly to and from a user's process. Most UNIX systems use a form of memory management called *virtual memory*. This means that the kernel manipulates the memory management unit (MMU) in such a way as to make it appear to the user's process that it has access to more memory than it has actually been allocated. The contents of the memory not currently allocated is stored on disk.

When the process accesses memory that has not actually been allocated, the process is suspended, an area of memory is allocated, and the contents of the memory loaded from disk. The process is then started again and continues as if the accessed memory had always been present.

Similarly, when the kernel runs out of memory, it looks at all of the memory allocated to each of the processes and determines which parts can be copied back to disk and de-allocated. This technique is called *paging*.

Now consider the needs of a device that performs direct memory access (DMA), such as the host adapter studied in the previous chapter. When it transfers data from the disk to the computer, it is given the physical address of the memory and copies the data from the disk directly to memory bypassing the MMU.

There are two problems that can develop. One is that with systems that support virtual memory (such UNIX System V, Release 3) processes are not usually allocated contiguous memory. What the process sees as contiguous logical addresses may be scattered throughout physical memory (see Figure 8-1 on the next page).

What if the buffer that the user's process has allocated to receive the incoming data spans a page boundary (see Figure 8-2)? The host adapter will transfer the data using the physical address (since it does not go through the MMU) and will place some of the data in memory allocated to some other process!

Another problem occurs when the kernel decides that the block of memory containing the buffer is no longer needed by the process and pages it out to disk. In this case the memory that was allocated to the process is assigned to another process. And when the host adapter starts copying the data directly to the physical address it has been provided, it writes over memory now assigned to a process different from the process that actually initiated the I/O request.

Clearly neither of these situations can be permitted to occur.

These problems did not arise in our earlier drivers for two reasons. Firstly, the transfers always occurred at task time when the user's process was the current process and secondly, the copyin/copyout routines handle the problems of virtual memory transparently to the driver.

With character drivers that perform DMA, we must ask the kernel to make special arrangements to ensure that DMA transfers (a) do not cross page boundaries and (b) do not reference pages of memory that are not loaded.

FIGURE 8-1

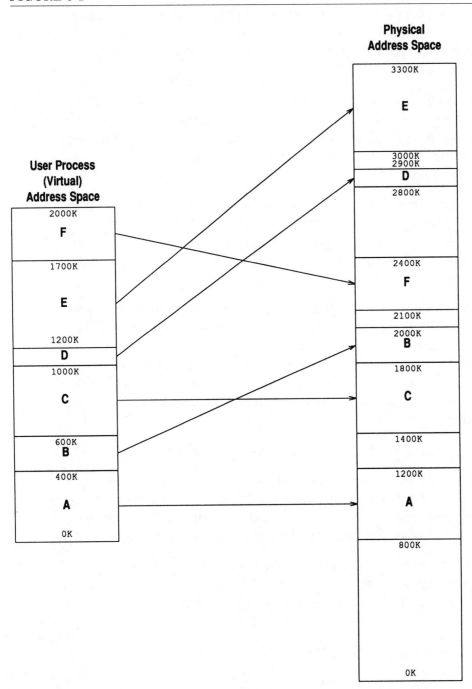

FIGURE 8-2

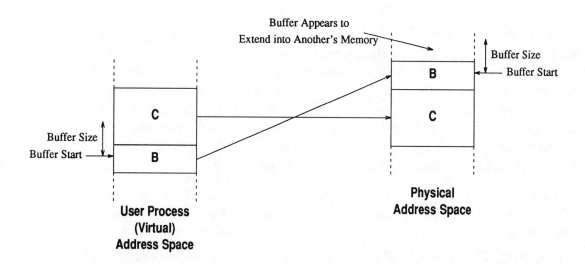

The General Structure

The general structure of all raw disk drivers is the same. The read and write routines call the kernel-supplied routine *physck* to validate the request and the routine *physio* (a) to ensure that the addressed memory is resident, (b) to convert the request into a block-type request by setting up a buffer header, and (c) to call the *strategy* entry point to perform the raw I/O, passing it a buffer header containing the details of the request.

```
xxread(dev)
dev_t dev;
{
    if (physck(xxdisksize, B_READ))
        physio(xxstrategy, NULL, dev, B_READ);
}

xxwrite(dev)
dev_t dev;
{
```

```
    if (physck(xxdisksize, B_WRITE))
        physio(xxstrategy, NULL, dev, B_WRITE);
}
```

The variable *xxdisksize* contains the number of 512-byte blocks on the disk and is used by physck to validate the request. The physio routine works by taking the request specified in the u.u_base, u.u_offset, and u.u_count variables and creating a buffer header that appears to make the same request. That is, the b_count field in the buffer header is set to u.u_count; the b_blkno field is set to u.u_offset after conversion to block numbers; and the pointer in the buffer header to the actual data area (i.e., paddr(bp)) is set up to point to the same place as u.u_base.

Physio then calls the specified strategy entry point to perform the actual I/O. As far as the strategy entry point is concerned the request appears the same as any other request from the kernel to empty or fill a buffer.

Physio performs a number of important functions in addition to obtaining and initialising the buffer header. It locks the referenced pages in memory so that they will not be paged out while the I/O request is being processed. It also breaks the request up if it should cross a page boundary or a 64K segment boundary. Some devices cannot perform DMA across a 64K segment boundary.

Special Considerations with Strategy Entry Points

With strategy routines that are only called to empty or fill buffers in the buffer cache, one need not be concerned with the b_count field, since it will always be for a single block (defined as BSIZE, usually 1Kb).

When we add a raw interface to the block driver and start calling strategy by way of physio, things change. The b_count field is set by physio and can be as large as the page size of the machine (usually 4Kb). Note that our SCSI and RAM disk drivers (covered in the previous two chapters) were designed to handle requests of any size, but the first block driver discussed cannot handle b_count values larger than 1K.

Another concern is that the memory address of the buffer (paddr(bp)) is now in a user address space rather than the kernel address space. This means that if the driver needs to obtain the physical address of the buffer, it must use *vtop* (which can handle user address space pointers) rather than *ktop* (which may not be able to in all cases). See line 369 of the SCSI disk driver in Chapter 7.

Exercises

1. Add a raw interface to each of the block drivers that has appeared earlier in this book.
2. Fix the block driver that appeared in Chapter 5 to handle requests with b_bcount larger than 1Kb properly.

Chapter 9

Terminal Drivers I: The COM1 Port

Terminal drivers are character drivers with attitude.

Although, strictly speaking, drivers for communications ports used to connect to user terminals are character drivers, there are a number of issues unique to these drivers that justifies discussing them as a separate category of beast.

Unlike almost any other type of driver, terminal drivers are responsible for a lot of the data processing. Most drivers only have to manage the flow of data to and from the device, leaving any processing to the kernel and the user process. Terminal drivers, on the other hand, must handle such things as the conversion of carriage returns to new lines, the conversion of tabs to spaces, the processing of erase and kill editing characters, and more. Fortunately, the kernel provides routines to perform most of the processing required of a terminal driver.

Line Disciplines

In early versions of UNIX the kernel provided one set of routines to assist terminal drivers with character processing. While this helped substantially, it meant that users were limited to one approach to terminal processing.

As UNIX evolved someone came up with the idea of collecting all of the routines related to terminal processing and referring to them as a *line discipline*. The system provides a standard line discipline and other systems programmers can add additional ones. Properly written terminal drivers merely reference the 'current' line discipline. In this manner it is possible to add other line disciplines without affecting existing drivers or line disciplines. We shall see in this driver how line disciplines are used.

TERMIO

The behavior of the general terminal interface including the standard line discipline is described in the UNIX reference manual under the heading *TERMIO* (terminal I/O). This section of the manual is required reading for anyone who wishes to develop or modify a terminal driver. It describes in detail all of the processing that must be performed by the terminal driver and the line discipline. Although much of the work required will be done by the line discipline code, it is still essential that the driver writer be familiar with the manner in which the processing is specified, even if he does not have to do it himself.

Casual readers of this chapter need not worry, however, as we shall describe those parts of TERMIO that are necessary for a cursory understanding of the driver discussed herein.

The Device

The communications ports that are used to connect terminals to UNIX systems use a form of data communications referred to as *asynchronous* serial communications. Asynchronous means that the data can be sent whenever it is ready to be transmitted without being synchronized to a clock signal. Serial means the data is sent one bit at a time (as opposed to parallel where eight or more bits of data are sent across eight or more wires, all in parallel).

Since UNIX systems deal with character information in units of bytes (eight bits), and serial communications requires the data to be sent a bit at a time; something has to take the byte and send it a bit at a time. Similarly, at the receiving end, something has to take the bits and collect them into a byte that can be handled by the computer. The chip that performs this job is usually referred to as a UART (universal asynchronous receiver/transmitter, pronounced "you-art").

The basic COM1 port on an industry-standard PC is nothing more than a UART and some support chips. Figure 9-1, shown on the next page, shows the layout of the registers of the 8250 UART which is the standard chip used for such COM ports.

The Driver

The Driver Prologue

The prologue for this driver is similar to ones we have seen for other drivers. The headers unique to terminal drivers are described below.

```
1    #include <sys/types.h>
2    #include <sys/param.h>
3    #include <sys/sysmacros.h>
4    #include <sys/dir.h>
5    #include <sys/signal.h>
6    #include <sys/user.h>
7    #include <sys/tty.h>
8    #include <sys/termio.h>
9    #include <sys/conf.h>
10   #include <sys/file.h>
11   #include <sys/errno.h>

12   static char SCCSid[]="@(#)COM1 Serial Device Driver 1.0\n";

13   #define TRUE     (1)
14   #define FALSE    (0)
```

FIGURE 9-1

Register	Bit 7	Bit 6	Bit 5	Bit 4	Bit 3	Bit 2	Bit 1	Bit 0
TXR (W) (0x3F8)	Transmit Data Port							
RXR (R) (0x3F8)	Received Data Port							
DIV LSB (W) (0x3F8)	LSB of Baud Rate Divisor							
DIV MSB (W) (0x3F9)	MSB of Baud Rate Divisor							
INTENB (W) (0x3F9)					Modem Status Change Channel 3	RX Status Change Int Enb	Transmitter Ready Int Enb	RX Data Ready Int Enb
IIR (R) (0x3FA)					Interrupt Identification Code			
LCR (W) (0x3FB)	Divisor Access Latch	Send Break Signal	Stuck Parity Enable	Even Parity	Parity Enable	Number of Stop Bits	Word Length	
MCR (W) (0x3FC)	Data Terminal Ready	Request to Send	Misc. Output Line 1	Misc. Output Line 2				
LSR (R) (0x3FD)		Transmitter Idle	Transmitter. Ready for Data	Break. Signal Detected	Framing Error	Parity Error	Data Overrun Error	Received Data Ready
MSR (W) (0x3FE)	Data Carrier Detect	Ring Indicate	Data Set Ready	Clear to Send	DCD has Changed	RI has Changed	DSR has Changed	CTS has Changed

The header file *<sys/termio.h>* (line 8) contains the definitions necessary to support the TERMIO commands. The other declarations (lines 12-14) are obvious and have been discussed in earlier drivers.

Now comes what can sometimes be the longest (and most boring) part of the driver, the definitions of the various device registers and their contents. We earlier described the structure of the COM1 port. These definitions describe in C what Figure 9-1 illustrated.

```
15   #define TXR      0x3F8    /* transmit reg (write, DLAB=0) */
16   #define RXR      0x3F8    /* receive reg (read, DLAB = 0) */
17   #define DIVLSB   0x3F8    /* divisor latch LSB (DLAB = 1) */
18   #define DIVMSB   0x3F9    /* divisor latch MSB (DLAB = 1) */
19   #define INTENB   0x3F9    /* interrupt enable (DLAB=0) */
20   #define IIR      0x3FA    /* interrupt identification reg */
21   #define LCR      0x3FB    /* line control register */
22   #define MCR      0x3FC    /* modem control register */
23   #define LSR      0x3FD    /* line status register */
24   #define MSR      0x3FE    /* modem status register */
```

Lines 15-24 define the address of each of the registers in the COM1 port. If we wanted to make the driver more useful, we would define these registers as offsets from a base address and then store a list of base addresses for the various communication ports we wished to support. This way, a single driver could handle many different COM ports. (See Exercise 2 at the end of this chapter.)

```
25   #define LCR5B    0x00    /* word length: 5 bits */
26   #define LCR6B    0x01    /* word length: 6 bits */
27   #define LCR7B    0x02    /* word length: 7 bits */
28   #define LCR8B    0x03    /* word length: 8 bits */
29   #define LCR1SB   0x00    /* stop bits: 1 */
30   #define LCR2SB   0x04    /* stop bits: 1.5 (for 5) or 2 */
31   #define LCRPEN   0x08    /* parity enable */
32   #define LCREVP   0x10    /* even parity */
33   #define LCRSTP   0x20    /* stuck parity, par=LCRSTP */
34   #define LCRBRK   0x40    /* set break */
35   #define LCRDLAB  0x80    /* divisor latch access (DLAB) */
```

Lines 25-35 define the bits of the line control register.

```
36   static short Divisors[] =
37   {
38        0, 2304, 1536, 1047, 857, 768, 576, 384,
39      192,   96,   64,   48,  24,  12,   6,   3
40   };
```

Lines 36-40 declare and initialize an array of divisors. These are the numbers that, when loaded in the divisor registers (*DIVLSB* and *DIVMSB*), will generate the proper clock signals for the various baud rates. The baud rates (in order) that ought to be supported are: 0, 50, 75, 110, 134, 150, 200, 300, 600, 1200, 1800, 2400, 4800, 9600, 19200, and 38400 (from <sys/termio.h>). The sixteen values in the *Divisors* array specify the values that will generate each of these 16 baud rates. The actual divisor values are obtained from the technical documentation for the COM1 port.

```
41   #define LSRDR   0x01    /* data ready (i.e. data in RXR) */
42   #define LSROER  0x02    /* overrun error */
43   #define LSRPER  0x04    /* parity error */
44   #define LSRFER  0x08    /* framing error */
45   #define LSRBI   0x10    /* break interrupt */
46   #define LSRTHRE 0x20    /* xmtr holding reg mt (TX rdy) */
47   #define LSRTSRE 0x40    /* xmtr shift reg mt (TX idle) */

48   #define IERRX   0x01    /* receiver data ready int enb */
49   #define IERTX   0x02    /* transmitter data ready int enb */
50   #define IERRST  0x04    /* receiver status interrupt enb */
51   #define IERMST  0x08    /* modem status interrupt */
```

Lines 41-47 define the line status register and lines 48-51 the interrupt enable register.

```
52   #define MCRDTR  0x01    /* data terminal ready */
53   #define MCRRTS  0x02    /* request to send */
54   #define MCROUT1 0x04    /* misc. modem control line 1 */
55   #define MCROUT2 0x08    /* misc. modem control line 2 */

56   #define MSRDCTS 0x01    /* delta CTS */
57   #define MSRDDSR 0x02    /* delta DSR */
58   #define MSRTERI 0x04    /* trailing edge ring indicator */
59   #define MSRDDCD 0x08    /* delta DCD */
60   #define MSRCTS  0x10    /* CTS status */
```

```
61   #define MSRDSR   0x20    /* DSR status */
62   #define MSRRI    0x40    /* RI status */
63   #define MSRDCD   0x80    /* DCD status */
```

Lines 52-55 define the modem control register and lines 56-63 define the modem status register. One quirk of most PC COM ports is that the OUT1 bit must be set to enable data to be transmitted. This is not always documented.

```
64   struct tty com1_tty[1]; /* tty structure for COM1 */

65   #define ON      (MCRDTR | MCRRTS | MCROUT1 | MCROUT2)
66   #define OFF     0x00

67   #define com1dcd()      (inb(MSR) & MSRDCD)
68   #define com1dtr(state)  outb(MCR, state)

69   #define spldev()     spltty()
```

Line 64 defines an array of tty structures. One of these structures is required for each communications port. The structure itself is defined in the header <sys/tty.h>. Since our driver supports only one port, we declare the array to have only one member. Obviously we could have just declared a single structure but by declaring it as an array of one the rest of the code will use array references that will better reflect the style of most terminals drivers (which usually control multiple ports). Lines 65 and 66 define the modem control bits to set to turn the port 'ON' and 'OFF'. Line 67 defines a trivial macro that returns TRUE if the data carrier detect (DCD) modem control signal is detected.

Line 68 defines a simple macro for setting the state of the data terminal ready (DTR) and related modem control lines. This macro is used with the defines on lines 65 and 66 (e.g., *com1dtr(ON)*).

Line 69 defines the CPU priority that this driver will operate at. *Spltty* is defined within the kernel as the priority at which all tty devices (and related kernel routines) may operate at without fear of being interrupted.

The Init Entry Point

```
70  com1init()
71  {
72      printf(&SCCSid[4]);
73      outb(INTENB, 0);
74  }
```

Our init entry point for this driver merely announces its presence (line 72) and then disables interrupts (line 73). A proper init routine would verify the existence of the COM1 port hardware. (See Exercise 1 at the end of this chapter.)

The Open Entry Point

The open entry point of a terminal driver is responsible for the following:

- verifying the minor device number;
- initializing the appropriate tty structure if the port is not already open or blocked waiting to open;
- waiting for the carrier detect modem control signal (if appropriate);
- invoking the open routine for the line discipline; and
- initializing the hardware.

```
75      open entry point:
81          if (minor device number != 0)
82-84           set error code and return

86          if (this port is not already open)
88-89           initialize the tty structure for this port
90              set the port's communication parameters

92          increase CPU priority thus disabling interrupts
93          enable the port's DTR signal
94          if (terminal is local OR DCD signal is present)
95              mark carrier as being present
96          else
97              mark carrier as not being present

98          if (device was opened without the no-delay flag)
99              while (carrier is not present)
```

```
101              mark device as waiting for carrier
102              go to sleep (waiting for carrier)

104      call line discipline code to complete open
105      enable device's interrupts
106      restore processor priority
```

```
75  com1open(dev, flag)
76  int dev, flag;
77  {
78      short x;
79      extern void com1proc();
80      extern void com1param();

81      if (minor(dev) != 0)
82      {
83          u.u_error = ENXIO;
84          return;
85      }

86      if (!(com1_tty[0].t_state & (ISOPEN | WOPEN)))
87      {
88          ttinit(&com1_tty[0]);
89          com1_tty[0].t_proc = com1proc;
90          com1param(dev);
91      }

92      x = spldev();
93      com1dtr(ON);


94      if ((com1_tty[0].t_cflag & CLOCAL) || com1dcd())
95          com1_tty[0].t_state |= CARR_ON;
96      else
97          com1_tty[0].t_state &= ~CARR_ON;

98      if (!(flag & FNDELAY))
99          while (!(com1_tty[0].t_state & CARR_ON))
100         {
101             com1_tty[0].t_state |= WOPEN;
102             sleep((caddr_t) &com1_tty[0], TTIPRI);
103         }
104     (*linesw[com1_tty[0].t_line].l_open)(&com1_tty[0]);
```

```
105        outb(INTENB, IERRX | IERTX | IERRST | IERMST);
106        splx(x);
107    }
```

On line 81 we check to see if the minor device number is valid and if not we set the error flag and return (lines 83 and 84).

We next check to see if this device is already open or waiting to open (line 86) and if not, we initialize the com1_tty structure using the kernel routine *ttinit* (lines 88 and 89) and call com1param to set the hardware parameters (baud rate, parity, etc.).

We then disable interrupts (line 92) and make sure the data terminal ready modem control signal is asserted (line 93).

Line 94 checks to see if this is a local terminal (i.e., modem control signals are to be ignored), or if data carrier detect is present. If either condition is true, we consider carrier to be on (line 95). If neither condition is true, then carrier is absent (line 97).

If the device has not been opened in "no delay" mode (line 98), then we wait until carrier is detected (lines 99-103). In detail, we check the carrier on flag (line 99) and loop until it is set. Within the loop we set a flag indicating we are waiting for carrier (line 101) and go to sleep (line 102). The wakeup that corresponds to this sleep is found on line 212.

Finally: we call the line discipline to perform any processing it wishes to do to complete the processing associated with the open (line 104); we enable all interrupts from the device (line 105); and we restore the processor priority (line 106).

The Close Entry Point

The close routine of a terminal driver is responsible for several things:

- if the HUPCL (hang up on close) flag is set, then the driver must drop the data terminal ready (DTR) modem control signal (which will cause the modem to hang up the line);
- the line disciplines close routine must be invoked; and
- the hardware must be shut down (i.e., interrupts disabled).

```
108   close entry point:
111       if ('hang up on close' flag is set)
113           drop the DTR signal (will cause modem to hang up line)
114           delay for two seconds to make sure line is hung up
116       call line discipline to perform processing related to close
117       disable device's interrupts
```

```
108   com1close(dev)
109   int dev;
110   {
111       if (com1_tty[0].t_cflag & HUPCL)
112       {
113           com1dtr(OFF);
114           delay(2 * HZ);
115       }
116       (*linesw[com1_tty[0].t_line].l_close)(&com1_tty[0]);
117       outb(INTENB, 0);
118   }
```

On line 111 we check to see if the hang up on close flag (HUPCL) has been set. If so, we turn the data terminal ready (DTR) modem control signal off (line 113) and delay for two seconds (line 114). The delay is necessary since it is possible that on a fast machine the *init* process could spawn a new *getty* on the terminal line quickly enough that the modem would not see DTR drop for long enough to cause it to hang up the phone.

The line discipline's close routine is invoked on line 116 to handle the cleaning up of the buffers and finally we disable interrupts on line 117, effectively shutting down the hardware.

The Read and Write Entry Points

As we have seen in previous drivers, the *read* and *write* entry points are called to manage the transfer of data to and from the driver. In terminal drivers this task is handled entirely by the line disciplines and hence the read and write entry points collapse into single-line routines.

```
119   com1read(dev)
120   int dev;
121   {
122       (*linesw[com1_tty[0].t_line].l_read)(&com1_tty[0]);
```

```
123  }

124  com1write(dev)
125  int dev;
126  {
127      (*linesw[com1_tty[0].t_line].l_write)(&com1_tty[0]);
128  }
```

The Ioctl Entry Point

The ioctl entry point is responsible for handling ioctl requests from the user processes. In terminal drivers this task is handled entirely by a kernel-supplied routine (*ttiocom*).

```
129  com1ioctl(dev, cmd, arg, mode)
130  int dev, cmd, mode;
131  faddr_t arg;
132  {
133      extern void com1param();

134      if (ttiocom(&com1_tty[0], cmd, arg, mode))
135          com1param(dev);
136  }
```

On line 134 we call ttiocom to perform the processing of the ioctl request. If changes to the hardware parameters are called for, ttiocom returns *true* and we call com1param to reset the hardware.

The Com1param Routine

Almost every terminal driver has an *xx*param routine that is responsible for setting the hardware parameters. The communication parameters that are usually handled by the hardware are stored in the *t_cflag* member of the tty structure for this port. The *xx*param routine must examine the flags of interest and set the hardware appropriately.

```
137  com1param routine:

142      if (parity is enabled)
143          if (odd parity is requested)
144              set parity enable bit (odd is default) in lcr
```

```
145          else
146               set parity enable and even parity bits in lcr

147          switch (based on number of data bits (5, 6, 7 or 8))
148-161          set the number of bits appropriately in lcr

162          if (two stop bits requested)
163               set two stop bits in lcr

164          increase CPU priority thus disabling interrupts
165          call the proc routine to suspend output
166          write lcr to the device's line control register
             enable the 'divisor latch access bit'
168-170      set the two divisor registers based on requested baud rate
171          clear the 'divisor latch access bit'
172          enable the modem control signals
173          enable interrupts
174          call the proc routine to resume output
175          restore processor priority
```

```
137  static void com1param(dev)
138  int dev;
139  {
140      register short lcr = 0;
141      int x;

142      if (com1_tty[0].t_cflag & PARENB)
143          if (com1_tty[0].t_cflag & PARODD)
144              lcr = LCRPEN;
145          else
146              lcr = LCRPEN | LCREVP;

147      switch (com1_tty[0].t_cflag & CSIZE)
148      {
149      case CS5:
150          lcr |= LCR5B;
151          break;
152      case CS6:
153          lcr |= LCR6B;
154          break;
155      case CS7:
156          lcr |= LCR7B;
```

```
157              break;
158         case CS8:
159              lcr |= LCR8B;
160              break;
161         }

162         if (com1_tty[0].t_cflag & CSTOPB)
163              lcr |= LCR2SB;

164         x = spldev();

165         (*(com1_tty[0].t_proc))(&com1_tty[0], T_SUSPEND);

166         outb(LCR, lcr | LCRDLAB);
167         outb(DIVLSB,
168                  Divisors[com1_tty[0].t_cflag & CBAUD] & 0xff);
169         outb(DIVMSB,
170                  (Divisors[com1_tty[0].t_cflag & CBAUD] >> 8) &
                     0xff);
171         outb(LCR, lcr);
172         outb(MCR, ON);
173         outb(INTENB, IERRX | IERTX | IERRST | IERMST);

174         (*(com1_tty[0].t_proc))(&com1_tty[0], T_RESUME);

175         splx(x);
176    }
```

The first part of this routine is involved in examining specific bits in the
t_cflag member and setting the appropriate bits in the variable *lcr* which
will eventually be written to the line control register of the UART.

Lines 142-146 handle parity, lines 147-161 handle character size, and
lines 162-163 handle the number of stop bits. On lines 164 and 165 we
disable interrupts and output to ensure that the hardware is not touched
while we reset the parameters. On line 166 we load the new line control
register parameters and set the divisor latch access bit. The DLAB bit
enables us to load new values into the baud rate divisor register, which is
done on lines 167-170. Note that we take the baud rate value (a number
from 0 to 15) from t_cflag and use it as an index into the *Divisors* array
(see line 36) to obtain the proper value to place in the divisor register.

Because the divisor is a 16-bit value and the device registers are only 8 bits wide, we have to chop the divisor value up into its high and low bytes and load them separately.

On line 171 we clear the DLAB bit, on line 172 we enable the modem control signals, on line 173 we enable interrupts, and on lines 174 and 175 we re-enable output and lower the processor priority so that interrupts can be fielded.

The Intr Entry Point

With most terminal communication devices, interrupts can be caused by several events:

- a character has been received;
- a character has been sent and the transmit buffer is empty (and available for the next character to be sent); and
- a modem control line has changed state.

In this interrupt handling routine we first interrogate the device to determine the cause of the interrupt and then we branch to one of three routines to handle the interrupt. Since more than one interrupt can occur at the same time, we loop until the device indicates we have responded to all pending interrupts.

```
177   com1intr(vec)
178   int vec;
179   {
180       register int interrupt;
181       extern void com1rxintr();
182       extern void com1txintr();
183       extern void com1mdintr();

184       while ((interrupt = inb(IIR)) != 1)
185           switch (interrupt)
186           {
187           case 0x04:
188           case 0x06:
189               com1rxintr();
190               break;
```

```
191          case 0x2:
192              com1txintr();
193              break;
194          case 0x0:
195              com1mdintr();
196              break;
197          default:
198              printf("Unidentified flying interrupt.\n");
199          }
200  }
```

We first (line 184) read the contents of the interrupt identification register (IIR). This tells us what caused the interrupt. We then branch to one of three interrupt handling routines based on this value (line 185).

Note that all of this code is enclosed in a loop (see line 184) that continues until the IIR indicates that all interrupts have been processed.

The Com1mdintr Routine

The com1mdintr routine is called when the com1intr routine has determined that an interrupt has been caused by a change in one of the modem control lines. This is usually caused by the data carrier detect (DCD) line turning on or off.

```
201  com1mdintr routine:

205  if (port is local (i.e. ignore modem control signals)
206      return

207  if (we are waiting for the DCD signal)
209      if (the DCD signal is now present)
211          mark carrier as being present
212          wakeup everyone waiting for carrier
215  else if (port is currently open)
217      if (the DCD signal is now present)
218          mark carrier as being present
219      else (if carrier was present)
221          send everyone in this process group a hang-up signal
222          turn the DTR signal off (i.e. hang-up the modem)
223          flush the read and write queues
224          mark carrier as not being present
```

```
201   static void com1mdintr()
202   {
203       register short dcd;

204       dcd = com1dcd();

205       if (com1_tty[0].t_cflag & CLOCAL)
206           return;

207       if (com1_tty[0].t_state & WOPEN)
208       {
209           if (dcd)
210           {
211               com1_tty[0].t_state |= CARR_ON;
212               wakeup((caddr_t) &com1_tty[0]);
213           }
214       }
215       else if (com1_tty[0].t_state & ISOPEN)
216       {
217           if (dcd)
218               com1_tty[0].t_state |= CARR_ON;
219           else if (com1_tty[0].t_state & CARR_ON)
220           {
221               signal(com1_tty[0].t_pgrp, SIGHUP);
222               com1dtr(OFF);
223               ttyflush(&com1_tty[0], FREAD | FWRITE);
224               com1_tty[0].t_state &= ~CARR_ON;
225           }
226       }
227   }
```

On line 204 we get the current status of the DCD line. We then check to see if this line is local (line 205) in which case we do not care about the state of the modem control lines. Otherwise we check (line 207) to see if we are waiting to open the device (i.e., are waiting for DCD). If we were, and DCD is now on (line 209), we set the carrier detect flag (line 211) in the tty state variable (t_state) and wake up (line 212) any processes waiting for DCD (see line 102).

Otherwise, if this device has already been opened (line 215) and we have now lost DCD (line 219), we must handle the orderly shutting down of the device.

On line 221 we send a hang-up signal to all processes in the process group associated with this terminal. We then turn off the DTR signal (line 222), flush the buffers (line 223), and clear the carrier detect flag in the tty state variable.

Usually the hang up signal will cause all processes that have this device open to terminate, thus forcing a close of the device.

The Com1rxintr Routine

The receive-interrupt handler is responsible for taking the received character from the device and performing the preliminary processing prior to handing the character over to the line discipline for further processing.

```
228   com1rxintr routine:

236        while (there is still data in the device to be read)
238-239        read data and save it
240-244        if (no place to put the data)
242-243            report an error and return
245            if (7-bit mode is set)
246                strip the high bit from the read character
247            if (flow control is enabled)
249                if (output has been flow-controlled)
251                    if (received character is an X-ON OR
                                    any character may restart output)
252                        resume output
254                    else (received character is an X-OFF)
255                        suspend output

256            if (received character is either X-ON or X-OFF)
258                go to top of loop (line 236)

228   static  void com1rxintr(status)
229   short status;
230   {
231       register short iflag;
```

```
232          short ch7;
233          short data[3];
234          short ndata = 1;

235          iflag = com1_tty[0].t_iflag;

236          while ((status = inb(LSR)) & (LSRDR | LSRBI))
237          {
238              data[0] = inb(RXR) & 0xff;
239              ch7 = data[0] & 0x7f;

240              if (com1_tty[0].t_rbuf.c_ptr == NULL)
241              {
242                  printf("No COM1 receive buffer!\n");
243                  return;
244              }

245              if (com1_tty[0].t_iflag & ISTRIP)
246                  data[0] = ch7;

247              if (com1_tty[0].t_iflag & IXON)
248              {
249                  if (com1_tty[0].t_state & TTSTOP)
250                  {
251                      if ((ch7 == CSTART) ||
                             (com1_tty[0].t_iflag & IXANY))
252                          (*com1_tty[0].t_proc)(&com1_tty[0], T_RESUME);
253                  }
254                  else if (ch7 == CSTOP)
255                      (*com1_tty[0].t_proc)(&com1_tty[0], T_SUSPEND);

256                  if ((ch7 == CSTART) || (ch7 == CSTOP))
257                      continue;
258              }
```

Since we will be referring to *t_iflag* frequently, we make a copy of it in a register variable (line 235). We then embark on a loop (line 236) that encompasses the entire routine. The loop continues as long as the line status register indicates that data is ready (LSRDR) or that a break interrupt has been received (LSRBI).

On line 238 we take the character from the receive register and immediately make a copy of it, masking out the lower seven bits (for reasons that will become obvious). On line 240 we check to make sure we have a clist buffer in which to put the incoming data. On line 245 we check to see if the ISTRIP bit is set indicating that the eighth bit of all received data is to be stripped off. If so, we replace the received character with the "stripped" copy we made earlier (line 246).

Lines 248 through 259 handle flow control and are executed only if flow control is enabled (line 247). If flow control is enabled and output has been stopped (line 249) and the received character is the start character or the IXANY flag is set (line 251) (which indicates any received character ought to restart output), then output is resumed (line 252).

Otherwise, if output is not stopped and the received character is the stop character (line 254), then we stop output (line 255).

In any case, whenever flow control is enabled we discard any start or stop characters that are received (lines 256 and 257).

```
259          if (break interrupt was detected)
261               if (break interrupts are to be ignored)
262                    go to top of loop (line 236)
263               if (break interrupts are to cause a BREAK signal)
265                    call line discipline to handle
266                    go to top of loop (line 236)

269          if (parity checking is turned off)
270               clear the parity error bit from the status

271          if (status indicates parity, framing, or overrun error)
273               if ('ignore characters with errors' is set)
274                    go to top of loop (line 236)
275          if ('mark parity errors' is set)
276-280          mark character by prepending with 0xff and 0x00
282          else if ('mark parity errors' is set AND char is 0xff)
283-286          mark character by prepending with 0xff

287-292      place char (and marks, if any) in temporary read buffer
                  and pass to line discipline
```

```
259            if (status & LSRBI)
260            {
261                if (com1_tty[0].t_iflag & IGNBRK)
262                    continue;
263                else if (com1_tty[0].t_iflag & BRKINT)
264                {
265                    (*linesw[com1_tty[0].t_line].l_input)
                                (&com1_tty[0], L_BREAK);
266                    continue;
267                }
268            }

269        if (!(com1_tty[0].t_iflag & INPCK))
270            status &= ~LSRPER;
271        if (status & (LSRPER | LSRFER | LSROER))
272        {
273            if (com1_tty[0].t_iflag & IGNPAR)
274                continue;

275            if (com1_tty[0].t_iflag & PARMRK)
276            {
277                data[1] = 0;
278                data[2] = 0xff;
279                ndata = 3;
280            }
281        }
282        else if ((com1_tty[0].t_iflag & PARMRK) &&
                    (data[0] == 0xff))
283        {
284            data[1] = 0xff;
285            ndata = 2;
286        }

287        while (ndata)
288        {
289            *com1_tty[0].t_rbuf.c_ptr = data[--ndata];
290            com1_tty[0].t_rbuf.c_count--;
291            (*linesw[com1_tty[0].t_line].l_input)
                        (&com1_tty[0], L_BUF);
292        }
293    }
294 }
```

On line 259 we check to see if a break has been received. If so, we see if breaks are to be ignored (line 261) or if breaks are to cause a signal to be generated (line 263). In the former case, we continue the loop, thus ignoring the break (line 262). In the latter case, we call the line discipline routine to handle the break (line 265).

The last thing we handle before passing on the data to the line discipline are parity errors (lines 269 through 286). If parity checking on incoming characters is disabled (line 269), we clear any parity error bits from the status.

Otherwise, we check (line 271) to see if an error was detected. (We actually consider of parity, framing, or overrun errors to be 'parity' errors.) If there has been an error with this received character then we check to see if we ought to ignore it (lines 273-274) or mark it (lines 275-280). Marking a parity error involves adding the characters 0xff and 0x00 immediately before the character in error. Note that the data array is read out in reverse order so that the 0x00 and 0xff will appear before the received character.

If no error was detected but parity marking is enabled (line 282) and the received character is 0xff, we must insert a duplicate 0xff in the data stream so that the single 0xff is not mistaken for a parity error marker (lines 284-285).

Finally, we transfer the character (and any parity markers) to the raw buffer (line 289) and call the line discipline routine to further process the input (line 291).

The Com1txintr Routine

The transmit interrupt handler for a terminal device is responsible for handling the front-line flow control tasks as well as informing the proc routine that more data can be output to the device.

```
295  com1txintr routine:
297      if (waiting to send X-ON)
299          mark device as busy
300          send X-ON
301          clear 'waiting to send X-ON' flag
```

```
303         else if (waiting to send X-OFF)
305             mark device as busy
306             send X-OFF
307             clear 'waiting to send X-OFF' flag
309         else
311             clear busy flag
312             call proc routine to send more output to the device
```

```
295  static void com1txintr()
296  {
297      if (com1_tty[0].t_state & TTXON)
298      {
299          com1_tty[0].t_state |= BUSY;
300          outb(TXR, CSTART);
301          com1_tty[0].t_state &= ~TTXON;
302      }
303      else if (com1_tty[0].t_state & TTXOFF)
304      {
305          com1_tty[0].t_state |= BUSY;
306          outb(TXR, CSTOP);
307          com1_tty[0].t_state &= ~TTXOFF;
308      }
309      else
310      {
311          com1_tty[0].t_state &= ~BUSY;
312          com1proc(&com1_tty[0], T_OUTPUT);
313      }
314  }
```

We first check (line 297) to see if the TTXON flag is set indicating that we ought to send a START character to cause the far-end device to resume output. If so, we set the busy bit in the state variable (line 299), put a START character in the transmit register (line 300), and clear the TTXON bit from the state variable.

Otherwise, we check to see if the TTXOFF flag is set indicating that we must send a STOP character to cause the far-end device to stop its output. If so, we set the busy bit in the state variable (line 305), put a STOP character in the transmit register (line 306), and clear the TTXOFF bit from the state variable.

Finally, if none of the above two conditions hold, we clear the BUSY bit indicating that the device is ready to send more data and we call the *com1proc* routine to transfer more output to the device (line 312).

The Com1proc Routine

The proc routine is the do-it-all of a terminal driver. It is called both by the line discipline and other parts of the driver to handle various functions. The possible commands that the routine must handle are listed in the <sys/tty.h> header file.

The routine consists of two parts. The first part (lines 324 to 380) handles most of the commands. The second part (lines 381 to 402) handles any output that needs to be sent.

```
315   com1proc routine:

323       increase CPU priority thus disabling interrupts
324       switch (based on command passed to routine)

326        T_BREAK: (start sending a break)
327           start sending a break
328           set flag indicating a break is in progress
329           set a timeout to restart output in a quarter of a second
330           break out of switch statement

331        T_TIME: (stop sending a break)
332           clear flag indicating a break is in progress
333           stop sending a break
334           set flag indicating output may be sent to device
335           break out of switch statement

336        T_WFLUSH: (flush write buffers)
337-338       clear temporary output buffer
              (fall into the next case)

340        T_RESUME: (resume previously suspended output)
341           clear flag indicating output is suspended
              (fall into the next case)

343        T_OUTPUT: (send output to device)
```

344   **set flag indicating output is to be sent to device**
345   **break out of switch statement**

```
315   static void com1proc(tp, command)
316   register struct tty *tp;
317   int command;
318   {
319       register struct ccblock *ccp;
320       int flag = FALSE;
321       extern ttrstrt();
322       short x;

323       x = spldev();

324       switch (command)
325       {
326       case T_BREAK:
327           outb(LCR, inb(LCR) | LCRBRK);
328           tp->t_state |= TIMEOUT;
329           timeout(ttrstrt, tp, HZ/4);
330           break;

331       case T_TIME:
332           tp->t_state &= ~TIMEOUT;
333           outb(LCR, inb(LCR) & ~ LCRBRK);
334           flag = TRUE;
335           break;

336       case T_WFLUSH:
337           tp->t_tbuf.c_size -= tp->t_tbuf.c_count;
338           tp->t_tbuf.c_count = 0;
339           /* fall into next case */

340       case T_RESUME:
341           tp->t_state &= TTSTOP;
342           /* fall into next case */

343       case T_OUTPUT:
344           flag = TRUE;
345           break;
```

The first step after disabling interrupts (line 323) is to branch based on the received command (line 324).

The T_BREAK command causes a break signal to be transmitted. This is done by setting the break bit (LCRBRK) of the line control register (line 327), setting a flag indicating that we are waiting for a timeout to complete (line 328), and requesting timeout to call the routine *ttrstrt* in a quarter of a second. Ttrstrt will call the *proc* routine passing it the T_TIME command.

The T_TIME command (line 331) causes the driver to clear the TIMEOUT flag (line 332), clear the break bit in the line control register, and set the flag variable true indicating that normal output may proceed. In this manner, a break signal is sent for about 250 millseconds.

The T_WFLUSH command causes the output queues to be flushed. This is done by clearing the internal transmit buffer (lines 337-338) and falling into the code for the T_RESUME command.

The T_RESUME command causes the driver to resume output that may have been previously suspended. The 'output is stopped' flag TTSTOP is cleared (line 342) and the code falls into the T_OUTPUT command.

The T_OUTPUT command (line 343) indicates that an attempt ought to be made to transfer data from the temporary transmit buffer to the device. All that is done here is the variable *flag* is set. This variable will be checked in the second part of the routine and will cause the driver to perform the actual output.

```
346        T_SUSPEND: (suspend transmission)
347            set flag indicating output is to be suspended
348            break out of switch statement

349        T_BLOCK: (send flow-control character to block input)
350            clear 'send X-ON' flag
351            set 'input is blocked' flag
352            if (device is busy)
353                set 'send X-OFF' flag
354            else
356                set 'device is busy' flag
```

```
357              transmit an X-OFF character
359          break out of switch statement

360      T_RFLUSH: (flush read queue)
361          if (input is not blocked)
362              break out of switch statement
             (else fall into next case)

364      T_UNBLOCK: (send flow-control character to unblock input)
365          clear 'input is blocked' and 'send X-OFF' flag
366          if (device is busy)
367              set 'send X-ON' flag
368          else
370              set 'device is busy' flag
371              transmit an X-ON character
373          break out of switch statement

374      T_PARM: (set device parameters)
375          call com1param routine
376          break out of switch statement

377      T_DISCONNECT: (disconnect from modem)
378          drop DTR signal
379          break out of switch statement

346      case T_SUSPEND:
347          tp->t_state |= TTSTOP;
348          break;

349      case T_BLOCK:
350          tp->t_state &= ~TTXON;
351          tp->t_state |= TBLOCK;
352          if (tp->t_state & BUSY)
353              tp->t_state |= TTXOFF;
354          else
355          {
356              tp->t_state |= BUSY;
357              outb(TXR, CSTOP);
358          }
359          break;

360      case T_RFLUSH:
```

```
361                if (!(tp->t_state & TBLOCK))
362                    break;
363                /* fall into next case */
364        case T_UNBLOCK:
365                tp->t_state &= ~(TTXOFF | TBLOCK);
366                if (tp->t_state & BUSY)
367                    tp->t_state |= TTXON;
368                else
369                {
370                    tp->t_state |= BUSY;
371                    outb(TXR, CSTART);
372                }
373                break;

374        case T_PARM:
375                com1param(0);
376                break;

377        case T_DISCONNECT:
378                com1dtr(OFF);
379                break;
380        }
```

The T_SUSPEND command causes the driver to suspend output (this is usually in response to a flow control request). All we do here is set the TTSTOP flag indicating that output is to be stopped (line 347). This flag will prevent the driver from transferring any more data to the device. It will also cause the receive interrupt handler to watch for START characters which indicate that output may be resumed (see lines 249-253).

The T_BLOCK command is a request to block (stop) input by sending a flow control character (X-OFF) to the terminal that is transmitting data to us. This command is called by the line discipline when (a) the receive buffers within the line discipline are about to overflow, and (b) the user has requested input flow control (the IXOFF bit in TERMIO).

We start (line 350) by clearing the flag that indicates that we are to send an X-ON when we get an opportunity (see lines 297-302). We then set a flag indicating that input is blocked (line 351) and check to see if the device is currently busy (line 352). If the device is busy, we set a flag (line

353) indicating that we are to send an X-OFF when we get an opportunity (see lines 303-308). If the device is idle, we mark the device as busy (line 356) and send the X-OFF character immediately (line 357).

The T_RFLUSH command is a request to flush the receive buffers. Since we do not buffer any data within the driver itself all we need do is check (line 361) to see if input is blocked. If so, we must re-enable it. We accomplish this by falling into the T_UNBLOCK command.

The T_UNBLOCK command causes the driver to restart input that was previously blocked (see lines 349-359). This is done by sending an X-ON flow-control character. We clear the flag that indicates input is blocked and the flag that indicates we are to send an X-OFF character as soon as possible (line 365). We then try to send the X-ON. If the device is currently busy (line 366) we set a flag (line 367) that means an X-ON ought to be sent as soon as possible (see lines 297-302). Or else we mark the device as busy (line 370) and send the X-ON right now (line 371).

The T_PARAM command is a request to reset the device parameters. This is done by calling the com1param routine (see lines 137-176).

Lastly, the T_DISCONNECT command causes the driver to drop the DTR signal (line 378). This will cause the modem (if any is attached) to hang-up the phone line.

```
381        if (flag is set (indicating output ought to be attempted))
383            if (device is busy, or a break is in progress,
                                        or output is suspended)
385                restore processor priority
386                return

388-389        if (temporary output buffer is missing or empty)
391                if (temporary output buffer is empty)
392                    reset pointer to start of buffer
393                call line discipline to fill temporary buffer
               if (nothing to put into buffer)
395                    restore processor priority
396                    return

399        mark device as busy
```

```
400          transmit next character in buffer
401          decrement count of characters in buffer

403      restore processor priority

381      if (flag)
382      {
383          if (tp->t_state & (BUSY | TIMEOUT | TTSTOP))
384          {
385              splx(x);
386              return;
387          }

388          ccp = &tp->t_tbuf;
389          if ((ccp->c_ptr == NULL) || (ccp->c_count == 0))
390          {
391              if (ccp->c_ptr)
392                  ccp->c_ptr -= ccp->c_size;
393              if (!(CPRES & (*linesw[tp->t_line].l_output)(tp)))
394              {
395                  splx(x);
396                  return;
397              }
398          }
399          tp->t_state |= BUSY;
400          outb(TXR, *(ccp->c_ptr++));
401          ccp->c_count--;
402      }
403      splx(x);
404  }
```

The flag tested in line 381 is set whenever the driver should to send data to the device.

The first check (line 383) is to see if the device is currently busy (BUSY), if we are in the midst of waiting for a timeout to expire (TIMEOUT), or if output has been halted (TTSTOP). If so, we restore the CPU priority (line 385) and exit (line 386).

On line 388 we make a copy of the pointer to the transmit character control block (the buffer of characters waiting to be transmitted). If the pointer into the buffer is NULL or there is no data in the buffer (line 389) we must attempt to obtain more data. One line 391 we check to see if the pointer is not NULL and if not, we move it back to point to the start of the buffer (line 392). We call the line discipline's output routine (line 393) to put more data in the transmit buffer. If this fails, then we restore the processor priority (line 395) and return (line 396).

By line 399 we are assured that there is data to transmit so we set the BUSY flag indicating the device is active and take the next character from the line discipline's transmit buffer and pass it to the device to transmit (line 400). We decrement the count of characters in the buffer (line 401) and restore the processor priority (line 403) in preparation for leaving this routine.

Beyond Line Disciplines

As UNIX developed and became used more and more in networked system (both local and wide area) it became apparent that the character driver model—including the terminal driver model and line disciplines—could not meet the needs of all communications devices adequately.

As a result, Dennis Ritchie at Bell Laboratories developed an extension to UNIX referred to as STREAMS. STREAMS and STREAMS drivers provide a more flexible method for implementing communications protocols and drivers. In Release 4 of UNIX System V all terminal drivers are (supposed to be) implemented using the STREAMS model. In Chapter 12 we explore such a STREAMS driver for the COM1 port.

Summary

In this chapter we explored a sub-class of character drivers called terminal drivers. These drivers are used to support communications devices that connect users' terminals to the UNIX system. As we saw, the character model has been extended to provide additional support for the terminal I/O (TERMIO) functions. We also learned how the work is shared between the driver and the line discipline(s).

The structure of this driver is similar to all terminal drivers.

Exercises

1. Modify the init entry point to properly verify properly that the COM1 port exists and is responding.

2. Modify the driver to handle the COM2 port (hex address 2f8) as minor device 1 *in addition* to the COM1 port supported already. This will require: changing the register definitions to offsets; adding the definition of an array of base addresses for COM1 and COM2; and changing references to registers from the simple form *LSR* to something like *base_addr[minor(dev)] + LSR* .

   The macros defined on lines 67 and 68 will also have to be changed to accept a base address.

Chapter 10

Character Drivers V: A Tape Drive

In this chapter we shall examine a device driver for a SCSI tape drive. As you will recall, we discussed in depth the details of driving a SCSI disk in Chapter 7 and examined how to handle a SCSI host adapter at that time. Since the details of interfacing to a SCSI bus with the Adaptec 154x host adapter are the same regardless of the device being controlled, we shall concentrate here on the details related to the tape drive.

A SCSI Tape Drive

For the most part, a SCSI tape drive is a SCSI tape drive is a SCSI tape drive. Or in other words, once you have seen one SCSI tape drive, you have seen 80% of all SCSI tape drives. And it is the 80% to which we shall direct our attention.

The tape drive we have chosen for this chapter is based on the helical scan technology developed for Digital Audio Tape (DAT) drives. The drive uses small cartridges (about half the size of a standard audio cassette) and can store about 1.3 gigabytes (i.e., 1,300 megabytes) of data on a single

DAT cartridge. The actual model is the Wangtek 6130FS OEM drive which is incorporated in several available products such as the Tallgrass FS1300 product.

Although the DAT drive supports a number of extended features, we shall concentrate for now on the basic tape drive functions. The SCSI command set defines a number of standard commands for sequential access (i.e., tape) devices:

- TEST UNIT READY—verify that the tape drive is connected to the SCSI bus, is powered up, has a tape loaded, and is ready to respond to read and write commands.
- REWIND—cause the tape to be positioned at the beginning.
- ERASE—cause the tape to be erased.
- LOAD/UNLOAD/RETENTION—cause the tape to be loaded, unloaded, or retentioned.
- READ—transfer data from the tape to the host adapter.
- WRITE—transfer data from the host adapter to the tape.
- WRITE FILEMARK—write a mark on the tape that indicates the end of the current file.
- SPACE—move the tape forward the specified number of blocks or filemarks.

We shall see how these commands are used when we consider the driver.

As mentioned earlier, one of the special considerations when using a tape device is the size of the data blocks that are to be written. Most tape drives place a fixed-sized gap between data blocks. Obviously the smaller the data blocks the larger the amount of space wasted on inter-record gaps. To minimize this inefficiency, most tape devices are implemented as character drivers so they are not limited to the small fixed-sized blocks used by most disk drives. As we shall see shortly, we have selected a maximum block size of 10 Kbytes.

The Driver

As mentioned, this driver presents the tape-drive-specific portion of the complete driver. We assume that a driver exists which supports the SCSI host adapter that provides a routine called *scsi_command* which takes the following arguments:

- a pointer to a SCSI command block;
- the number of bytes in the SCSI command block (usually 6 for the SCSI commands listed above);
- an indication of whether data is to be read or written;
- the number of bytes that is to be read or written; and
- a pointer to the buffer to be read or written.

Such a driver would be very similar to the one presented in Chapter 7.

The Driver Prologue

```
 1   #include <sys/param.h>
 2   #include <sys/errno.h>
 3   #include <sys/types.h>
 4   #include <sys/signal.h>
 5   #include <sys/dir.h>
 6   #include <sys/user.h>
 7   #include <sys/tty.h>
 8   #include <sys/sysmacros.h>
 9   #include <sys/file.h>
10   #include <sys/tape.h>

11   #include "scsi.h"

12   #define MIN(a, b)    ((a) < (b) ? (a) : (b))

13   #define MAXBSIZE    10240
14   static unsigned char tbuf[MAXBSIZE];

15   static short flags;

16   #define OPEN  0x01
17   #define DIRTY 0x02
```

```
18   void writefm(), readfm();
19   int rewind();

20   #define TAPE_ID    ID_2
```

The only header file in our prologue that we have not encountered so far in our studies is *<sys/tape.h>*. This file defines some standard ioctl commands that are used to manipulate tape drives. We shall discuss these further when we reach this driver's ioctl entry point.

Since it is expected that our system might have drivers for a number of different SCSI devices, we place all of the definitions related to the common SCSI support in a separate file *scsi.h* which we shall examine in a moment.

As mentioned earlier, one of the special considerations when using a tape device is the size of the data blocks that are to be written. Our driver will support any size of data block up to 10 Kbytes. Recall from Chapter 7 that the host adapter uses direct memory access (DMA) to transfer data to and from memory. In other words, the host adapter will access the memory directly, bypassing the memory management unit. This means that the buffer which is being read or written must be contiguous in *physical memory*. Normally, if we allocate memory dynamically within the driver (see the driver in Chapter 6), the memory will be virtually contiguous but may not be physically contiguous. This is illustrated in Figure 10-1. If we attempt to perform DMA to a buffer that is not physically contiguous we risk overwriting memory that is not allocated to us (since the DMA circuitry bypasses the memory management unit and only deals in physical addresses).

In this driver we get around the problem by declaring a fixed-sized buffer within the driver (line 14). With all 3.2 UNIX machines, such array declarations are assured of being allocated contiguous physical memory when the kernel is first loaded into memory. And since the kernel is never paged, the array will remain contiguous. We shall discuss the issue of contiguous buffers further at the end of the chapter.

On line 15 we declare a local status variable that can contain the flags defined on lines 16 and 17. OPEN marks the driver as currently open and

DIRTY indicates that at least one block of data has been written to the device. Lines 18 and 19 provide forward declarations for routines we wish to use before defining them.

FIGURE 10-1

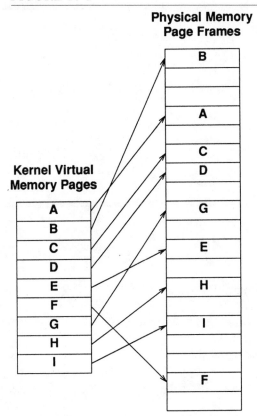

Line 20 defines the SCSI target id for the tape drive (in this case ID #2).

The scsi.h File

```
1   #define G0READ                0x08
2   #define G0TEST_UNIT_READY     0x00
3   #define G0LOAD_UNLOAD         0x1b
4   #define G0WRITE_FILEMARK      0x10
5   #define G0SPACE               0x11
6   #define G0REWIND              0x01
```

```
 7  #define G0WRITE              0x0a
 8  #define G0ERASE              0x19
    #define G1GETSZ              0x25

 9  #define DATAOUT              0x10
10  #define DATAIN               0x08

11  #define ID_0                 0x00
12  #define ID_1                 0x20
13  #define ID_2                 0x40
14  #define ID_3                 0x60
15  #define ID_4                 0x80
16  #define ID_5                 0xa0
17  #define ID_6                 0xc0
18  #define ID_7                 0xe0

19  #define LOAD_BIT             0x01
20  #define RETEN_BIT            0x02

21  #define LONG_BIT             0x01

22  struct group0
23  {
24      uchar_t opcode;       /* SCSI operation code */
25      uchar_t lun_lba;      /* LUN + LBA */
26      uchar_t lba_mid;      /* more logical block address */
27      uchar_t lba_lsb;      /* more logical block address */
28      uchar_t length;       /* transfer length */
29      uchar_t misc;         /* miscellaneous bit fields */
30      uchar_t sense[14];    /* sense data from adapter */
31  };

32  struct group1
33  {
34      uchar_t opcode;       /* SCSI operation code */
35      uchar_t lun;          /* logical unit number */
36      uchar_t lba_msb;      /* logical block address - MSB */
37      uchar_t lba_nmsb;     /* lba - next most sig. byte */
38      uchar_t lba_lmsb;     /* lba - least MSB */
39      uchar_t lba_lsb;      /* lba - least significant byte */
40      uchar_t pad;          /* reserved */
41      uchar_t len_msb;      /* transfer length (for I/O cmds) */
```

```
42        uchar_t len_lsb;      /* transfer length - LSB */
43        uchar_t misc;         /* miscellaneous bit fields */
44        uchar_t sense[14];    /* sense data from adapter */
45    };

46    typedef union scsi
47    {
48        struct group0 group0;
49        struct group1 group1;
50    } scsi_t;

51    extern int scsi_command(scsi_t *sp, long slen, long dlen
                              int datIO char *bp);
```

The scsi.h file contains definitions and declarations common to all SCSI drivers that use the scsi_command interface. Lines 1 to 8 define the various SCSI command operation codes. Lines 9 and 10 define the direction of data transfer (with respect to the host adapter) while lines 11 through 18 are the SCSI target id numbers for the desired target. These are ored in with DATAIN or DATAOUT to provide the third argument to scsi_command indicating the direction of data transfer and the device to access. Lines 19 through 21 define various option bits that can be used in certain SCSI commands. Lines 22 to 50 define the structure of the SCSI command block that is passed to the scsi_command routine. These declarations are the same as those first used in Chapter 7. Finally, we provide an external declaration of the scsi_command routine and its arguments (line 51).

The Init Entry Point

We assume that the driver for the SCSI host adapter has verified that the host adapter itself is present. Given that the tape drive may not normally be powered up, it would be premature for us to attempt to verify the presence of the tape drive at this point. So we simply announce our presence.

```
21    datinit()
22    {
23        printf("SCSI DAT Tape Device Driver v1.0\n");
24    }
```

The Open Entry Point

The open routine is the earliest point when we can reasonably check for the presence of the tape drive. We also check to see if the tape drive is already open. If so, we return an error since it makes little sense to permit two users to read or write the same tape drive at the same time.

```
25  open entry point:
29      if (device is already open)
31          set error code
32          return

34-39    prepare a 'Test Unit Ready' SCSI command block
40       send command to tape device
         if (command fails)
42           send command to tape device (again)
43           if (command fails)
45               print an error message
46               set error code
48           else
49               set flag indicating device is open
51       else
52           set flag indicating device is open
```

```c
25  int datopen(dev_t dev, int flag)
26  {
27      scsi_t scmd;
28      int retval;

29      if (flags & OPEN)
30      {
31          u.u_error = EBUSY;
32          return;
33      }

34      scmd.group0.opcode = G0TEST_UNIT_READY;
35      scmd.group0.lun_lba = 0;
36      scmd.group0.lba_mid = 0;
37      scmd.group0.lba_lsb = 0;
38      scmd.group0.length = 0;
39      scmd.group0.misc = 0;
```

```
40          if (scsi_command(&scmd, 6, 0, TAPE_ID, NULL))
41          {
42              retval = scsi_command(&scmd, 6, 0, TAPE_ID, NULL);
43              if (retval)
44              {
45                  printf("DAT ERR: Device Not Ready (%d)\n", retval);
46                  u.u_error = EIO;
47              }
48              else
49                  flags = OPEN;
50          }
51          else
52              flags = OPEN;
53  }
```

If the device is already open (line 29), then return an error indicating the device is busy (lines 31 and 32). Otherwise, create a SCSI command block with the 'test unit ready' command. As defined in the manual for the tape drive, "the TEST UNIT READY command provides a means to determine if the logical unit is powered-on, the medium (cartridge) is in place and loaded, and [the] logical unit is ready to accept a medium access command".

On line 40 we pass the SCSI command block to scsi_command indicating that it is six bytes long (the standard length for a group 0 SCSI command) and that no data is to be transferred. If the first attempt (line 40) fails, we try again (line 42). The attempt will always fail with a 'unit attention' error the first command after the drive has been powered up or the tape cartridge has been changed. Rather than bothering to check the reason for the error, we just reissue the command. If it fails a second time then we assume that the drive is really not ready (line 46).

If either attempt at issuing the command succeeds we mark the drive as successfully opened (line 49 or 52).

The Close Entry Point

With a tape drive there are a couple of things that must be done when the user is finished with the drive. If any data has been written to the device then a file mark must be written out to mark the end of the data. Also, a

check must be made to determine if the tape is to be rewound after use
and if so, the appropriate command is issued to rewind the tape.

```
54  close entry point:
56      if (tape has been written to)
57          write file mark

58      if (tape was accessed in 'rewind mode')
60          if (tape has been written to)
61              write (another) file mark
62          rewind tape

64      clear flag indicating device was open
```

```
54  int datclose(dev_t dev)
55  {
56      if (flags & DIRTY)
57          writefm();

58      if (minor(dev) == 0)
59      {
60          if (flags & DIRTY)
61              writefm();
62          rewind();
63      }

64      flags = 0;
65  }
```

We shall see shortly that the DIRTY flag is set whenever a block of data
has been written to the tape. When we are about to close the device, we
check to see if anything has been written (line 56). If it has, we call a routine (discussed below) to write a single file mark.

We now consider whether or not to rewind the tape. Usually the user
wants to write only a single file (i.e., the output of a single *tar* or *cpio* command) to tape and then wants the tape to be rewound in preparation for
being removed from the drive.

On most drives, however, it is possible to read and write multiple data file
on the tape. For example, the user could save some files in one directory

to the tape drive using tar and request that the tape not be rewound when closed. Then the user could save some other files to the tape. This could continue many times. On the last write the user would request that the tape be rewound after use. The resulting tape would look something like Figure 10-2.

FIGURE 10-2

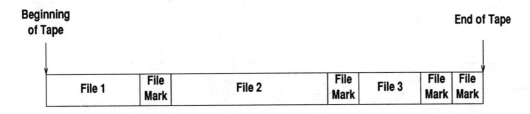

The question arises as to how the user can tell the tape drive and driver not to rewind the tape when it is closed. The convention with most UNIX systems is to define two entries in the /dev directory, one for the tape in 'rewind upon close mode,' and one for 'no rewind mode'. The two entries would have the same major device number but would have a different minor device number. For example, the minor device number might be divided up as shown in Figure 10-3. This would allow up to eight tape drives on the system, each with a rewind and no-rewind device.

Our driver only supports a single tape drive and so we can take the simpler approach of assuming that if the minor device is zero (line 58), then the device is to be rewound (line 62) when closed. If the minor device number is anything else, we treat it as a no-rewind device.

Note that we again check to see if the tape has been written to (line 60) and if so, we write another file mark (line 61). By convention, the last file on the tape is terminated by a set of two file marks. In this way a program reading the tape can tell when it has to read the last file. So if we are about to rewind the tape and have written to it, we write two tape marks indicating the furthest extent of data on the media.

FIGURE 10-3

No Rewind On Close				Tape Drive Number (0..7)

```
crw-r--r--  1 root  root   15,  0 Oct 10 21:04 /dev/dat0
crw-r--r--  1 root  root   15,128 Oct 10 21:04 /dev/dat0nr
crw-r--r--  1 root  root   15,  1 Oct 10 21:04 /dev/dat1
crw-r--r--  1 root  root   15,129 Oct 10 21:04 /dev/dat1nr
crw-r--r--  1 root  root   15,  2 Oct 10 21:04 /dev/dat2
crw-r--r--  1 root  root   15,130 Oct 10 21:04 /dev/dat2nr
crw-r--r--  1 root  root   15,  3 Oct 10 21:04 /dev/dat3
crw-r--r--  1 root  root   15,131 Oct 10 21:04 /dev/dat3nr
crw-r--r--  1 root  root   15,  4 Oct 10 21:04 /dev/dat4
crw-r--r--  1 root  root   15,132 Oct 10 21:04 /dev/dat4nr
crw-r--r--  1 root  root   15,  5 Oct 10 21:04 /dev/dat5
crw-r--r--  1 root  root   15,133 Oct 10 21:04 /dev/dat5nr
crw-r--r--  1 root  root   15,  6 Oct 10 21:04 /dev/dat6
crw-r--r--  1 root  root   15,134 Oct 10 21:04 /dev/dat6nr
crw-r--r--  1 root  root   15,  7 Oct 10 21:04 /dev/dat7
crw-r--r--  1 root  root   15,135 Oct 10 21:04 /dev/dat7nr
```

Before leaving we clear the flags (line 64) to indicate that the device is not open.

The Write Entry Point

The *write* routine is relatively straightforward. We accept requests up to the size of our internal buffer (see line 14), copy the data from the user process's buffer to our internal buffer, and then send a command to the tape drive to copy that data to the tape.

Remember that we have to perform this extra copy operation to make sure that the data is physically contiguous before writing it to the tape.

```
66   write entry point:

71        copy data from user process to driver buffer
          if (transfer fails)
73            set error code
74            return

76-81     prepare a 'Write' SCSI command block
82        send command to tape device
          if (command fails)
84            set error code
85        else
87-89         update u. variables to indicate a successful operation
90            set flag indicating the tape has been written to
```

```
66   int datwrite(dev_t dev)
67   {
68       long count = MIN(u.u_count, MAXBSIZE);
69       scsi_t scmd;
70       int retval;

71       if (copyin(u.u_base, tbuf, count) == -1)
72       {
73           u.u_error = EFAULT;
74           return;
75       }

76       scmd.group0.opcode = G0WRITE;
77       scmd.group0.lun_lba = 0;
78       scmd.group0.lba_mid = (count >> 16) & 0xff;
79       scmd.group0.lba_lsb = (count >> 8) & 0xff;
80       scmd.group0.length = count & 0xff;
81       scmd.group0.misc = 0;

82       retval = scsi_command(&scmd,6, count, DATAOUT|TAPE_ID, tbuf);

83       if (retval != 0)
84           u.u_error = EIO;
85       else
```

```
86      {
87              u.u_count -= count;
88              u.u_base += count;
89              u.u_offset += count;
90              flags |= DIRTY;
91      }
92  }
```

We initialize the count variable (line 68) to the lesser of the number of bytes requested to be written and the size of our internal buffer. We then use the kernel routine copyin (line 71) to copy the data from the user process to our buffer. If copyin fails, we return an error (lines 73 and 74).

On lines 76 through 81 we create a SCSI command block. The first byte of the block is the op code for a WRITE command (line 76). The next byte (line 77) specifies the logical unit number of the tape drive (among other options).

It is important to note that the LUN is not the same as the target id. A SCSI bus may have up to eight targets. Each target may support up to eight separate logical units, although most tape devices only support a single logical unit (LUN 0).

The third, fourth, and fifth bytes contain the size of the transfer in bytes (lines 78-80). Finally, the last byte of the SCSI command block is not used (line 81).

On line 82 we pass this command block to the host adapter driver to send to the tape drive. If an error is detected (line 83), we set the error return code (line 84). If everything goes smoothly, we then update the u_count, u_base, and u_offset variables to reflect the size of the actual transfer (lines 87-89) and we mark the device as dirty (line 90).

The Read Entry Point

The *read* entry point is an almost perfect mirror of the write. A SCSI command block is built to read the data from tape to our internal buffer and then copyout is summoned to transfer that data to the user process.

93   read entry point:

98-103 prepare a 'Write' SCSI command block
104   send command to tape device
         if (command fails)
106   set error code
107   else
109   copy data from user process to driver buffer
         if (transfer fails)
110   set error code
111   else
113-115   update u. variables to indicate a successful operation

```
 93   int datread(dev_t dev)
 94   {
 95       long count = MIN(u.u_count, MAXBSIZE);
 96       scsi_t scmd;
 97       int retval;

 98       scmd.group0.opcode = G0READ;
 99       scmd.group0.lun_lba = 0;
100       scmd.group0.lba_mid = (count >> 16) & 0xff;
101       scmd.group0.lba_lsb = (count >> 8) & 0xff;
102       scmd.group0.length = count & 0xff;
103       scmd.group0.misc = 0;

104       retval = scsi_command(&scmd, 6, count, DATAIN|TAPE_ID, tbuf);

105       if (retval != 0)
106           u.u_error = EIO;
107       else
108       {
109           if (copyout(tbuf, u.u_base, count) == -1)
110               u.u_error = EFAULT;
111           else
112           {
113               u.u_count -= count;
114               u.u_base += count;
115               u.u_offset += count;
116           }
117       }
118   }
```

Given the strong similarity between this and the previous entry point, no additional discussion is necessary.

The Ioctl Entry Point

Just as the user process's read and write system calls become calls to a driver's read and write entry point, so too do user ioctl calls become calls to a driver's ioctl entry point. We have discussed in earlier chapters how the association is made and how the kernel knows which driver's entry point to call. What is of concern to us now is the purpose and nature of ioctl system calls.

The ioctl system call is an essentially unlimited back door for device requests that are not reads or writes. The general form of an ioctl system call is:

```
retval = ioctl(fildes, request, arg);
```

In this call *fildes* is the file descriptor returned by the open system call; *request* is a number representing the type of ioctl request; and *arg* contains additional information (either an integer or a pointer to a buffer). The request and the arg are passed directly to the driver when its ioctl entry point is called (as the second and third arguments to the entry point).

The request number is an arbitrary integer that is agreed upon between the writer of the device driver and the user of the device driver. In the case of typical devices, there may be a series of ioctl requests already defined. For example the <sys/tape.h> header file (see line 10) defines a number of ioctl request values such as REWIND, which is defined as the value (('m' << 8) | 3).

The reason for this strange expression is to lessen the likelihood that an ioctl request intended for another class of device is misinterpreted if accidentally passed to an inappropriate device. Consider if the definition of the REWIND ioctl request were just a simple integer, say 3. Further suppose the hard disk driver had an ioctl called FORMAT which did a low-level format of the disk and destroyed all of the data on the disk drive. If the FORMAT request were also defined as the same simple integer (3), then the stage is set for a disaster when some systems manager makes a mistake and runs the tape utility on the hard disk and requests the tape be rewound. The REWIND request is nothing more than a request value of 3 which the disk drive interprets as a request to do a low-level format.

To reduce the possibility of such problems the convention is to select a different letter of the alphabet for each class of device. Then each ioctl request for that calls of devices is assigned a number (i.e., 3 in the case of REWIND) combined with the unique letter (shifted up one byte). The result is an integer value that is probably unique among all ioctl requests.

As mentioned the arg can be an integer or a pointer value. In this driver we do not use the arg value but it can be used to pass additional information in either direction. If arg is a pointer then the driver's ioctl entry point can use the kernel routines *copyin* or *copyout* to access the buffer pointed to by the arg value.

```
119   ioctl entry point:

123       switch (based on ioctl command)
125          MT_RETEN:  (retention tape)
126-131         prepare a 'Retention Tape' SCSI command block
132             send command to tape device
                if (command fails)
135                 set error code
136             break out of switch statement

119   int datioctl(dev_t dev, int cmd, caddr_t arg, int mode)
120   {
121       scsi_t scmd;
122       int retval;

123       switch (cmd)
124       {
125          case MT_RETEN:
126            scmd.group0.opcode = G0LOAD_UNLOAD;
127            scmd.group0.lun_lba = 0;
128            scmd.group0.lba_mid = 0;
129            scmd.group0.lba_lsb = 0;
130            scmd.group0.length = RETEN_BIT | LOAD_BIT;
131            scmd.group0.misc = 0;
```

```
132         if ((retval =
                      scsi_command(&scmd, 6, 0, TAPE_ID, NULL)) != 0)
135            u.u_error = EIO;
136         break;
```

This ioctl entry point is one large switch statement (line 123) which branches depending on the ioctl request (cmd). The retention ioctl (line 125) is a request to issue a LOAD/UNLOAD command with the retention and load bits on (line 130). The appropriate SCSI command block is built (lines 126-131) and then passed to the host adapter driver (line 132). If scsi_command reports a problem we set the error return (line 135).

```
125       MT_ERASE:  (erase tape)
139           call `rewind tape' routine
              if (rewind fails)
140              break out of switch statement
141           else
143-144          prepare an `Erase Tape' SCSI command block
145           send command to tape device
              if (command fails)
148              set error code
              (fall into next case)

152       MT_REWIND:  (rewind tape)
153           call `rewind tape' routine

138      case MT_ERASE:
139       if (rewind())
140            break;
141       else
142       {
143           scmd.group0.opcode = G0ERASE;
144           scmd.group0.lun_lba = LONG_BIT;

145           if ((retval =
                      scsi_command(&scmd, 6, 0, TAPE_ID, NULL)) != 0)
148              u.u_error = EIO;
150       }

151       /*  fall into next case  */
```

```
152          case MT_REWIND:
153           rewind();
154           break;
```

The MT_ERASE ioctl (line 138) is a request to erase the entire tape. The first step is to rewind the tape so that the erase operation will start with the beginning of the tape (line 139). Rewind is a routine defined later in this driver.

Once a successful rewind has been performed, we set up a SCSI command block with the ERASE command combined with the LONG_BIT. This indicates that the entire tape is to be erased (lines 143-144). If this command fails, we set an error indication (line 148). In any case, we fall into the next case and attempt to rewind the tape. This is necessary since the tape drive documentation states that the position of the tape is undefined after an erase command and that the tape must be rewound before further I/O is attempted.

The MT_REWIND command is handled by calling our rewind routine (line 152-153).

```
155          MT_WFM:   (write file mark)
156              call 'write file mark' routine

158          MT_RFM:   (read file mark)
159              call 'read file mark' routine

161          default:
162              set error code
```

```
155            case MT_WFM:
156             writefm();
157             break;

158            case MT_RFM:
159             readfm();
160             break;

161            default:
162             u.u_error = EIO;
163             break;
```

```
164        }
165   }
```

The remaining two ioctl requests, write file mark and read file mark, are
handled by calling simple routines that will issue the appropriate SCSI
command block.

If we do not understand the ioctl request (i.e., do not support it) we set an
error return code (lines 161-162).

The Support Routines

In order to make the code more manageable we have taken a number of
the tape operations and packaged them into simple routines that create a
SCSI command block to perform the operation and to pass it to the host
adapter driver to handle.

```
166   static int rewind()
167   {
168        scsi_t scmd;
169        int retval;

170        scmd.group0.opcode = G0REWIND;
171        scmd.group0.lun_lba = 0;
172        scmd.group0.lba_mid = 0;
173        scmd.group0.lba_lsb = 0;
174        scmd.group0.length = 0;
175        scmd.group0.misc = 0;

176        if ((retval = scsi_command(&scmd, 6, 0, TAPE_ID, NULL)) != 0)
177        {
179             u.u_error = EIO;
180             return (1);
181        }
182        return (0);
183   }

184   static void readfm()
185   {
186        scsi_t scmd;
187        int retval;
```

```
188        scmd.group0.opcode = G0SPACE;
189        scmd.group0.lun_lba = 1;
190        scmd.group0.lba_mid = 0;
191        scmd.group0.lba_lsb = 0;
192        scmd.group0.length = 1;
193        scmd.group0.misc = 0;

194        if ((retval = scsi_command(&scmd, 6, 0, TAPE_ID, NULL)) != 0)
197            u.u_error = EIO;
199    }

200    static void writefm()
201    {
202        scsi_t scmd;
203        int retval;

204        scmd.group0.opcode = G0WRITE_FILEMARK;
205        scmd.group0.lun_lba = 0;
206        scmd.group0.lba_mid = 0;
207        scmd.group0.lba_lsb = 0;
208        scmd.group0.length = 1;
209        scmd.group0.misc = 0;

210        if ((retval = scsi_command(&scmd, 6, 0, TAPE_ID, NULL)) != 0)
213            u.u_error = EIO;
215    }
```

Since we have already examined code similar to that employed in each of these routines, the detailed study of this code is left as an exercise for the reader.

Possible Enhancements

There are a number of improvements that would need to be made to this driver to turn it into a production quality driver.

The driver only supports a single tape drive with a fixed SCSI target ID number. A proper tape driver would handle as many tape drives as the SCSI bus could support (seven) and would take the SCSI target ID from the minor device number (say the low three bits).

As with almost all of our drivers there is little useful information returned when an error occurs. The tape drive will return detailed information in the sense vector attached to the SCSI command block (lines 30 and 44 of scsi.h). The driver ought to examine this information and determine the detailed reasons for the error, perhaps printing a meaningful message or selecting a more meaningful error number to return. Also some errors need to be reported (e.g. end of file, media changed, drive powered up, etc.).

The DAT tape drive supports a number of options that this driver ignores. DAT tapes can be formatted with two partitions. The driver at the very least ought to support the special commands to switch partitions, if not also support the command to format a tape with two partitions (the default is one partition).

There are also several performance issues that could be addressed:

- the driver's buffer is permanently allocated and consumes space even when the driver is not in use;
- the maximum block size is small considering the transfer speed of most tape drives; and
- the data is copied twice (once from the user process to the driver and once from the driver to the tape driver) instead of being transferred directly.

The first two problems could be resolved by allocating physically contiguous memory dynamically when the device is opened. While there is no standard way of allocating physically contiguous memory within a driver, some UNIX implementations provide special kernel routines to support this feature. Another possibility is to allocate non-contiguous memory dynamically and to use the scatter-gather capability of some SCSI host adapters to transfer a single large block of data from several smaller, discontinuous buffers.

To resolve the third problem we not only need to generate scatter-gather type requests, we need to ask the kernel to lock in memory (prevent paging) of the user's buffer so we can safely access it using DMA. This is not always possible, so most tape drivers make the extra copy and try to compensate by allocating large buffers (e.g., a megabyte or more) dynamically.

These are some of the details that we have left out of our driver so that we could easily illustrate the key features of a tape device driver.

Summary

Most of this driver is an obvious extension of what we have learned to date studying the SCSI disk driver in Chapter 7 and the other previous character drivers. The only item that is relatively new with this driver is the processing of ioctl requests.

We learned that ioctl system calls are a mechanism to pass requests to a driver other than the traditional read and write commands. Because the ioctl command provides two arguments that are passed untouched to the driver, the possibilities are endless. By convention the first argument is an integer that indicates the type of ioctl request being made. The second argument can be a pointer to a buffer of any size that the driver can access using copyin or copyout. Indeed, by defining READ and WRITE ioctl one could do away with the traditional read and write entry points and do everything (except open and close the device) through the ioctl entry point.

Exercises

1. As mentioned at the beginning of the chapter, this driver requires a SCSI host adapter driver that supports a routine called *scsi_command* which handles the details of passing the SCSI command block to the host adapter and waiting for a response. Your mission, should you choose to accept it, is to rewrite the driver presented in Chapter 7 to provide such a routine.
2. On a related note, rewrite the disk-related portions of the driver in Chapter 7 to use the same *scsi_command* routine as the interface to the host adapter driver.

Chapter 11

STREAMS Drivers I: A Loop-Back Driver

STREAMS drivers are a relatively recent addition to the architecture of the UNIX kernel. They were developed by Dennis Ritchie at Bell Laboratories in the mid 1980s and first appeared in a commercial version of UNIX with Release 3. STREAMS were designed to address some of the limitations of the character driver model, especially in the area of networking and communications.

You will recall that the character driver has a relatively direct connection with user processes as illustrated in Figure 11-1 (shown on the next page). As we have seen, this model works well with many types of devices. The problems arise, however, when one tries to support a communications device that requires additional processing of the data stream between the process and the device.

Take a simple example such as remote terminals connected to a UNIX system. As we discussed in Chapter 9, there is a significant amount of processing that is done before the user process receives data from the communications device. Figure 11-2 shown on the next page; shows the user's view of this process schematically while Figure 11-3 (shown on the next page) represents how we implemented this architecture with our driver in Chapter 9.

FIGURE 11-1

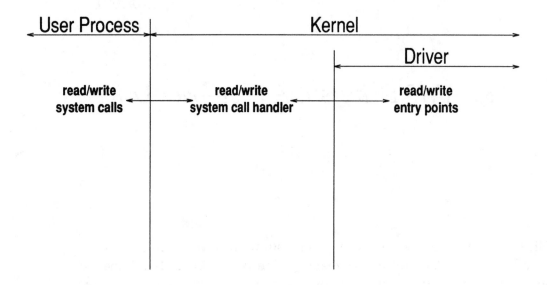

FIGURE 11-2

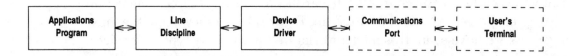

FIGURE 11-3

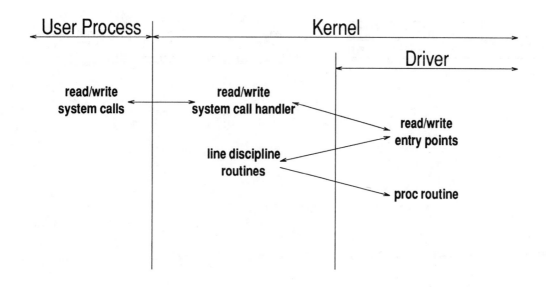

Although this approach works for a simple protocol stack such as the line discipline example, it becomes rapidly untenable as the protocol stack increases in complexity. Consider the protocol stack required to log onto a remote computer over ethernet using TCP/IP (see Figure 11-4). Although this can be implemented using an approach similar to that illustrated in Figure 11-5 we can see that as protocols become more complex and networks more ubiquitous, the need for a driver model more suited to layered procotols is needed.

It was these considerations that drove the development of STREAMS. The essence of the STREAMS model is an implementation that mimics the protocol stacks illustrated earlier. A typical STREAMS stack (shown in Figure 11-6) consists of: a STREAMS driver at the bottom that handles the interface to the hardware; zero or more STREAMS modules that implement the various procotol layers; and a stream-head that handles the interface between the stream and the user process.

FIGURE 11-4

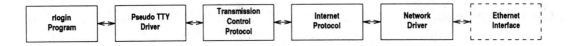

FIGURE 11-5

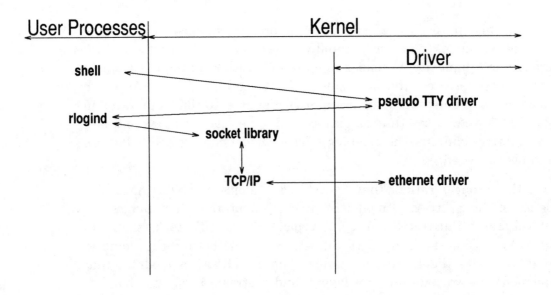

Data from a user's process flows *downstream* from the Stream head through the stacked protocol modules to the driver. Also, received data flows *upstream* from the driver through the STREAMS modules to the Stream head and from there to the user process. As data flows through the STREAMS module,s the necessary protocol processing is performed. In addition to data, control messages can also flow up and down the stream.

FIGURE 11-6

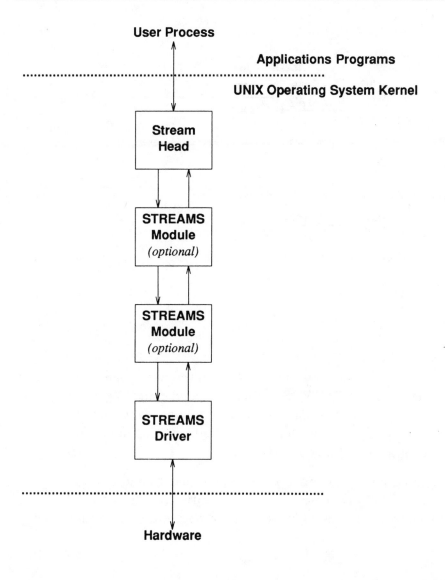

Figure 11-7 shows in detail the architecture of a stream. Note that the primary data structure is the *queue* which is used to buffer messages (data and control) as they wait to be processed by a module and passed up- or down-stream. Each module or driver has a read and a write queue where messages are stored prior to being processed by the module.

FIGURE 11-7

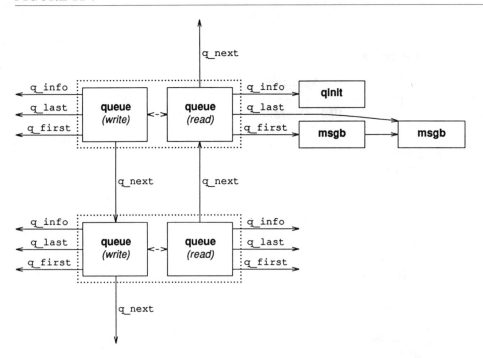

The structure of a message is shown in Figure 11-8 (on the next page). As can be seen, the structure of a STREAMS message is such that it is easy to prepend or append protocol information without having to copy the body (data) of the message. This allows for the efficient addition of protocol information to the data as it flows downstream.

The STREAMS model supports a number of message types. In addition to the basic data message, there are messages sent to control the driver and device, messages to control the Stream head, and messages to implement *ioctl* system calls. We shall further explain the message types that our drivers support when we consider the drivers themselves.

FIGURE 11-8

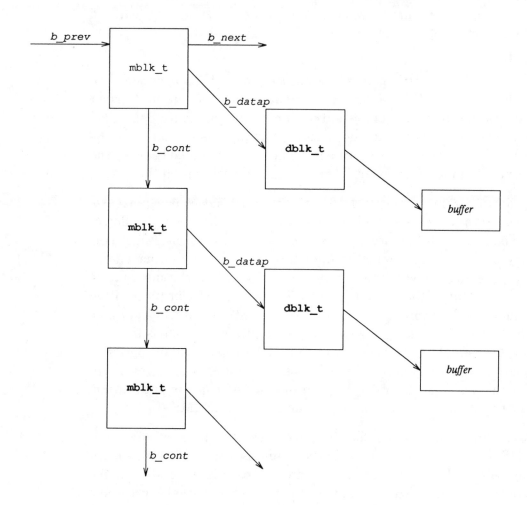

STREAMS drivers have some similarities with the character drivers we have already studied. As with character drivers, STREAMS drivers may include init, start, halt, and intr entry points. They must include open and close entry points. In addition, there are entry points that are specific to STREAMS drivers: read and write queue service (*xxsrv*) and read and write queue put (\(*flxxput)* functions. The put entry points are required (with the exception of the read-side of a driver). The service entry points are optional.

The put and service entry points are associated with each queue, and since each module and driver has two queues, each module and driver may have two put and two service entry points. The put routine is called to place a message on a queue and perform any processing that must be done immediately; the service routine is called on a scheduled basis by the kernel to perform less time-sensitive processing of messages on the queue.

Looking downstream in Figure 11-6, the Stream head converts a *write* system call into a message and invokes the put routine for the down-stream module's write queue. This routine examines the message, per-forms any processing that must be done immediately, and either passes the urgent message downstream immediately by calling the put routine for the write queue of the module next in line downstream or places it on its own queue for later processing by the service entry point. On a periodic basis, the kernel schedules the queue service routines for queues that are not empty for execution. The service routines are responsible for perform-ing the less time-critical processing of messages and passing them down-stream to the next module or driver by calling its write queue put routine. The same thing works on the upstream side of the STREAMS stack.

STREAMS device drivers are for the most part the same as any other STREAMS module. On the write side they must provide a put entry point that may be called by the upstream module to pass messages down the stream to the driver. The driver may (but usually does not) also provide a write-side service routine. Normally, the driver takes the data directly from the queue and passes it to the device.

On the read side the driver usually does not provide a put routine since there are no modules downstream to invoke it. Rather, the interrupt or poll routine takes the data from the device and either places it on the driver's read queue or passes it directly to the read queue of the first module upstream from the driver. If the driver places the data on its own queue then it must provide a service entry point to process this data further and pass it up the stream.

The Design Issues

The prime purpose of this chapter is to introduce the changes to the kernel/driver interface and the internal operation of the driver because of the STREAMS approach.

We shall see that the changes to the kernel/driver interface are substantial. In place of the *read* and *write* entry points of the character driver we have *put* and *srv* (service) entry points that manage messages on queues.

No less are the changes to the internal operation of the driver. Instead of accessing information in the *u.* area we shall receive all data and control information in the form of messages. We shall dispense with *copyin* and *copyout* and rely on a number of kernel-supplied routines to manage the queues and messages. And we shall not be responsible for process scheduling any more (i.e., the *sleep* and *wakeup* routines). The kernel will handle all of the process scheduling issues for us.

Some of these changes will be discussed in this chapter and more in the next.

A Loop-Back STREAMS Driver

As an introduction to STREAMS drivers we shall examine a simple driver that echoes or loops back any message written to it. Data written to the Stream head will be passed to the driver's write queue and the driver's write service routine will take the message and pass it back up the read side to the Stream head.

In many ways this driver operates like a named pipe. A process may open the device for reading and will be suspended until another process has opened the device for writing and has written some data.

The device can be tested by running a simple process that consumes data (i.e., cat) on one terminal and running a process that generates data (i.e., ls) on another terminal.

On terminal 1:

```
$ cat < /dev/slop
```

And on terminal 2:

```
$ ls -l /bin > /dev/slop
```

The output of the *ls* command ought to appear on terminal 1.

Note that unlike the drivers presented earlier in this book which were written for UNIX System V Release 3.2, the drivers in this, the next, and the last chapter (Chapters 11, 12, and 15) are written for UNIX System V Release 4. This is because the support for STREAMS is more complete in Release 4. With minor changes to the prologues these drivers would, however, compile and run on most Release 3.x systems. As mentioned in the preface, all of these drivers have been tested on 386/486 machines.

The Driver Prologue

The prologue for STREAMS drivers differs somewhat from those we have seen earlier in that many of the entry points of the driver are not externally visible but rather referenced through a data structure that is visible to the kernel.

```
 1   #include "sys/types.h"
 2   #include "sys/param.h"
 3   #include "sys/sysmacros.h"
 4   #include "sys/errno.h"
 5   #include "sys/stream.h"
 6   #include "sys/stropts.h"
 7   #include "sys/dir.h"
 8   #include "sys/signal.h"
 9   #include "sys/user.h"
10   #include "sys/errno.h"
11   #include "sys/cred.h"
12   #include "sys/cmn_err.h"
```

```
13   int nodev(), slopopen(), slopclose(), slopput(), slopsrv();

14   static struct module_info m_info =
         { 41, "slop", 0, 256, 512, 256 };

15   static struct qinit rinit =
         { NULL, NULL, slopopen, slopclose, NULL, &m_info, NULL };

16   static struct qinit winit =
         { slopput, slopsrv, NULL, NULL, NULL, &m_info, NULL };

17   struct streamtab slopinfo =
         { &rinit, &winit, NULL, NULL };

18   int slopdevflag;
```

The header files that are distinctive to STREAMS drivers are
<sys/stream.h>, which contains definitions of the STREAMS data structures and *<sys/stropts.h>*, which contains definitions of ioctl messages
and various defines for different message types. The header file
<sys/cred.h> is distinctive of Release 4 drivers and is not used in this
driver except to declare certain parameters to entry points. It includes
definitions of the credentials structure that can be used to verify the identity and authorization of users attempting certain restricted operations.

Line 13 provides a forward declaration of the routines that we shall be
referencing in the initialization of the STREAMS data structures.

The remainder of the prologue declares and initializes the various data
structures that describe a STREAMS module or driver. Figure 11-9 on the
next page, provides a diagram of the relationship between these various
data structures.

Starting from the bottom up, we declare and initialize the *module_info*
structure on line 14 (see Figure 11-10). Although both the read and write
queues reference a module_info structure, they may share the same one,
as is done in this driver. The module_info structure provides the kernel
with information to identify the module or driver as well as default values
for various limits on messages on the queue.

FIGURE 11-9

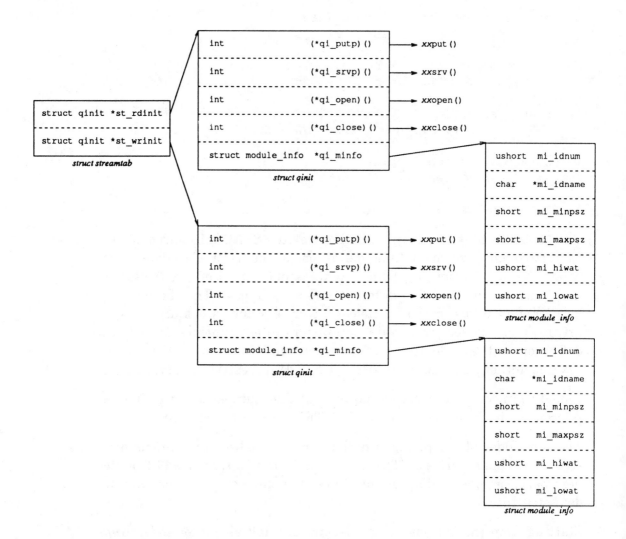

The module id number ought to be unique but since one cannot determine the module id numbers of other modules and drivers this is somewhat of a guess. The number is used for logging and tracing only so it is not critical to the operation of the system or the driver.

FIGURE 11-10

struct module_info m_info			
Member Type	*Member Name*	*Description*	*Initial Value*
ushort	mi_idnum	ID Number	41
char *	mi_idname	ID Name	"slop"
short	mi_minpsz	Minimum Packet Size	0
short	mi_maxpsz	Maximum Packet Size	256
ushort	mi_hiwat	High Water Mark	512
ushort	mi_lowat	Low Water Mark	256

The module name must be unique and is the same as the prefix used when installing the module or driver in the system. Since the names of all other modules are part of the system configuration files it is possible to check the name before using it.

The minimum and maximum packet sizes as well as the low and high water marks (all specified in bytes) in the module_info structure are used to initialize the queue limits when the module or driver is first opened and the actual queue data structure is created by the kernel. The low and high water marks are used for flow control. Once copied to the queue structure they may be modified directly by the driver.

The *qinit* structure contains pointers to the put, srv, open, and close, entry points as well as a pointer to the module_info structure (see Figure 11-11). The pointer to the *admin* entry point and the statistics structure are currently unused.

On line 15 we declare and initialize the qinit structure for the read queue and on line 16 the write-side qinit structure. Note that the open and close entry points are always taken from the read queue's qinit structure and need not be referenced in the write side qinit structure (hence the first two NULLs in line 16). Both an open and close entry must be provided even if the entry points contain no code (see lines 29-32).

FIGURE 11-11

struct qinit rinit			
Member Type	*Member Name*	*Description*	*Initial Value*
`int (*) ()`	`qi_putp`	**Pointer to Put Entry Point**	`NULL`
`int (*) ()`	`qi_srvp`	**Pointer to Service Entry Point**	`NULL`
`int (*) ()`	`qi_qopen`	**Pointer to Open Entry Point**	`slopopen`
`int (*) ()`	`qi_qclose`	**Pointer to Close Entry Point**	`slopclose`
`int (*) ()`	`qi_qadmin`	*Reserved (Not Used)*	`NULL`
`struct module_info`	`qi_minfo`	**Pointer to Module Info**	`&m_info`
`struct module_stat`	`qi_mstat`	*Reserved (Not Used)*	`NULL`

Our driver does not use the read queue and hence there is no need for either a put or service entry point for the read qinit structure. We therefore specify NULL pointer values for the first two members of the read qinit initialization (see line 15).

In both the read and write qinit structure we reference the shared module_info structure (see the second to last member in lines 15 and 16).

Finally, we tie it all together with the declaration and initialization of the *streamtab* structure on line 17. This structure contains pointers to the read and write qinit structures (the first two members). The other two members are pointers to structures used for modules that operate as multiplexors and are not usually used for STREAMS drivers. This declaration must be externally accessible (i.e., not declared static) so that it may be accessed directly by the kernel.

The *devflag* variable declared on line 18 must be externally visible (i.e., not static) and is used by the kernel to recognize the presence of a Release 4 driver. There are some small differences between Release 3 and Release 4 drivers in the open and close routines and the presence of this variable alerts the kernel to use the Release 4 interface.

The Init Entry Point

In addition to the special open, close, srv, and put entry points available, STREAMS drivers may also use the initialization entry points available to character drivers such as init and start. This driver defines an init point solely to announce its presence. Since this is a pseudo-device driver there is no hardware to verify or initialize.

```
19  void slopinit()
20  {
21      (void) cmn_err(CE_NOTE, "Test Streams Loop Driver v1.0");
22  }
```

Line 21 calls the cmn_err routine (preferred over printf for Release 4 drivers) to display information about this driver.

The Open and Close Entry Points

The open and close entry points for STREAMS drivers differ somewhat from those entry point we have studied for character drivers. Also, unlike character drivers, the open and close entry points are mandatory for STREAMS drivers.

The first argument points to the read queue for the driver. The *dev* and *flag* arguments are the same as for the character drivers we studied earlier. The *sflag* parameter indicates whether this is a normal open, a clone open, or a module open. While the details of clone drivers are beyond the scope of this book it is sufficient to know that this driver cannot handle anything but a normal open. Lastly, the credentials structure pointer references information that may be used to verify the identity of the user who is performing the request.

```
23   static int slopopen(queue_t *q, dev_t dev, int flag,
                          int sflag, cred_t *cp)
24   {
25       if (sflag)
26            return (ENXIO);

27       return (0);
28   }
```

As mentioned, our driver only handles normal driver opens, hence on line 25 we verify that the *sflag* argument is zero and return an error if it is not. Note that with Release 4 drivers errors are indicated by the return value of the entry point rather than by direct reference to the user structure.

Our close entry point has nothing to do so it merely returns a value indicating success.

```
29   static int slopclose(queue_t *q, int flag, cred_t *cp)
30   {
31       return (0);
32   }
```

The Put Entry Point

A driver's put entry point is responsible for accepting messages from the module immediately upstream, performing the initial processing of the message, and disposing the message. The put routine may dispose of a message by:

- placing it on its own queue;
- returning the message to the upstream module; or
- destroying the message and returning the memory associated with it to the kernel.

Usually the put routine processes only the urgent messages and places the less important messages on the queue to be processed later by the service entry point.

```
33  put entry point:
35      switch (based on message type)
37-38      M_DATA or M_IOCTL:
39            put message on queue for later processing
40            break out from switch statement

41      M_FLUSH:
42          if ('flush write q' flag is set)
43              flush write q
44          if ('flush read q' flag is set)
46              clear 'flush write q' flag (may not be set)
47              send message back up write queue
49          else
50              destroy message
51          break out from switch statement

52      default:
53          destroy message
```

```
33  static int slopput(queue_t *q, mblk_t *mp)
34  {
35      switch (mp->b_datap->db_type)
36      {
37        case M_DATA:
38        case M_IOCTL:
39          putq(q, mp);
40          break;

41        case M_FLUSH:
42          if (*mp->b_rptr & FLUSHW)
43              flushq(q, FLUSHDATA);

44          if (*mp->b_rptr & FLUSHR)
45          {
46              *mp->b_rptr &= ~FLUSHW;
47              qreply(q, mp);
48          }
49          else
```

```
50                    freemsg(mp);
51              break;

52          default:
53              freemsg(mp);
54              break;
55      }

56      return (0);
57  }
```

Normally a driver that performs as little processing on messages as this driver does would handle all messages in the put routine. It would not use the queue or need a service routine. In this driver, however, we have divided processing between the put and the server routine in order to demonstrate several aspects of STREAMS drivers.

On line 35 we examine the message type to determine the type of processing required. The processing of data and ioctl messages is deferred until service time by placing these messages on the queue (line 39). The *putq* routine is provided by the kernel and is used to place a message on a queue.

Flush messages are sent downstream to force all modules and the driver to delete any messages that are on the queues managed by the modules and driver. The message may request either one or both of the read and write queues be flushed. In the case of a request to flush the write queue (line 42) the driver uses the kernel-supplied routine *flushq* (line 43) to empty the driver's write queue. In the case of a request to flush the read queues (line 44), the driver must flush its own read queue (if it has one—this driver has not) and then send the message back up the read side (line 47) to cause all modules upstream to flush their read queues. If the message is to flush the write queue only, then the message must be destroyed after the write queue has been flushed (line 50).

Messages that are not understood (line 52) are destroyed (line 53).

The Service Entry Point

The service routine is called by the kernel on a periodic basis to handle the less urgent messages on the queue. When invoked, service routines must process all the messages on the queue before returning. Service routines dispose of messages in the following ways:

- passing the message to another module or driver upstream or downstream; or
- destroying the message and returning the memory associated with it to the kernel.

```
58   srv entry point:
61       while (there are messages still on the queue)
62           switch (based on type of message)
64               M_DATA
65                   send message back up write-side queue
66                   break out from switch statement
67               M_IOCTL:
68                   change message into a negative acknowledgment
69                   send message back up write-side queue
70                   break out from switch statement
```

```
58   static int slopsrv(queue_t *q)
59   {
60       mblk_t *mp;

61       while ((mp = getq(q)) != NULL)
62           switch (mp->b_datap->db_type)
63           {
64             case M_DATA:
65               qreply(q, mp);
66               break;

67             case M_IOCTL:
68               mp->b_datap->db_type = M_IOCNAK;
69               qreply(q, mp);
70               break;
71           }
```

```
72        return (0);
73    }
```

The service routine loops until all messages have been processed (lines 61-71). The kernel-supplied routine *getq* returns the next message from the queue or NULL if no more messages are left to process. The switch statement that starts on line 62 is similar to the one in the put routine.

The only types of messages we shall have to process are data and ioctl messages since these are the only types of messages that the put routine defers by placing on the read queue. Data messages are sent back upstream by using the kernel-supplied routine *qreply* (line 65).

Ioctl messages must always be acknowledged (either positively or negatively). Our driver does not handle any ioctl messages so all such messages are acknowledged negatively. We do this by overwriting the message type with the *M_IOCNAK* (line 68) and then sending the revised message back upstream (line 69).

Summary

As can be seen by the many figures in this chapter, the STREAMS model for I/O provides flexibility and modularity at the cost of some complexity. By making it possible to layer STREAMS modules on top of drivers cleanly, it becomes much easier to support communications protocols and to re-use the same procotol modules with different communications devices. This power, however, requires a number of data structures that make STREAMS drivers more involved than character drivers for the same functionality.

In this chapter we reviewed the various data structures and examined the changes to the kernel/driver interface as well as to the internal structure of the driver that are involved with the STREAMS. We saw how a driver can defer immediate processing of messages by placing them on its own queue. And we considered some of the kernel-supplied functions that are used to manage messages.

This chapter provided a brief introduction to STREAMS drivers by way of a simple pseudo-driver. The next chapter completes our presentation of

STREAMS drivers with a complete STREAMS driver for an actual communications device.

Exercises

1. We mentioned in discussions of this driver that the processing of the messages was sufficiently simple that we really did not need to defer some of the processing for processing by the service routine. Rewrite this driver to perform all of the processing in the put routine and remove all of the references to the service routine.

2. Currently this driver does not perform any processing on the data that it echoes back upstream. Modify this driver to treat all messages as text data and perform some simple transformation on each byte (i.e., reverse the case of each letter, change every 'A' to 'B', every 'B' to 'C', etc.).

Chapter 12

Streams Drivers II: The COM1 Port (Revisited)

The previous chapter described the general architecture of STREAMS drivers and the advantages this approach has over character drivers when supporting communications drivers. You will also recall that the terminal driver in Chapter 9 relied on kernel-supplied routines to provide support for the TERMIO functions required of a terminal device. Figure 11-3 illustrated this approach. Since STREAMS were designed to implement protocol stacks cleanly, it is an obvious application to use them to support terminal devices as well.

With Release 4 of UNIX, the old character driver approach with the driver calling various line discipline routines directly was discarded in favour of a STREAMS approach. All terminal devices under Release 4 are supported using STREAMS drivers and a STREAMS module called LDTERM that implements the line discipline and termio processing. This clean separation of functions makes it easy to change line discipline modules and to use existing line discipline modules on other protocol stacks.

This chapter takes the driver for a PC COM1 communications port that
we studied in Chapter 9 and rewrites it as a STREAMS driver for Release
4. Since the device has already been explained in depth we shall concentrate here on the driver itself.

The Driver

This driver has been written for UNIX System V/386 Release 4.

The Driver Prologue

```
 1   #include <sys/types.h>
 2   #include <sys/param.h>
 3   #include <sys/systrtty.h>
 4   #include <sys/errno.h>
 5   #include <sys/stream.h>
 6   #include <sys/stropts.h>
 7   #include <sys/dir.h>
 8   #include <sys/signal.h>
 9   #include <sys/user.h>
10   #include <sys/errno.h>
11   #include <sys/cred.h>
12   #include <sys/cmn_err.h>
13   #include <sys/fcntl.h>
14   #include <sys/termio.h>

15   #define spldev()    splstr()

16   extern int sttyopen(), sttyclose(), sttywput(), sttyrsrv();

17   static struct module_info rm_info =
18        { 47, "stty", 0, INFPSZ, 0, 0 };

19   static struct qinit rinit =
20        { NULL, sttyrsrv, sttyopen, sttyclose, NULL, &rm_info, NULL};

21   static struct module_info wm_info =
22        { 47, "stty", 0, INFPSZ, 256, 64 };

23   static struct qinit winit =
24        { sttywput, NULL, NULL, NULL, NULL, &wm_info, NULL };
```

```
25  struct streamtab sttyinfo =
26       { &rinit, &winit, NULL, NULL };

27  int sttydevflag;
```

We have seen all of these header files (lines 1 through 14) before so no further comment is necessary. The declarations and initialization on lines 16 through 27 are part of every STREAMS driver prologue and were discussed extensively in Chapter 11. The main difference here is that we have a a service routine for the read queue. Drivers never need a put routine for the read queue since no module can exist downstream from a driver. Even if the driver uses its own read queue to defer processing (as this driver does) the driver places the messages on the queue directly and does not need to use (or provide) a standard put routine.

```
28  #define STOP_WRITE   0x001    /* suspend output */
29  #define STOP_READ    0x002    /* suspend input */
30  #define OPENED       0x004    /* device is already open */
31  #define BREAK_IP     0x008    /* break in progress */
32  #define DCDWAIT      0x010    /* waiting for carrier detect */
33  #define DRAINW       0x020    /* waiting for output to drain */
34  #define CARRIER      0x040    /* waiting for output to drain */
35  #define SEND_STOP    0x080    /* send STOP character */
36  #define SEND_START   0x100    /* send START character */
37  #define DELAY_IP     0x200    /* delay in progress */

38  struct strtty
39  {
40      queue_t *wq;            /* write queue pointer */
41      queue_t *rq;            /* write queue pointer */
42      struct termio t;        /* termio information */
43      int     flags;
44  };

45  static struct strtty ststate;
```

We define a structure *strtty* (lines 38-44) and use it to contain pointers to both queues, a copy of the current termio flags, and a set of flags that reflect the internal state of the driver. Lines 28-37 define the various internal state flags that may be set. We shall discuss these flags as we use them in this driver.

```
46   #define TXR     0x3F8    /* transmit reg (write, DLAB=0) */
47   #define RXR     0x3F8    /* receive reg (read, DLAB = 0) */
48   #define DIVLSB  0x3F8    /* divisor latch LSB (DLAB = 1) */
49   #define DIVMSB  0x3F9    /* divisor latch MSB (DLAB = 1) */
50   #define INTENB  0x3F9    /* interrupt enable (DLAB=0) */
51   #define IIR     0x3FA    /* interrupt identification reg */
52   #define LCR     0x3FB    /* line control register */
53   #define MCR     0x3FC    /* modem control register */
54   #define LSR     0x3FD    /* line status register */
55   #define MSR     0x3FE    /* modem status register */

56   #define LCR5B   0x00     /* word length: 5 bits */
57   #define LCR6B   0x01     /* word length: 6 bits */
58   #define LCR7B   0x02     /* word length: 7 bits */
59   #define LCR8B   0x03     /* word length: 8 bits */
60   #define LCR1SB  0x00     /* stop bits: 1 */
61   #define LCR2SB  0x04     /* stop bits: 1.5 (for 5) or 2 */
62   #define LCRPEN  0x08     /* parity enable */
63   #define LCREVP  0x10     /* even parity */
64   #define LCRSTP  0x20     /* stuck parity, par=~LCRSTP */
65   #define LCRBRK  0x40     /* set break */
66   #define LCRDLAB 0x80     /* divisor latch access (DLAB) */

67   static short Divisors[] =
68   {
69       0, 2304, 1536, 1047, 857, 768, 576, 384,
70       192,  96,   64,   48,  24,  12,   6,   3
71   };

72   #define LSRDR   0x01     /* data ready (i.e. data in RXR) */
73   #define LSROER  0x02     /* overrun error */
74   #define LSRPER  0x04     /* parity error */
75   #define LSRFER  0x08     /* framing error */
76   #define LSRBI   0x10     /* break interrupt */
77   #define LSRTHRE 0x20     /* xmtr holding reg mt (TX rdy) */
78   #define LSRTSRE 0x40     /* xmtr shift reg mt (TX idle) */

79   #define IERRX   0x01     /* receiver data ready int enb */
80   #define IERTX   0x02     /* transmitter data ready int enb */
```

```
81   #define IERRST   0x04   /* receiver status interrupt enb */
82   #define IERMST   0x08   /* modem status interrupt */

83   #define MCRDTR   0x01   /* data terminal ready */
84   #define MCRRTS   0x02   /* request to send */
85   #define MCROUT1  0x04   /* misc. modem control line 1 */
86   #define MCROUT2  0x08   /* misc. modem control line 2 */

87   #define MSRDCTS  0x01   /* delta CTS */
88   #define MSRDDSR  0x02   /* delta DSR */
89   #define MSRTERI  0x04   /* trailing edge ring indicator */
90   #define MSRDDCD  0x08   /* delta DCD */
91   #define MSRCTS   0x10   /* CTS status */
92   #define MSRDSR   0x20   /* DSR status */
93   #define MSRRI    0x40   /* RI status */
94   #define MSRDCD   0x80   /* DCD status */

95   #define ON        (MCRDTR | MCRRTS | MCROUT1 | MCROUT2)
96   #define OFF       0x00

97   #define com1dcd()        (inb(MSR) & MSRDCD)
98   #define com1dtr(state)   outb(MCR, state)
```

The definition of the various device registers and register bits (lines 46-98) is taken directly from our earlier driver (Chapter 9) and need not be discussed again here.

```
99    static void sttyrestart();
100   static void sttyrxintr();
101   static void sttytxintr();
102   static void sttymdintr();
103   static void sttyparam(struct strtty *stp);
104   static void doioctl(queue_t *q, mblk_t *mp);
105   static int getmc(mblk_t **mpp);
```

In order to permit us to discuss the driver in a top-down approach we have placed some of the routines internal to this driver at the end of the listing. We therefore must provide forward declarations (lines 99-105) so we may reference these routines before we define them.

The Init Entry Point

The init routine here is the same as in our previous COM1 driver with the exception that we use the *cmn_err* routine instead of the *printf* routine to announce our presence. Although supported on most SVR4 systems, the use of the printf routine is deprecated and drivers ought to use cmn_err instead.

```
106   void sttyinit()
107   {
108       cmn_err(CE_NOTE, "Streams TTY Driver v1.0");
109       outb(INTENB, 0);
110       com1dtr(OFF);
111   }
```

The Open Entry Point

The open routine for this driver is a combination of the open routine from our previous COM1 driver and the open routine for the STREAMS driver in the previous chapter.

```
112   open entry point:

116       if (not a simple open)
117           return (error code)

118       if (device is not already open)
120-126       initialize device state structure
127           set device parameters (call sttyparam)
128           enable the DTR modem control line
129           enable device interrupts

132       raise the processor priority (disabling interrupts)

134       while (device opened NOT in no-delay or non-block mode AND
135               device is NOT a local terminal AND
136               the DCD signal is NOT present)
138           set flag indicating we are waiting for DCD
139           go to sleep
              if (sleep is rudely awakened)
141               clear flag indicating we are waiting for DCD
142               return (interrupted sleep error code)
```

```
145      restore processor priority
146      mark device as open
147      return (success)

112  static int sttyopen(queue_t *q, dev_t dev, int flag,
                         int sflag, cred_t *cp)
113  {
114      int x;
115      struct msgb *mp;

116      if (sflag)
117          return (ENXIO);

118      if ((ststate.flags & OPENED) == 0)
119      {
120          ststate.rq = q;
121          ststate.wq = WR(q);

122          ststate.t.c_iflag = BRKINT;
123          ststate.t.c_oflag = OPOST | ONLCR | TAB3;
124          ststate.t.c_cflag = B9600 | CS8 | CREAD;
125          ststate.t.c_lflag = ISIG | ICANON | ECHO | ECHOK;
126          ststate.t.c_line = 0;
127          sttyparam(&ststate);
128          com1dtr(ON);
129          outb(INTENB, IERRX | IERTX | IERRST | IERMST);
130      }
131
132      x = splstr();
133
134      while ((((flag & (O_NDELAY | O_NONBLOCK)) == 0) &&
135              ((ststate.t.c_cflag & CLOCAL) == 0) &&
136              (com1dcd() == 0))
137      {
138          ststate.flags |= DCDWAIT;
139          if (sleep((caddr_t) &ststate, STIPRI | PCATCH))
140          {
141              ststate.flags &= DCDWAIT;
142              return (EINTR);
143          }
144      }
```

```
145      splx(x);
146      ststate.flags |= OPENED;

147      return (0);
148   }
```

As with our earlier STREAMS driver, we check the sflags argument to verify that this is a normal open (line 116). If not, we fail the open (line 117).

If the device is not already open (line 118), we initialize the ststate structure (lines 120-126). We copy the pointers to the read (line 120), write (line 121) queues, and then set reasonable initial values for the TERMIO communications parameters (lines 122-126). We then initialize the hardware by calling our internal *sttyparam* routine (line 127), turning the *data terminal ready* (DTR) signal on (line 128), and enabling the device to generate interrupts (lines 129).

In all cases, we raise the processor priority to ignore interrupts temporarily (line 132) and then check to see if we ought to wait for *data carrier detect* (DCD). If the open has not set either of the 'no delay' flags (line 134), and the device is not flagged as a local (i.e., non-modem) device (line 135), and the DCD signal from the modem is not present (line 136), then we must wait until DCD is detected. We set a flag in our local status structure indicating we are waiting for DCD (line 138) and then we go to sleep (line 139). Note that we *or* PCATCH with the priority argument to sleep. This tells sleep that if the sleep is interrupted, it is still to return to the driver. Interrupted sleeps, however, return a value of one while normally terminated sleeps (i.e., terminated by a call to wakeup) return a value of 0. If the sleep is interrupted we clear the DCDWAIT flag (line 141) and return an error (line 142). Otherwise we loop (line 134-144) until we are convinced that the conditions are proper to continue with the open. We will see later (lines 391-398) how we detect the change in the state of the DCD signal and issue the wakeup that terminates this sleep.

Before we leave the open routine we restore the previous processor priority (line 145), note that the device has been successfully opened (line 146), and return with a value that indicates success (line 147).

The Close Entry Point

The responsibilities of the close routine are: to wait until all of the output
has been transmitted; to hang up the phone (if requested); and to put the
hardware in a quiescent state.

```
149  close entry point:
152      raise the processor priority (disabling interrupts)
153-154  while (there is work still to do)
156          set flag indicating we are waiting for output to complete
157          go to sleep
             if (sleep is rudely awakened)
                 break out of loop (i.e. go to line 160)
160      restore processor priority

161      if ('hang up phone on close' flag is set)
163          drop the DTR modem control signal
164          wait for two seconds

166      disable interrupts
167      clear the 'device is open' flag
168      return success
```

```
149  static int sttyclose(queue_t *q, int flag, cred_t *cp)
150  {
151      int x;

152      x = splstr();
153      while ((qsize(ststate.wq) > 0) ||
154              (ststate.wq->q_ptr != NULL))
155      {
156          ststate.flags |= DRAINW;
157          if (sleep((caddr_t) &ststate, STIPRI | PCATCH))
158              break;
159      }
160      splx(x);

161      if (ststate.t.c_cflag & HUPCL)
162      {
163          com1dtr(OFF);
164          delay(2 * HZ);
165      }
```

```
166        outb(INTENB, 0);

167        ststate.flags = 0;

168        return (0);
169  }
```

We check to see if there is any data still in the queue waiting to be transmitted (lines 153 and 154). Note that the queue pointer passed to the close routine is for the read queue and we must check the state of the write queue. We could either access the write queue by using the kernel supplied routine *WR* (see line 121) or by using the previously stored queue pointer as is done here.

As we will see later in the driver, the message data block that is currently being transmitted is pointed to by the *q_ptr* member of the write queue. So even if the queue is empty (qsize == 0) there could still be one last message block waiting to be sent, hence the second test on line 154.

If there is data still to be sent, we set a flag indicating that we are waiting for output to drain (line 156). We shall see later that this flag is checked when the last character is sent to determine if a wakeup is in order (lines 318-319). With the flag set, we go to sleep (line 157). Again we *or* in the PCATCH flag to ensure that the sleep call will always return. If the sleep is interrupted, we exit the loop waiting for the output to drain.

Remember that, as has been our practice in previous drivers, we bracket the loop with *spl* calls (lines 152 and 160) to ensure that an interrupt cannot happen between our test (lines 153 and 154) and our going to sleep (lines 156 and 157).

Once the output has been drained, we check to see if the HUPCL flag is set (line 161). If so, we must arrange to hang up the phone line (lines 163-164). This is exactly the same as in our earlier COM1 driver.

We then turn off interrupts from the device (line 166), clear all internal status flags (line 167), and return a value indicating a successful close (line 168).

The Write-Side Put Entry Point

Recall from our discussion of STREAMS drivers in Chapter 11 that the put routine is responsible for performing the initial urgent processing of messages and then: passing them to another queue; placing them on the local queue for later processing; or disposing of the message altogether.

In this entry point we will see examples of all three options.

```
170   write-side put entry point:

175       switch (based on message type)
177         M_DATA or M_BREAK or M_DELAY:
178           put message on queue
179           call sttyrestart to process
180           break out of switch statement

181         M_IOCTL:
182           if (ioctl command is not TCSETAW)
183               put message on queue
184               call sttyrestart to process
185           else
186               call doioctl to process immediately
```

```
170   static int sttywput(queue_t *q, mblk_t *mp)
171   {
172       struct iocblk *ip;
173       int x;
174       struct copyresp *csp;

175       switch (mp->b_datap->db_type)
176       {
177         case M_DATA: case M_BREAK:  case M_DELAY:
178           putq(q, mp);
179           sttyrestart();
180           break;

181         case M_IOCTL:
182           if (((struct iocblk *)mp->b_rptr)->ioc_cmd != TCSETAW)
                  {
183               put(q, mp);
```

```
184               sttyrestart();
           }
185        else
186            doioctl(q, mp);
187        break;
```

We branch based on the type of message we have been passed (line 175). Messages that are not of high priority or ought to be processed in sequence with data messages are placed on the queue. In this driver this means that M_DATA, M_BREAK, and M_DELAY messages are placed on the driver's write queue without any processing (line 177). Sttyrestart is called in order to make sure that work is being done to process messages on the queue (line 179).

If the M_IOCTL message contains a TCSETAW command (i.e., set communications once output has drained—line 182), it is placed on the queue (line 183) to be processed in sequence with the data messages and sttyrestart is called (line 184). Otherwise (line 186), it is passed to the internal routine *doioctl* for immediate action. We shall consider this routine later.

```
188        M_CTL:
189-190       change command to 'please do all TERMIO processing'
191           send message back upstream

193        M_FLUSH:
194           if ('flush write q' flag is set)
195               flush write q
196           if ('flush read q' flag is set)
198               clear 'flush write q' flag (may not be set)
199               send message back up write queue
201           else
202               destroy message
203           break out from switch statement
```

```
188        case M_CTL:
189            ip = (struct iocblk *)mp->b_rptr;
190            ip->ioc_cmd = MC_DO_CANON;
191            qreply(q, mp);
192            break;
```

```
193          case M_FLUSH:
194             if (*mp->b_rptr & FLUSHW)
195                     flushq(q, FLUSHDATA);

196             if (*mp->b_rptr & FLUSHR)
197             {
198                     *mp->b_rptr &= ~FLUSHW;
199                     qreply(q, mp);
200             }
201             else
202                     freemsg(mp);
203             break;
```

High-priority messages must be dealt with immediately. The M_CTL message (line 188) is sent downstream by the LDTERM module to determine what termio processing the device and its driver can handle. Our response (MC_DO_CANON—line 190) indicates that we cannot perform any line discipline processing and that we expect the LDTERM module to handle everything. This response is generated by changing the message to return MC_DO_CANON and sending the message back using the qreply routine which places the message on the first upstream queue (line 191).

The M_FLUSH message (line 193) must be handled by all drivers and is an instruction to flush the read and/or write queues of the driver. A request to flush the write queue is acted upon immediately (lines 194 and 195) while a request to flush the read queues is sent back upstream (lines 196 and 200) where it will cause all upstream modules to flush their queues. A message requesting the flushing of the write queues only is destroyed once acted upon (line 202).

```
204          M_STOP:
205             set 'suspend output' flag
206             destroy message
207             break out of switch statement

208          M_START:
209             clear 'suspend output' flag
210             call sttyrestart to resume output
211             destroy message
212             break out of switch statement
```

```
204          case M_STOP:
205             ststate.flags |= STOP_WRITE;
206             freemsg(mp);
207             break;

208          case M_START:
209             ststate.flags &= ~STOP_WRITE;
210             sttyrestart();
211             freemsg(mp);
212             break;
```

The M_START and M_STOP messages are commands to start and stop output respectively. When the driver receives an M_STOP message, it sets the STOP_WRITE flag so that output will be suspended (line 205). It then frees the message (line 206).

In the case of the M_START message we clear the STOP_WRITE flag (line 209) and call the sttyrestart routine (line 210) to resume output. This routine will be examined shortly. Once handled, we free the message (line 211).

```
213          M_STOPI:
214             set 'suspend input' and 'send X-OFF' flags
215             raise the processor priority (disabling interrupts)
216             call sttytxintr to try to send X-OFF
217             restore processor priority
218             destroy message
219             break out of switch statement

220          M_STARTI:
221             clear 'suspend input' flag
222             set 'send X-ON' flag
223             raise the processor priority (disabling interrupts)
224             call sttytxintr to try to send X-ON
225             restore processor priority
226             destroy message
227             break out of switch statement

213          case M_STOPI:
214             ststate.flags |= STOP_READ | SEND_STOP;
```

```
215              x = spldev();
216              sttytxintr();
217              splx(x);
218              freemsg(mp);
219              break;

220          case M_STARTI:
221              ststate.flags &= ~STOP_READ;
222              ststate.flags |= SEND_START;
223              x = spldev();
224              sttytxintr();
225              splx(x);
226              freemsg(mp);
227              break;
```

In contrast to the stop output messages just considered, the M_STOPI and M_STARTI messages are instructions to stop and resume input, respectively. In the case of an M_STOPI message, we set flags (line 214) to indicate that input ought to be halted and that a STOP character (usually an X-OFF) ought to be sent to stop the connected device from sending us data. To ensure that the STOP character is sent we simulate the arrival of a transmit interrupt by (a) disabling interrupts (line 215), (b) calling the transmit interrupt handler (line 216), and (c) re-enabling interrupts (line 217). On line 218 we dispose of the M_STOPI message since it has been completely processed.

The handling of the M_STARTI message is similar (lines 220-227).

```
228          M_IOCDATA:
230            switch (based on type of command)
232              TCGETA:
233                  set return code based on success of copy
234                  reply (send message back upstream)
235                  break out of inner switch statement

226-237          TCSETA or TCSETAW:
238                  if (copy failed)
240                      destroy message
241                      break out of inner switch statement
243                  copy TERMIO parameters into local structure
244                  set device parameters
```

```
245-251              modify message to acknowlege receipt of data
252                  reply (send message upstream)
254            break out of outer switch statement

255        default:
256            destroy message

259     return (success)

228         case M_IOCDATA:
              ip = (struct iocblk *)mp->b_rptr;
229           csp = (struct copyresp *)mp->b_rptr;
230           switch (csp->cmd)
231           {
232             case TCGETA:
233               mp->b_datap->db_type =
                                    (cp->cp_rval ? M_IOCNAK : M_IOCACK);
234               qreply(q, mp);
235               break;

236             case TCSETA:
237             case TCSETAW:
238               if (csp->cp_rval)
239               {
240                   freemsg(mp);
241                   break;
242               }
243               ststate.t = *((struct termio *)mp->b_cont->b_rptr);
244               sttyparam(&ststate);
245               mp->b_datap->db_type = M_IOCACK;
246               mp->b_wptr = mp->b_rptr + sizeof(struct termio);
247               freemsg(mp->b_cont);
248               mp->b_cont = NULL;
249               ip->ioc_count = 0;
250               ip->ioc_error = 0;
251               ip->ioc_rval = 0;
252               qreply(q, mp);
253           }
254         break;

255     default:
256         freemsg(mp);
```

```
257              break;
258       }

259       return (0);
260  }
```

The M_IOCDATA message is sent by the Stream head in response to a M_COPYOUT or M_COPYIN message from the driver. These messages are generated by the driver to return or to obtain the information related to an ioctl request. This is discussed in depth later when we consider the *doioctl* routine in this driver.

In the case of a TCGETA ioctl command, the driver sends an M_COPYOUT message with the information necessary to respond to the TCGETA ioctl. The M_IOCDATA message is sent to the driver to indicate the success or failure of the Stream head in copying the data to the user process. In turn (line 233) the driver acknowledges the ioctl either positively (IOCACK) or negatively (IOCNAK) depending on the return value in the M_IOCDATA message.

With the TCSETA or TCSETA ioctl commands, the M_IOCDATA message contains the detailed parameter information to complete the ioctl request. We first check to see if the M_COPYIN request was successful (lines 238-242). If it was, we copy this information into our local status structure (line 243) and then call sttyparam to change the hardware parameters to reflect the new information (line 244).

We then convert the message into a positive acknowledgment (line 245), adjust the write pointer to indicate that we have read the data (line 246), free any associated data blocks (lines 247 and 248), clear various fields that were used when the message was an M_IOCDATA message (lines 249-251) and send the message back upstream (line 252).

If we receive a message we do not understand (line 255), we merely dispose of it by returning the message block(s) to the kernel (line 256).

The Read-Side Service Entry Point

The *read* service entry point is called by the operating system to process messages that have been placed on the driver's *read* queue (by the driver).

Read messages contain data that has been received by the communications device. Although the driver could immediately pass the message upstream by calling the put routine of the module immediately upstream, it is preferable for the driver to do as little as possible during interrupt time (when the data is received). Therefore we place the data on our own queue and wait for the kernel to schedule the service routine to process it. As we shall see, the processing required is nothing more than passing it upstream.

```
261   read-side service routine:

264       while (messages on queue)
266           if (room to pass message upstream)
267               pass message upstream
268           else
270               put message back on own queue
271               break out of loop
```

```
261   static int sttyrsrv(queue_t *q)
262   {
263       mblk_t *mp;

264       while ((mp = getq(q)) != NULL)
265       {
266           if (canput(q->q_next))
267               putnext(q, mp);
268           else
269           {
270               putbq(q, mp);
271               break;
272           }
273       }
274   }
```

This is a relatively simple service routine that loops (starting at line 264) as long as there are messages on the queue. The *getq* kernel routine returns the next message on the queue or NULL if there are none.

If we have a message we then check, using the kernel routine *canput*, to see if there is room on the upstream *read* queue. If there is, we put the message on that queue (line 267). If not, we place the message *back* on our own queue (line 270) and exit the loop (line 271). The kernel will reschedule our service routine once the upstream queue has room to accept more messages from us.

The Restart Routine

The restart routine is called from within our driver to try to restart output. It is called whenever an interrupt arrives that indicates a character has been transmitted (and hence there is room in the device's transmit buffer) or whenever the driver wishes to make sure the device is busy. Note that since it may be called when the device is already busy or when there is actually no work to be done, the routine must be able to handle these cases. The restart routine also ought to do as much work as possible before exiting.

```
275  sttyrestart routine:

283      raise the processor priority (disabling interrupts)

284      while (work to do)
286          if (no current data message to process)
287              try to get another message from queue
                 if (no more messages)
289                  if (someone is waiting for output to complete)
290                      wakeup waiting process(es)
291                  return
293              else
294                  save pointer to message
```

```
275  static void sttyrestart()
276  {
277      register queue_t *q = ststate.wq;
278      register mblk_t *mp;
279      char c;
280      int period;
281      int working = 1;
282      int x;

283      x = spldev();
```

```
284        while (working)
285        {
286            if ((mp = (mblk_t *)q->q_ptr) == NULL)
287                if ((mp = getq(q)) == NULL)
288                {
289                    if (ststate.flags & DRAINW)
290                        wakeup(&ststate);
291                    return;
292                }
293                else
294                    q->qptr = (caddr_t)mp;
```

We ignore interrupts for the duration of our processing by increasing the processor priority (line 283). We then loop (lines 284 to 335) while there is still work to do. The variable *working* is initialized to 1 (line 281) and will be set to zero when we know there is no more work to be done.

Every queue has a pointer (q_ptr) that can be used by the driver for internal purposes. In this driver we use the q_ptr for the write queue to point to the message we are currently processing. We check on line 286 to see if q_ptr points to a message. If not, we try to obtain the next message on the queue (line 287).

If there is no message pointed to by q_ptr and no messages on the queue then there is no work to be done. Before leaving the restart routine, however, we check to see if someone is waiting for all of the output to be transmitted (line 289). If the DRAINW flag is set this indicates that the driver is waiting for all of the output to be sent before closing the device (refer back to lines 153-159). We issue a wakeup (line 290) to permit the close entry point to complete. Then we exit this routine (line 291).

If, on the other hand, there is no message pointed to by q_ptr but there is a message on the queue, we set q_ptr to point to the message (line 294).

```
295        switch (based on message type)
297            M_DATA:
298                if (output is not possible)
300                    clear 'work to do' flag
301                    break out of switch statement

303                while (device can take data AND
```

```
304                              there is data to send)
205                    transmit data
306             clear 'work to do' flag if device is busy
307             break out of switch statement

295        switch (mp->b_datap->db_type)
296        {
297          case M_DATA:
298            if (ststate.flags & (STOP_WRITE|BREAK_IP|DELAY_IP))
299            {
300                working = 0;
301                break;
302            }

303            while ((inb(LSR) & LSRTHRE) &&
304                   ((c = getmc((mblk_t **)&q->q_ptr)) != -1))
305                  outb(TXR, c);
306            working = (inb(LSR) & LSRTHRE);
307            break;
```

We check the message type and branch accordingly (line 294). In case of a data message, we check to see if we are currently prohibited from transmitting data (the STOP_WRITE flag) or are waiting for a break or delay to end (line 298). If any of these conditions hold, then we clear the working flag (line 300) and exit the switch statement (line 301).

On line 303 we check to see if the device has room for another character in its Transmit Holding Register. If so, we call our *getmc* routine to return the next character from the message (line 304). If a character is available then we place it in the Transmit Register (line 305). We continue the loop (lines 303-305) until either the device has no more room or there is no more data in the message. If the device has no more room, then there is nothing more to do. If, however, there *is* room (i.e., we left the loop because there was no more data in the message) then we will want to continue the main loop (lines 284-335) in search of more work. We therefore set *working* based on the test on line 306 to see if there is room in the device...if there is...there is work to be done!

```
308            M_BREAK:
309              if (device is not transmitting)
```

```
311                 set `break in progress' flag
312                 start sending break
313                 request sttybreak be called in 0.25 seconds
314                 destroy message
315                 clear pointer to `current message'
317             clear `work to do' flag if device is busy
318             break out of switch statement

319         M_DELAY:
320             if (device is not transmitting)
322                 set `delay in progress' flag
323                 obtain delay period from body of message
324                 request sttytimeout be called after delay
325                 destroy message
326                 clear pointer to `current message'
328             clear `work to do' flag if device is busy
329             break out of switch statement

308         case M_BREAK:
309             if (inb(LSR) & LSRTSRE)
310             {
311                 ststate.flags |= BREAK_IP;
312                 outb(LCR, inb(LCR) | LCRBRK);
313                 timeout(sttybreak, 0, HZ/4);
314                 freemsg(mp);
315                 q->q_ptr = NULL;
316             }
317             working = 0;
318             break;

319         case M_DELAY:
320             if (inb(LSR) & LSRTSRE)
321             {
322                 ststate.flags |= DELAY_IP;
323                 period = *(int *)mp->b_rptr;
324                 timeout(sttytimeout, 0, period);
325                 freemsg(mp);
326                 q->q_ptr = NULL;
327             }
328             working = 0;
329             break;
```

Handling M_BREAK and M_DELAY messages is somewhat similar. The M_BREAK message is a request to send a break signal. We first check (line 309) to see if the device is busy transmitting data. Since it has some internal buffering it might have room for another character but still be busy transmitting. But we cannot start sending a BREAK signal until the device is completely idle. So we check the TSRE bit in the LSR register which indicates that the device is not transmitting. If it is not set, then the device is busy and we just leave the routine. When the device is completely idle we will receive an interrupt and will perform this test again.

If the device is idle we set a bit in our internal status flag (line 311) indicating that a break signal is in progress. We then set the 'send break' bit in the LCR register (line 312) and then request a timeout to be delivered in a quarter of a second (line 313). When the timeout has elapsed, the routine *sttybreak* will be called. As we shall see in a moment, this routine clears the BREAK_IP flag, clears the 'send break' bit from the LCR register, and calls the restart routine to get things going again.

Having handled the M_BREAK message, we free the message (line 314) and clear q_ptr (line 315) to indicate that there is no current message to process.

The processing of the M_DELAY message is very similar (line 319). The M_DELAY message is a request to delay output for a specified number of clock ticks. Again we check to make sure the device is not currently sending any data (line 320). This is to ensure that the delay is accurately timed (i.e., does not include the time to transmit previous characters). We set a flag indicating that output ought to be suspended because we are waiting for a delay to expire (line 322) and then access the delay period specified in the body of the message (line 323). We then request a timeout for the specified period (line 324), free the message (line 325), and clear q_ptr (line 326).

We will encounter the routine *sttytimeout* shortly. This routine is called when the timeout expires and is responsible for clearing the DELAY_IP flag and restarting output.

```
330             M_IOCTL:
331                 call doioctl to process message
```

```
332                   clear pointer to 'current message'

336    restore previous processor priority

330                case M_IOCTL:
331                    doioctl(q, mp);
332                    q->q_ptr = NULL;
333                    break;
334            }
335        }
336    splx(x);
337 }
```

If the message is an ioctl request we pass it to our *doioctl* routine for processing (line 331). We then clear q_ptr to indicate that the current message has been handled and that a new message must be obtained from the queue (line 332).

The loop that started on line 284 extends to line 335 continues while there is still work to be done (and a device ready to transmit).

After leaving the loop we restore the processor priority (line 336) before leaving the restart routine.

The Sttybreak and Sttydelay Routines

The sttybreak and sttydelay routines are scheduled to be called when the time for a break and delay have expired. We have already seen where arrangements were made to have these routines called (lines 313 and 324). As discussed, they are responsible for terminating the break or delay condition and restarting output (by calling sttyrestart).

```
338 sttybreak routine:
340     stop sending break signal
341     clear 'break in progress' flag
342     call sttyrestart to resume output

344 sttytimeout routine:
346     clear 'delay in progress' flag
347     call sttyrestart to resume output
```

```
338   static void sttybreak()
339   {
340       outb(LCR, inb(LCR) & ~LCRBRK);
341       ststate.flags &= ~BREAK_IP;
342       sttyrestart();
343   }

344   static void sttytimeout()
345   {
346       ststate.flags &= ~DELAY_IP;
347       sttyrestart();
348   }
```

When the end of the break signal occurs, we clear the 'send break' bit from the LCR register (line 340), clear the 'break in progress' flag from our internal status variable (line 341) and restart output (line 342).

When a delay ends, we clear the 'delay in progress' flag (line 346) and restart output (line 347).

The Intr Entry Point

The intr entry point is called whenever the device signals a hardware interrupt. The entry point is responsible for determining the reason for the interrupt and handling it appropriately.

```
349   void sttyintr(int vec)
350   {
351       register int interrupt;

352       while ((interrupt = inb(IIR)) != 1)
353           switch (interrupt)
354           {
355             case 0x04:
356             case 0x06:
357               sttyrxintr();
358               break;
359             case 0x2:
360               sttytxintr();
361               break;
362             case 0x0:
```

```
363                 sttymdintr();
364                 break;
365             default:
366                 printf("Unidentified flying interrupt.\n");
367         }
368  }
```

Our interrupt handler here is taken directly from our earlier COM driver
in Chapter 9. We query the interrupt identification register (IIR) on line
352 and loop as long as there are interrupts to process. We branch (line
353) to the appropriate routine based on the interrupt id code.

The Sttymdintr Routine

The sttymdintr routine is responsible for handling interrupts related to
the modem control signals.

```
369   sttymdintr routine:
372       obtain state of DCD modem control line
373       if (someone is waiting for DCD)
375           if (DCD now present)
377               wakeup all processes waiting for DCD
378               set 'carrier is present' bit
381       if (device is currently open)
383           if (DCD now present)
384               set 'carrier is present' bit
385           else if (carrier was present AND
386                           terminal is not local)
388               drop DTR signal
389               allocate a new message buffer
                  if (buffer is allocated)
391                   set message type to 'hangup'
392                   send message upstream
```

```
369   static void sttymdintr()
370   {
371       register short dcd;

372       dcd = com1dcd();
373       if (ststate.flags & DCDWAIT)
374       {
375           if (dcd)
```

```
376                {
377                    wakeup((caddr_t) &ststate);
378                    ststate.flags |= CARRIER;
379                }
380            }
381        else if (ststate.flags & OPENED)
382        {
383            if (dcd)
384                ststate.flags |= CARRIER;
385            else if ((ststate.flags & CARRIER) &&
386                    ((ststate.t.c_cflag & CLOCAL) == 0))
387            {
388                com1dtr(OFF);
389                if ((mp == allocb(0, BPRI_HI)) != NULL)
390                {
391                    mp->b_datap->db_type = M_HANGUP;
392                    putq(ststate.rq, mp);
393                }
394            }
395        }
396    }
```

We obtain the current state of the data carrier detect (DCD) signal (line 372) and check to see if our open routine (lines 134-144) is waiting for the DCD signal. If it is waiting and DCD is now present (line 375) we generate a wakeup (line 377) and set the carrier present flag 378.

On the other hand, if the device is already open (line 381) then we check to see if DCD is present (line 383). If it is, we set the carrier present flag (line 384). If not, we check to see if the carrier was present (line 385) and the device is not a local terminal (line 386). If both these conditions hold then it means we are connected to a modem and have lost the connection. We hang up the phone (line 388), allocate a message block (line 389), and place a 'hangup' message (line 396) on the read queue (line 392). This message will be sent upstream to notify the Stream head and user process that the modem connection has been lost. The Stream head will take care of generating the SIGHUP signal that we had to handle ourselves in our earlier driver (Chapter 9).

The Sttyrxintr Routine

The *sttyrxintr* routine is called when the interrupt handler has determined that the interrupt has been caused by a character being received or a receive error being detected. This routine is responsible for processing this interrupt and handling the received data, if any. A brief comparison with the *com1rxintr* routine in Chapter 9 will reveal many similarities.

```
397  sttyrxintr routine:

406      while (device has data to be read)
408          read and save data

409          if (break interrupt detected)
411              if (break interrupts are to be ignored)
412                  go back to top of loop (line 406)
413              else if (breaks are to generate signals)
415                  if (can allocate message buffer)
417                      set message type to BREAK
418                      send message upstream
420              go back to top of loop (line 406)
```

```
397  static void sttyrxintr()
398  {
399      short status;
400      short iflag;
401      short data[3];
402      short ndata = 1;
403      register char *cp;
404      register mblk_t *mp;

405      iflag = ststate.t.c_iflag;

406      while ((status = inb(LSR)) & (LSRDR | LSRBI))
407      {
408          data[0] = inb(RXR) & 0xff;

409          if (status & LSRBI)
410          {
411              if (ststate.t.c_iflag & IGNBRK)
412                  continue;
413              else if (ststate.t.c_iflag & BRKINT)
```

```
414                     {
415                             if ((mp == allocb(0, BPRI_HI)) != NULL)
416                             {
417                                     mp->b_datap->db_type = M_BREAK;
418                                     putq(ststate.rq, mp);
419                             }
420                             continue;
421                     }
422             }
```

The routine is essentially a giant *while* loop extending from line 406 to 447. The loop continues as long as there is either data to be read from the device (LSRDR) or a break has been detected (LSRBI). We start by reading the data register (line 408). We then check to see if the device has detected a break condition (line 409). If so, we check to see if break conditions are to be ignored (line 411) and if so, continue the loop from the top again (line 412). If break conditions are not to be ignored, then we check to see if they are to generate an interrupt signal (line 413). If so, we attempt to allocate a message block (line 415) and send an M_BREAK message upstream (lines 417 and 418).

```
423             if (parity checking is turned off)
424                     clear the parity error bit from the status

425             if (status indicates parity, framing, or overrun error)
427                     if ('ignore characters with errors' is set)
428                       go to top of loop (line 406)
429                     if ('mark parity errors' is set)
430-434                     mark character by prepending with 0xff and 0x00
436             else if ('mark parity errors' is set AND char is 0xff)
437-440                     mark character by prepending with 0xff

441             attempt to allocate message block to contain data
                if (successful)
443-444                 place char (and marks, if any) into message buffer
445                     send message upstream

423             if (!(ststate.t.c_iflag & INPCK))
424                     status &= ~LSRPER;
425             if (status & (LSRPER | LSRFER | LSROER))
426             {
```

```
427                if (ststate.t.c_iflag & IGNPAR)
428                      continue;

429                if (ststate.t.c_iflag & PARMRK)
430                {
431                     data[1] = 0;
432                     data[2] = 0xff;
433                     ndata = 3;
434                }
435          }
436          else if ((ststate.t.c_iflag & PARMRK) &&
                        (data[0] == 0xff))
437          {
438               data[1] = 0xff;
439               ndata = 2;
440          }

441          if ((mp == allocb(ndata, BPRI_MED)) != NULL)
442          {
443               while (ndata)
444                    *(mp->b_wptr)++ = data[--ndata];
445               putq(ststate.rq, mp);
446          }
447     }
448 }
```

By line 423 we know we have a character to process (it may of course be a null character caused by the break condition). We check to see if input parity checking is enabled (line 423) and if not, we clear any indication of a parity error from our copy of the line status register (line 424). On line 427 we check to see if any of a parity, framing, or overrun error has been detected. If so, we then check to see if characters with such errors are to be ignored (lines 427 and 428). If not, we check to see if characters received with errors are to be 'marked' (line 429). Marking a character means inserting the sequence '0xff 0x00' before the offending data. We place these bytes in the data array in opposite order since we read out the contents of the data array from data[2] to data[0].

On line 436 we check to see if a legitimate 0xff has been received and if so, we insert an additional 0xff (lines 438 and 439) so that the real 0xff character is not confused with the first byte of a parity mark sequence.

Finally, we attempt to allocate a data block (line 441) and copy into it the data we have received (lines 443 and 444). We then place the message on our read queue (line 445) to be sent upstream later by our service routine (refer to the section in this chapter on *sttyrsrv*, lines 261-274).

This loop (lines 406-447) continues as long as there is received data in the device to be extracted and sent upstream.

The Sttytxintr Routine

The *sttytxintr* routine is called by our interrupt entry point to handle transmit interrupts. These are generated when the device has transmitted a character. We need to check to see if a special flow control (i.e., X-ON or X-OFF) character must be sent, otherwise we merely call *sttyrestart* to obtain more data to transmit. As with the earlier routine there are strong similarities to the *com1txintr* routine in the character driver from Chapter 9.

```
449  com1txintr routine:
451      if (waiting to send X-OFF)
453          send X-OFF
454          clear 'waiting to send X-OFF' flag
457      else if (waiting to send X-ON)
459          send X-ON
460          clear 'waiting to send X-ON' flag
462      else
463          call sttyrestart routine to send more output to device

449  static void sttytxintr()
450  {
451      if (ststate.flags & SEND_STOP)
452      {
453          outb(TXR, ststate.t.c_cc[VSTOP]);
454          ststate.flags &= SEND_STOP;
456      }
457      else if (ststate.flags & SEND_START)
458      {
```

```
459              outb(TXR, ststate.t.c_cc[VSTART]);
460              ststate.flags &= ~SEND_START;
461      }
462   else
463        sttyrestart();
464 }
```

We first check to see if we are to send a 'stop' or 'start' flow control character (lines 451 and 457). If so, send the character and clear the flag that
indicated that the character had to be sent (lines 453-455 and 459-460).
Otherwise, call *sttyrestart* to obtain more data and transmit it.

The Getmc Routine

The *getmc* routine returns the next character from a data message that
may contain many attached data blocks. It is called from *sttyrestart* to
obtain the next character to be transmitted.

```
465  getmc routine:
470      mp = pointer to message block
471      while (no more data in this message block)
473          get next message block in chain
             if (there are no more message blocks)
475              free original message block
476              set pointer to message pointer to NULL
                     (indicating entire message gas vbbeen processed)
477              return (error indication)
479          else
481              free original message block
482              set pointer to message pointer to next block in chain
483              mp = next message block
```

```
465  static int getmc(mblk_t **mpp)
466  {
467      char c;
468      register mblk_t *mp;
469      register mblk_t *nmp;

470      mp = *mpp;

471      while (mp->b_rptr == mp->b_wptr)
472      {
```

```
473              if ((nmp = unlinkb(mp)) == NULL)
474              {
475                  freeb(mp);
476                  *mpp = (mblk_t *)NULL;
477                  return (-1);
478              }
479              else
480              {
481                  freeb(mp);
482                  *mpp = nmp;
483                  mp = nmp;
484              }
485          }
```

If the message's rptr is the same as its wptr then there is no more data in this message block (line 471). We call the kernel routine *unlinkb* to obtain a pointer to the next message block (line 473). If there are no more message blocks then we free the message block we have just finished (line 475) and return with an indication that there is no more data to be obtained from this message (lines 476 and 477).

If there is another message block, then we free the block we have just finished (line 481) and update the pointers to refer to the new message block (lines 482-483).

```
486      c = next character in message block

487      while (no more data in this message block)
489          get next message block in chain
             if (there are no more message blocks)
491              free original message block
492              set pointer to message pointer to NULL
                     (indicating entire message gas vbbeen processed)
493              return (error indication)
495          else
497              free original message block
498              set pointer to message pointer to next block in chain
499              mp = next message block

502      return (character obtain on line 486)
```

```
486        c = *mp->b_rptr++;

487        while (mp->b_rptr == mp->b_wptr)
488        {
489            if ((nmp = unlinkb(mp)) == NULL)
490            {
491                freeb(mp);
492                *mpp = (mblk_t *)NULL;
493                return (c);
494            }
495            else
496            {
497                freeb(mp);
498                *mpp = nmp;
499                mp = nmp;
500            }
501        }
502        return (c);
503    }
```

The next character in the message block is pointed to by b_rptr and we access it on line 486. We then check again to see if there is any more data in this block, and if not, attempt to obtain the next message block in the chain. The code on lines 487 to 501 is essentially the same as that just examined on lines 473 to 584. At the end, we return with our character (line 502).

The Doioctl Routine

Ioctl processing with STREAMS drivers is far more complex than with character drivers. As we saw earlier in a couple of character drivers, the normal method of handling ioctls is to process the command directly and, if necessary, use *copyin* and *copyout* to transfer additional information between the user process and the driver.

With STREAMS things become more complex since the ioctl issued by the user process must be turned into a message by the Stream head, a message that could take a while to flow downstream to the driver. By the time the driver has received the ioctl message, the user process that issued the ioctl may not be the current process. This means that the driver cannot simply reach out and exchange data using *copyin* or *copyout*. It must instead send messages to the Stream head requesting the data be transferred to and from the user process. If data is being requested from the user process, we must use an M_COPYIN message. Otherwise we use an M_COPYOUT message.

Since drivers do not necessarily handle all possible ioctl commands we must explicitly acknowledge every ioctl message either positively (we can and have handled it) or negatively (we cannot and have not handled it). This will become somewhat clearer once we have examined this routine

To make things easier the Stream head will sometimes recognize the ioctl command and realize that either additional data must be sent to the driver or that additional data is required from the driver. These ioctl messages contain an indication that additional data is attached as part of the message or that additional data must be attached to the acknowledgment. Ioctl messages that do not contain or expect the additional data (and that require the use of M_COPYIN and M_COPYOUT messages to exchange the additional information) are called *transparent* ioctl requests.

```
504   doioctl routine:

509       switch (based on type of ioctl command)
511-512     TCSETA or TCSETAW:
513           if (request is a transparent ioctl command)
515               obtain pointer to message buffer
516               set user address in copy request
517-518           free chained message block
519-522           set up remainder of COPYIN message
523               send upstream to obtain data associated with ioctl
525           else
527-528           if (message buffer contains a termio structure)
530                   copy over the termio data
531                   call sttyparam to set the device parameters
532-533               change the message into a positive acknowlegement
534                   send reply upstream
536               else
538                   change the message into a negative acknowlegement
539                   send reply upstream
542           break out of switch statement
```

```
504   static void doioctl(queue_t *q, mblk_t *mp)
505   {
506       struct iocblk *ip = ((struct iocblk *)mp->b_rptr);
507       struct copyreq *cp;
508       int transparent = 0;

509       switch (ip->ioc_cmd)
510       {
511         case TCSETA:
512         case TCSETAW:
513           if (ip->ioc_count == TRANSPARENT)
514           {
515               cp = (struct copyreq *)mp->b_rptr;
516               cp->cq_addr = (caddr_t) *(long *)mp->b_cont->b_rptr;
517               freemsg(mp->b_cont);
518               mp->b_cont = NULL;
519               cp->cq_size = sizeof(struct termio);
520               cp->cq_flag = 0;
521               mp->b_datap->db_type = M_COPYIN;
522               mp->b_wptr = mp->b_rptr + sizeof(struct termio);
523               qreply(q, mp);
524           }
525           else
526           {
527               if ((ip->ioc_count == sizeof(struct termio)) &&
528                   (mp->b_cont != NULL))
529               {
530                   ststate.t =
                              *((struct termio *)mp->b_cont->b_rptr);
531                   sttyparam(&ststate);
532                   mp->b_datap->db_type = M_IOCACK;
533                   iocp->ioc_count = 0;
534                   qreply(q, mp);
535               }
536               else
537               {
538                   mp->b_datap->db_type = M_IOCNAK;
539                   qreply(q, mp);
540               }
541           }
542           break;
```

We branch depending on the ioctl command (line 509). The TCSETA and TCSETAW commands (lines 511 and 512) are requests to set the parameters for the communications line. If the request is a transparent request (line 513) then we must explicitly request the parameter information by sending an M_COPYIN message upstream. We do this by converting the received M_IOCTL message into an M_COPYIN message. We save a copy of the pointer to the message buffer (line 515), copy over the address of the parameter block in the user process (line 516), free any attached message blocks (lines 517 and 518), indicate how much data we want copied in (line 519), clear the flag member (line 520), overwrite the message type to be M_COPYIN (line 521), update the write pointer (line 522), and send the message upstream.

If the message is *not* a transparent ioctl request then the parameter data must be in a data block attached to this message. We check that the amount of data attached is what we expected and that there is, in fact, an attached data block (lines 527-528). If everything looks good, we use a structure assignment to copy the data from the attached data block to the termio structure in the strtty structure (line 530). We then call our *sttyparam* routine to put the new parameters into effect (line 531). We then convert the ioctl message into a positive acknowledgment message (lines 532 and 532) and send it back upstream (line 534).

If the message was not a transparent ioctl request and yet did not contain the expected attached data block, then we convert the ioctl message into a negative acknowledgment and send it back upstream (lines 538 and 539).

```
543        TCGETA:
544            if (request is a transparent ioctl command)
546                set flag indicating this is a transparent request
547-550            set up request part of a COPYOUT message
552            if (there are chained message blocks)
553                free them
554            allocate a message to hold a termio struct
               if (allocation failed)
556                convert original message into a negative ack
557                set the error code to suggest trying again later
558                send nak reply upstream
559                break out of switch statement
```

561   **copy current termio structure into message**
562   **if (transparent request flag was set)**
564-565   **finish setting up message as a COPYOUT request**
567   **else**
569-570   **set up message as an IOCACK message**
                    (positive acknowledgement with data attached)
572   **send message upstream**
573   **break out of switch statement**

```
543     case TCGETA:
544         if (ip->ioc_count == TRANSPARENT)
545         {
546             transparent++;
547             cp = (struct copyreq *)mp->b_rptr;
548             cp->cq_size = sizeof(struct termio);
549             cp->cq_addr = (caddr_t) *(long *)mp->b_cont->b_rptr;
550             cp->cq_flag = 0;
551         }
552         if (mp->b_cont)
553             freemsg(mp->b_cont);
554         if ((mp->b_cont =
                    allocb(sizeof(struct termio), BPRI_MED)) == NULL)
555         {
556             mp->b_datap->db_type = M_IOCNAK;
557             ip->ioc_error = EAGAIN;
558             qreply(q, mp);
559             break;
560         }

561         *((struct termio *)mp->b_cont) = ststate.t;

562         if (transparent)
563         {
564             mp->b_datap->db_type = M_COPYOUT;
565             mp->b_wptr = mp->b_rptr + sizeof(struct termio);
566         }
567         else
568         {
569             mp->b_datap->db_type = M_IOCACK;
570             ip->ioc_count = sizeof(struct termio);
571         }
```

```
572              qreply(q, mp);
573              break;
```

The TCGETA command is a request to obtain the current communications parameters. If the message is a transparent ioctl request (line 543) then we remember it as such (line 546) and begin to convert the M_IOCTL message into an M_COPYOUT message. We set the number of bytes we are sending back (line 548), and take from the original M_IOCTL message the address of where in the user process the data is to be placed (line 549). We also clear the flag member of the structure (line 550).

Regardless of the type of M_IOCTL (transparent or not) we free any attached message blocks (lines 552 and 553) since we will have to allocate one of the appropriate size anyway (line 554).

If the attempt to allocate a message block fails we send upstream a negative acknowledgment (line 556) with an indication to try the request again (line 557), perhaps when more message blocks are available.

In line 561 we use a structure assignment to copy the current parameters into the message block. We then check to see if we are handling a transparent ioctl or not (line 562). If we are, then this is an M_COPYOUT message (line 564) and we adjust b_wptr to indicate how much data is actually in the attached data block (line 565). If not, then this is a positive acknowledgment (line 569) with attached data. The ioc_count member indicates the amount of attached data (line 570). In either case the response is sent upstream (line 572).

If the request was a transparent ioctl then the Stream head will process the M_COPYIN or M_COPYOUT messages and will send an M_IOCDATA message in response. In the case of the M_COPYIN message, the M_IOCDATA will contain the requested information or an indication that the information could not be obtained (i.e., the address in the user process was not valid). In the case of the M_COPYOUT message, the M_IOCDATA will contain only the indication of whether the attempt to copy the data to the user process was successful.

The processing of M_IOCDATA messages is handled by the write-side put entry point which has already been examined (refer to lines 228-254).

```
574        default:
575          convert original message into a negative ack
576          send nak reply upstream
```

```
574      default:
575        mp->b_datap->db_type = M_IOCNAK;
576        qreply(q, mp);
577        break;
578    }
579  }
```

If we do not understand the command part of the ioctl message then we return a negative acknowledgment upstream.

The Param Routine

The *sttyparam* routine is called from within the driver whenever the hardware parameters of the COM port must be changed. It takes the parameters from the termio structure member of the strtty structure pointed to by the single argument to this routine.

```
580  static void sttyparam(struct strtty *stp)
581  {
582      register short lcr = 0;
583      int x;

584      if (stp->t.c_cflag & PARENB)
585          if (stp->t.c_cflag & PARODD)
586              lcr = LCRPEN;
587          else
588              lcr = LCRPEN | LCREVP;

589      switch (stp->t.c_cflag & CSIZE)
590      {
591        case CS5:
592          lcr |= LCR5B;
593          break;
594        case CS6:
595          lcr |= LCR6B;
596          break;
597        case CS7:
598          lcr |= LCR7B;
```

```
599            break;
600          case CS8:
601            lcr |= LCR8B;
602            break;
603        }

604        if (stp->t.c_cflag & CSTOPB)
605            lcr |= LCR2SB;

606        x = spldev();

607        stp->flags |= STOP_WRITE;

608        outb(LCR, lcr | LCRDLAB);
609        outb(DIVLSB, Divisors[stp->t.c_cflag & CBAUD] & 0xff);
610        outb(DIVMSB, (Divisors[stp->t.c_cflag & CBAUD] >> 8) & 0xff);
611        outb(LCR, lcr);
612        outb(MCR, MCRDTR | MCRRTS | MCROUT1 | MCROUT2);
613        outb(INTENB, IERRX | IERTX | IERRST | IERMST);

614        stp->flags &= ~STOP_WRITE;

615        splx(x);
616  }
```

Since this routine has been taken directly from the *com1param* routine
with no significant changes it will not be discussed further. Please refer to
Chapter 9 for an explanation of this code.

Suggestions for Improvements

Here are some suggestions for enhancements to this driver that would
make it of production quality. We could modify the driver:

- to work with multiple devices of the same type (i.e., multiple communications ports) each with its own pair of queues;
- to be more efficient in allocating messages for received characters
  (see exercise 2 on the next page); and
- to perform some of the line discipline functions itself rather than
  depending on LDTERM to do everything. Recall that on line 190

we told the LDTERM module we were not prepared to perform any line discipline processing. We could have instead indicated that some functions would be handled by us. Refer to the STREAMS driver reference manual for your system to determine exactly how to do this.

Summary

As can be seen by comparing this driver to the earlier one in Chapter 9, STREAMS drivers are considerably more complex than the equivalent character mode driver. What that complexity buys us, however, is a much cleaner and more modular architecture for communications devices.

In our earlier driver we had intimate knowledge of both the device and the line discipline routines and directly managed the flow of data between the two. With STREAMS we need only concern ourselves with the device and the interface to STREAMS. The processing that may or may not be done upstream is of no concern to us. And indeed the STREAMS architecture makes it trivial to replace or augment the standard line discipline processing—something that could not be done as flexibly with the older character driver approach.

Exercises

1. In our discussion of the close entry point we recalled that it was standard practice to protect loops such as the one on lines 153-159 with *spl* calls. Describe what problems might arise in this driver if the pair of spl calls on lines 152 and 160 were omitted.

2. This driver is relatively inefficient when it comes to receiving data since it allocates a message for each single character received (see lines 444-446). Modify the driver to buffer received characters until either 64 characters have been received or three clock ticks have occurred since the last character has been received. Then create a message of the appropriate size and send it upstream. (Note that most UNIX systems support a *poll* entry point that is called every clock tick.)

Chapter 13

Driver Installation

Now that you have written your driver it is time to install and test it. This chapter will discuss how to install UNIX device drivers and the next will make some suggestions on testing and improving your driver.

Installing a device driver in a UNIX system involves the following steps:

- compiling the device driver;
- modifying the kernel configuration tables and files;
- linking the device driver with the kernel object files to produce a new kernel;
- creating the necessary entries in the /*dev* directory; and
- rebooting the system with the new kernel.

Although the installation of any UNIX device driver will require the above steps, the details vary widely between different versions of UNIX.

This chapter will outline the approach taken by Release 3.2 of UNIX. We first consider these steps in detail and then take the driver from Chapter 4 as an example and illustrate how to compile and install the driver on SCO UNIX System V/386 Release 3.2. Other systems such as XENIX and BSD UNIX take very different approaches, although the net result is the same as the list above.

In any case, the reader is strongly advised to consult the documentation for his particular UNIX system before proceeding to install his driver.

Compiling the Driver

Compiling the driver is similar to compiling any other C program. Since the driver is not a stand-alone program it is always compiled to produce an object (i.e., the -c flag on most C compilers) rather than a linked executable file.

Also on some systems special flags are needed to ensure that the correct parts of the include files are used and that the compiler generates a module appropriate for linking into the kernel. This information must be obtained from your system's documentation.

Configuring the Kernel

The next step is modifying the kernel configuration tables to reflect the addition of the new driver. Again, the method varies between different UNIX versions and you must consult the documentation for your system to determine the actual method to use. The examples below are taken from SCO UNIX System V Release 3.2 and apply to most SVR3.2 systems.

The two configuration files used by the system to generate a new kernel are the *mdevice* and *sdevice* files in the */etc/conf/cf.d* directory. The mdevice file contains an entry for each device driver that exists on the system. The sdevice file contains information for each driver that is to be incorporated into the kernel. Another way of looking at it is that the mdevice file represents the menu of possible drivers available to the system administrator while the sdevice file represents his selection of the drivers to be incorporated in the kernel.

The Mdevice File

The mdevice file consists of nine fields:

Device Name   This is the internal name of the device driver (up to eight characters long).

Function List   This specifies the entry points that are declared within the device driver. Each entry point is represented by a single letter (e.g., o = open entry point, c = close, r = read, w = write, i = ioctl, etc.).

Driver Characteristics   This specifies the characteristics of the driver. Again, the field consists of a list of letters with each letter representing a characteristic (e.g., i = the device driver is installable, c = the device is a character device, b = the device is a block device, t = the device is a tty, o = this device may have only one sdevice entry, D = this option indicates that the device driver can share its DMA channel, etc.).

Handler Prefix   This is the prefix used for each of the driver's entry points (e.g., 'lp' in the line printer driver in Chapter 4). This string may be up to four characters long and must be unique among all drivers installed on the system.

Block Major Number   This is the major device number used to reference the driver. This value is assigned automatically during the installation process and ought to be left as 0 by the driver writer.

Character Major Number   This is the major device number used to reference the driver. This value is assigned automatically during the installation process and ought to be left as 0 by the driver writer.

Minimum Units   This specifies the minimum number of these devices that can be specified in the sdevice file.

Maximum Units   This specifies the maximum number of these devices that can be specified in the sdevice file.

DMA Channel   This specifies the DMA channel that the device will use. If DMA is not used, set the field to '-1'. On some systems different devices may not share the same DMA channel (hence the value in the field must be unique).

The installation example at the end of this chapter will illustrate how to create a new entry in the mdevice file.

The Sdevice File

The *sdevice* file consists of ten fields:

Device Name   This is the internal name of the device driver (up to eight characters long). This must match the device name field for one of the entries in the mdevice file.

Configure   This indicates whether or not this driver ought to be incorporated in the kernel. Appropriate values are 'Y' or 'N'.

Unit   This specifies the number of units installed. The value must be between the limits specified in the mdevice file. The value is not used by the kernel or installation process directly, but is available to the driver. It is usually used to represent the number of subdevices on a controller.

Ipl   This specifies the CPU priority level at which interrupts will be processed (and which the driver's interrupt handler will run). If the driver has no interrupt handler, then put a 0 in this field.

Interrupt Type   This specifies the interrupt architecture used by this device. Appropriate values include:

- The device does not require an interrupt line.
- The device requires an interrupt line. If the driver supports more than one hardware controller, each controller requires a separate interrupt.
- The device requires an interrupt line. If the driver supports more than one hardware controller, each controller will share the same interrupt.
- The device requires an interrupt line. If the driver supports more than one hardware controller, each controller will share the same interrupt. Multiple device drivers having the same ipl level can share this interrupt.

Vector   This specifies the interrupt vector used by this device (0 if no interrupt vector). This number must match the hardware interrupt line used by the hardware. Although it is possible for more than one device to share an interrupt vector, some bus architectures (most notably the PC/AT ISA bus) make this almost impossible without explicit cooperation between the different devices.

Start I/O Address (SIOA)   This specifies the starting address on the I/O bus through which the device communicates. If the device does not respond to any I/O addresses, use 0.

End I/O Address (EIOA)   This specifies the ending address on the I/O bus through which the device communicates. If the device does not respond to any I/O addresses, use 0.

Start Controller Memory Address (SCMA)   This specifies the starting address of the device's dual-ported memory (memory accessible both to the device and to the host CPU). If the device does not respond to any memory addresses, use 0.

End Controller Memory Address (ECMA)   This specifies the ending address of the device's dual-ported memory (memory accessible both to the device and to the host CPU). If the device does not respond to any memory addresses, use 0.

Installing the New Driver

On some UNIX systems utilities are provided to make the process of installing drivers easier. These tools will update the mdevice and sdevice files and perform many of the other tasks needed to install a new driver and update the system configuration files.

On SVR3.2 systems, the *idinstall* command will take the name of the new driver as well as the driver object file and the new mdevice and sdevice entries and install them in preparation for generating a new kernel. The details of the use of the idinstall are described in the documentation that accompanies SVR3.2 systems and are illustrated later in this chapter.

Building a New Kernel

Once the kernel configuration tables have been modified then you can generate the new kernel. The command to build a new kernel varies between different UNIX systems. On SVR3.2 systems the utility to run is *idbuild*. This program will generate a new UNIX kernel.

On some SVR3.2 systems the idbuild utility will ask you if you want the new kernel to boot by default. On others, the new kernel will automatically be used during the next boot.

Creating Entries in /dev

In order to access your driver you will need to create the special files in the */dev* directory that reference your device driver. On some UNIX systems this must be done manually using the *mknod* command. On most SVR3.2 systems this is done automatically (or at least semi-automatically). When you install your device driver you may optionally provide a *Node* file that defines the entries in /dev that you need. This file contains four fields.

Device Name   This is the internal name of the device driver (up to eight characters long). It must match the device name field for the entry in the mdevice and sdevice files.

Node Name   This is the name of the special file to be created in the /dev directory.

Node Type   This specifies whether the special file is to be character ('c') or block ('b') type.

Minor Device Number   This specifies the minor device number for this special file.

The file may contain more than one entry (indicating that more than one special file will be created.)

Note that you do not need to specify the major device number of the driver. The device driver installation software will generate a unique major device number automatically and associate it with the device name given in the first field of the mdevice file. When the system examines the Node file and goes to create the special files in /dev, it will use the device name in the first field of the Node file to look up the major device number assigned to this driver.

On most systems that support the Node file the entries in /dev will be generated automatically when the system reboots with the new kernel. On some systems the /dev entries will be created as part of the idbuild process (and you may be asked if you want "the kernel environment rebuilt" which is kernel-speak for creating the /dev entries). You may also manually force the /dev entries to be created by using the *idmkenv* and *idmknod* utilities.

Rebooting the New Kernel

If you are testing a new driver that you have written it is imperative that before booting your new kernel you perform a complete and full system backup. Because your new driver will be running as part of the new kernel without any protection against wild pointers or other illegal operations, it is quite possible that a bug in your driver could erase the entire file system from your disk. Indeed, drivers that have been almost completely debugged are as dangerous as drivers being installed for the first time. So it is essential to make sure that everything is safe before you start testing your driver.

The second thing to ensure is that you have a copy of the old UNIX kernel available. Usually the kernel build process will automatically save a copy of the old kernel in */unix.old* but it is essential to make an additional copy of your own (called, say */unix.original*). This is necessary since the next rebuild of the UNIX kernel will overwrite /unix.old with the current kernel (i.e., the one containing the first version of your driver).

If you find that your new kernel fails catastrophically it is possible on most UNIX systems to tell the system bootstrap to boot the old (unix.old or unix.original) kernel and thus restore normal operation.

Another option that is possible on some systems is to generate a bootable tape or floppy. With this, one can boot the system and run a restricted version of UNIX without using the hard disk. It is sometimes possible to restore a damaged file system in this manner using *fsck* (file system check) or *fsdb* (file system debugger). It may also be possible to mount the hard disk and save any critical files that were on the hard disk.

Installation Example

As an example of an actual driver installation process let us examine the installation of one of the device drivers we studied earlier in this book. We shall use the line printer driver from Chapter 4 since it controls *real* hardware and will illustrate many of issues in driver installation.

The first step is to compile the driver. On SCO UNIX the command line we enter is simple:

```
cc -O -c lp.c
mv lp.o Driver.o
```

This invokes the C compiler telling it to generate 'optimised' code (-O) and to generate an object file (-c) only and not a linked executable. We rename the object file *Driver.o* so that the idinstall command will be able to locate the file.

The next step is to generate the entries for the mdevice and sdevice files. These are placed in files called Master and System, respectively. The Master file for our line printer driver is as follows:

```
lp   Iocrw   Hcio   lp   0   0   1   1   -1
```

Let us examine this in detail. The first field ('lp') specifies the driver's internal name. The second field ('Iocrw') indicates that the driver has init, open, close, read, and write entry points. The third field ('Hcio') specifies that the driver controls actual hardware, is a character driver, uses interrupts, and may only have one sdevice entry. The fourth field ('lp') indicates that the prefix for the entry point names is 'lp'.

The fifth and sixth fields ('0 0') are place holders for the block and character major device numbers, respectively. Since this is a character driver the fifth field (the block major number will never be used). The sixth field will be filled in automatically by the installation utility once it has determined the unique major device number to use for this driver.

The seventh and eighth field ('1 1') specify the minimum and maximum number of units this driver will support. And finally, the ninth field ('-1') indicates that no DMA channel is used by this device.

The System file for our line printer driver is as follows:

```
lp   Y   1   3   1   7   378   37f   0   0
```

The first field ('lp') specifies the driver's internal name. This must be the same as for the Master file. The second field ('Y') indicates that the driver is to be incorporated into the kernel. The third field ('1') indicates the number of units connected to the line printer controller. The fourth field ('3') specifies the priority to assign interrupts from this device. The fifth field ('1') indicates that this device requires exclusive use of its interrupt line. The sixth field ('7') specifies the interrupt line (vector) used by the line printer controller supported by this driver. The seventh and eighth fields ('378 37f') indicate the range of I/O addresses used by the line printer controller. The last two fields ('0 0') indicate that no memory addresses are used by this device.

We also create a Node file that defines the /dev entries we want created automatically:

```
lp   lp   c   0
```

This indicates that we would like a character special file with minor device 0 to be created with the name */dev/lp*.

Next, we create a scratch directory (say /tmp/driver) into which we copy the Driver.o, Master, System, and Node files. We then move into that directory and run the driver installation program *idinstall*, indicating that we are adding a new driver and giving the name of the new driver:

```
/etc/conf/bin/idinstall -a lp
```

The driver has now been installed in the system configuration files and directories. We build a new kernel by running the *idbuild* utility:

```
/etc/conf/bin/idbuild
```

When this command is finished, we shall have installed our driver and built a new kernel. When the system is rebooted, the new kernel with our driver will be ready to test.

Advanced Driver Installation

Recall that one of the fields in the sdevice (or System) file specified the number of units the driver was to handle. This raises two questions: How does the driver determine how many units it has been configured to support? How can the driver size arrays based on configuration information such as the number of units?

On SVR3.2 systems there is an elegant two-part solution to this problem. The first part is that the installation process allows the driver writer to include a short C program (called Space.c) along with the Driver.o, Master, System, and Node files used by idinstall. This C program can contain the declarations of arrays or other variables that the driver needs and that can only be declared once the system has been configured (the Space.c file is compiled and linked when the kernel is rebuilt).

The second part of the solution is the *config.h* file which is generated during the kernel build process and contains most of the information from the Master and System files in the form of C defines.

For example, if the driver prefix (field 4 of the mdevice/Master file) was called *blat*, then the define *BLAT_UNITS* in config.h would represent the number of units specified in the third field of the sdevice/System entry. An examination of the config.h file (in /etc/conf/cf.d) will show how other fields in the mdevice and sdevice fields are available to the driver writer.

Taking these two parts together, we can see that if the *blat* driver needed to size an array based on the number of units configured, the driver writer could include a Space.c file of the form:

```
#include "config.h"

int blat_units = BLAT_UNITS;

int blat_flags[BLAT_UNITS];
```

Exercises

1. Select one of the other device drivers discussed earlier in this book and write the Master, System, and Node files that could be used to install it.
2. Study the documentation on driver installation for your UNIX system and examine the directories that contain the configuration information for the drivers already installed on your UNIX system. On SVR3.2 systems the directories to examine are in */etc/conf.*

Chapter 14

Zen and the Art of Device Driver Writing

In Chinese painting it is said that the key to mastery is learning where *not* to paint, rather than where to paint. In this vein it might be appropriate to talk for a moment about when not to write a device driver. More accurately, this section is a short compendium of some of the wrong reasons for writing drivers.

At the top of the list is the unstated wish of almost every systems programmer: to try writing a device driver. As has been mentioned at the start of this book, device drivers are properly considered among the most challenging and demanding types of software to write. And what programmer can resist the challenge?

Don't get me wrong. There is nothing wrong with wanting to write a device driver. The challenge and frustration is more than compensated for by the feelings of accomplishment and triumph when the driver (and device) are finally beaten into submission. The risk, however, is that the programmer will try to justify developing the driver on other grounds in order to obtain management approval for his endeavour.

The problems are not over when the driver is done and working. Companies that rely on a single programmer to develop their drivers (either for in-house use or as part of their products) must consider the critical issue of support. The driver/kernel interface is not the subject of any POSIX or X/OPEN standards. New releases of UNIX are free to mess with this interface. And in the case of third-party products, the hardware engineers can't resist messing with the hardware interface. So with both interface subject to change, the poor device driver writer has to modify his driver continually just to maintain the same functionality. And this demand for maintenance can place a company in a sticky position should their sole driver wizard depart for other (possibly greener) pastures.

Again, this is not a reason to dismiss custom device drivers entirely but rather a plea to consider the entire life cycle of the product and driver.

Solutions to this problem involve training other people in the company to assist (and if necessary, replace) the primary driver writer. Another possibility is to use (or arrange to use) the services of a driver writing company that has internal redundancy (i.e., more than one driver programmer) and a long track record of successful drivers and satisfied customers.

One other reason sometimes used to justify the writing of a driver is the need for performance and functionality that cannot be obtained merely by writing an application program. While it is certainly true that drivers can do many things efficiently that applications programs can do slowly if at all, the gains are often illusory.

Given that machine performance is gaining so rapidly (and faster processors are so cheap), the performance improvements have to be substantial to justify the much higher development costs associated with writing a driver. And since the driver/kernel interface is not standardised (as is the kernel interface for applications software), the maintenance costs will be much higher and the portability much lower for drivers than for applications software. Sometimes moving parts of an application into a driver is justified by the gain in performance and functionality. Frequently, however, the gains are modest and the costs substantial.

Preparing to Write a Driver

One of the factors that makes device driver writing difficult is the lack of complete and accurate documentation. Not only is the documentation on the UNIX kernel and driver interfaces incomplete, the documentation on the hardware device you are trying to support is often incomplete and full of errors. This is a fact of life. While this section describes some things that can be done to mitigate these problems, they will probably always plague device driver writers.

The first step is to collect as much information as possible about all aspects of the task at hand. Obtain every possible document on: the machine you are using; the version of UNIX it runs (especially any device writing guides for that release); and the device you wish to support. The first rule of writing drivers is that you can never have too much documentation. (And while we're on the topic of rules, note that the first corollary to this rule is that significant portions of any document relied upon by a driver writer will have significant errors or apply to another release of the product. The second corollary is that at least one piece of information necessary to write a correctly functioning driver will be missing from the documents. The third corollary is that you will locate the support engineer who knows the critical piece of information only after you have worked it out for yourself.)

The next step is to locate the life boats *before* you need them. This means contacting the company that is responsible for the operating system you are using and the hardware you are planning to support and obtain the name(s) of the support engineers who know the system/device well enough to answer the technical questions you will inevitably have. In the case of some operating system vendors you may have to spend money to obtain an advanced support contract that permits you to access these engineers directly without delay. Spend it. This is money well invested.

The final step before picking up the pen (keyboard) and actually designing the driver is to get into the right frame of mind.

Mental Preparation

One of the rudest awakenings that programmers receive occurs when they start to write device drivers and learn (a) that hardware is not at all like software, (b) hardware behaviour is at best probabilistic and at worst random, and (c) that most hardware documentation is even less accurate and complete than most software documentation.

These realisations can be extremely stressful, especially to one who has a tight deadline, who has a conviction that computers (hardware included) work logically, and who thinks that all that is necessary to emerge victorious is a strong will.

If you approach device driver writing as a 'mind over machine' battle then the odds are with the machine. It is critical that you adopt a patient zen-like detachment from the problems at hand and approach the problems with an open mind, uncluttered with conventional wisdom such as logic, electronics, and the expectation that any piece of hardware will work the way its designers described.

As any experienced driver writer will attest, hardware is subject to timing and sequencing sensitivities that can cause the most dedicated programmer to begin to doubt his own sanity. When stuck, the master driver writer tries things that seem not to have any relation to the problem at hand.

The master driver writer will rearrange statements, change the order certain registers are read or written, and make other changes that are mathematically provable to have no effect whatsoever on the software. And the master driver writer will frequently find that the hardware responds differently.

In summary, preparing one's mind to become a master driver writer is easy. All you need is peace of mind, patience, and a mind unbound to conventional hang-ups about determinism, causal theory, and other tenets of Western thinking.

Writing the Driver

Here are two more rules for writing device drivers. One, never write a driver from scratch: find a driver that is somewhat similar and modify to suit. Two, Rome wasn't built in a day: do not try to write the complete driver during the first editing session.

Large parts of most drivers are similar to large parts of other drivers. Or to put it another way, if you've seen one disk driver, you've seen roughly 50% of all disk drivers. Select a driver that supports a device similar to the one at hand (either from this book or from other sources) and edit it into the driver you need.

As for the second rule, start with the simplest possible driver that elicits some sort of response from the device. And then iteratively refine this into the complete production driver that you need, *testing every step of the way*. Not only will this prevent you from having to rewrite large parts of your driver when you find out the device works differently from the documentation, it also breaks the testing down into manageable units.

The brute force approach involves writing a 2000-line driver in its entirety, compiling it, and installing it. And then wondering why nothing seems to work at all. The more productive and less stressful approach is to add or modify 20 to 100 lines each time, testing as you go. If the driver stops functioning, you know that it was working a little while ago and you probably have only 20 to 100 lines to examine to locate the problem.

Debugging Device Drivers

Debugging device drivers can be particularly time consuming and frustrating for several reasons. Firstly, it is not possible to use the same debugging tools available for applications software. In particular, since the kernel containing the driver under test is also running the system, it is usually not possible to use breakpoints or single-step the kernel. Secondly, the time it takes to recompile the driver, rebuild the kernel, and reboot the system is much longer than the edit-recompile-test cycle for applications software.

Finally, because of the asynchronous (interrupt-driven) nature of the kernel, device drivers can fall prey to timing-dependent bugs that are both unknown to applications software and extremely intermittent. It is not unheard of to have a driver bug that causes the kernel to crash only after several days of operation, and the event that actually caused the crash occurred hours before the actual crash. As mentioned earlier, problems like these can cause you to doubt your own sanity.

Since the tools that are available on different UNIX systems vary considerably, we shall limit our discussion to general approaches and widely available tools. Specific information must be obtained from the documentation for your particular system.

Printf Statements

Placing printf statements within your driver to trace the execution path and to display the values of key variables is one of the simplest and yet most widely used driver debugging techniques. The advantages are that it is simple to use (i.e., no need to learn how to use a debugger) and that it can provide almost any piece of information needed about the operation of the driver. The disadvantages are: it can produce too much information; the mere presence of the printf statements can affect the timing of the driver; and the time taken to change the printf statements, recompile, rebuild, and test can slow the debugging process substantially.

The effect on timing is something that needs to be considered carefully. It is surprisingly common to find that merely by adding or removing printf statements a driver will malfunction or even start to function correctly. Usually this will not be obvious at first and the change in behaviour with the driver as printfs statements are added or removed will cause a great deal of confusion and frustration. It is important always to be aware that the presence of the printf statements may affect the driver and that the behaviour of the driver with the printf statements may not be the same as without the statements. If you will, this is the Heisenberg Uncertainty Principle applied to device driver development (i.e., any attempt to measure a physical phenomenon will affect the phenomenon itself). Adding printf statements in order to trace the execution of the driver may affect the execution of the driver.

The best defence against this problem is to keep detailed notes of every testing session and copies of every driver that was tested so that when you start to suspect the printf statements of affecting the operation of the driver you can review your notes looking for additional information and any patterns.

Indeed, this recommendation (keeping detailed notes and copies of all drivers) is one of the most important in this section. Frequently when debugging software, the current hypothesis as to the reason the driver is failing blinds us to other possibilities. It is only once our pet theory has been proven wrong that we start really to consider other explanations. And it is then that reviewing earlier tests can provide insights that would otherwise require running more tests with the delays associated with the edit-build-test tedium of kernel driver development.

And as if it needed to be mentioned, do not rush it. Carefully plan the debugging sessions and the placement of the printf statements. Carefully consider the expected results and the actual results. And think before repeating the cycle. In applications development it is so convenient to rebuild the application that it is usually faster to try an idea in code than to think it through. And most of us have developed this experimental approach to debugging. With drivers, however, most systems take so long to rebuild and reboot that it is usually faster to think more about the changes and tests than when debugging an applications program.

There are a couple of techniques that can be used to control the output of debugging messages without having to recompile the driver. The first is to use unused bits in the minor device to control printf statements. For example, if your device normally uses only minor devices 0 through 7, then the top five bits of the minor device number can be used to control debugging output. We can assign each of these five bits to a different category of printf statements:

```
#define DEBUG_READ 0x40
```

   . . .

```
if (minor(dev) & DEBUG_READ)
    printf(...);
```

If we then create a new entry in /dev (manually using the *mknod* command) with minor device number 51, we will access minor device 3 with the DEBUG_READ printf statements enabled.

Using a Debugger

Some systems provide a kernel debugger that will permit you to monitor variables during the operation of the kernel and your driver. Sometimes the debugger can even be used to breakpoint or single-step your driver. If you have access to such a tool then things will be somewhat easier for you. Remember that anything that changes the timing of the driver (i.e., breakpoints and single-stepping), will change the execution path through your driver and affect its operation.

The vast majority of systems do not, unfortunately, provide a kernel debugger. In these cases the standard applications debugger *adb* can usually be used. *Adb* is normally used to analyze the stack trace and variables of a program that has terminated abnormally and produced a core image. When applied to the kernel, however, adb accesses the */dev/kmem* pseudo-device. This permits you to access the current values of any global variables within the kernel as well as to change these variables. It does not, however, permit you to trace the execution of your driver directly. This must be done either through printf statements or by changing variables (that are observed by adb).

Earlier in this book we recommended that all variables declared within the driver be of static scope so as to reduce the chance of conflicting with a variable in the kernel or another driver. As valid as this suggestion is, remember that static variables are not visible to debuggers such as *adb*. Therefore when using adb during the testing of drivers you will have to remove the static declaration from any variables that are declared outside of functions if you wish to examine them using *adb*.

Analyzing Kernel Crash Dumps

On some versions of UNIX the system will generate a crash dump of the entire system memory should a panic trap cause the system to crash. This dump can be analyzed using a program called *crash*. A detailed discussion of the output of *crash* is beyond the scope of this book since understanding the output of *crash* requires a detailed knowledge of the entire UNIX kernel. But even without such knowledge *crash* can produce useful information such as the state of the various kernel data structures at the time of the crash as well as a stack trace of the kernel and driver routines called just prior to the crash. This last bit of information can be invaluable in trying to determine what part of your driver was responsible for the panic.

Other Debugging Techniques

In some cases none of the above techniques will help. You know that something funny is happening within the driver but printf statements affect the timing too much and mask the problem. And the event happens too quickly to capture it using adb.

One possibility is to declare a large array and use it to buffer debugging information. Then dump the array at some later time once the event to be traced has occurred. For example, the array could be printed when a device with a strange minor device number is opened. Or you could access the array by reading it through /dev/kmem or by writing another small driver similar to that shown in Chapter 2.

Finally, when you have no idea what is causing the problem or how to fix it, try anything. Assume the most ridiculous possibility and change the code to handle it. Change the order of statements when the order of those statements obviously cannot affect anything. Try resetting a device that does not need to be reset. Try setting bits that are automatically set or do not need to be set. Try reading registers that do not need to be read. Try anything.

Hardware is not software. There are often unknown and undocumented aspects to reading and writing device registers that can cause no end of problems...problems that are resolved merely by writing the registers in a different order...or by reading an interrupt register that returns no useful value merely to reset the interrupt logic (a point not mentioned in the documentation).

And try not to lose your sanity.

Driver Performance

The first and most important thing that can be said about device driver performance is that the fastest driver in the world is not worth bat dung if it is not reliable and robust.

Do not start tweaking and poking your driver in an attempt to get higher throughput before you have absolutely convinced yourself that your driver is bullet proof. Unreliable drivers do not improve when modified to increase performance and the last time you want to start debugging the fundamental operation of your driver is when you are in the middle of cranking the utmost out of it. Get it right...*then* get it fast.

Many of the general considerations with regard to driver performance are the same as for any other piece of software. For example, beware of assumptions. All too often programmers will assume that they know what is consuming all of the CPU time and what needs to be rewritten only to make significant changes and find a marginal difference in performance. Another trap often fallen into by neophyte programmers is optimising code that is rarely executed. Most programmers are paid to develop software. That means that the programmer must continually trade off the cost of developing his code with the cost of running it. It is possible to write code that is too efficient. Code that takes a long time to write, test, and debug because it is unnecessarily complex in the mistaken attempt to wring the last drop of performance out of the code. Code that is executed so infrequently that the cost of developing and maintaining the code far outweigh the savings in performance.

Software performance can be viewed at two levels. *Micro-performance* issues include the use of register variables where possible, use of machine-preferred constructs like *$*a$++* on an M68000 rather than *$*$++$a*, recoding certain functions in assembler, etc. *Macro performance* issues include selecting a heap sort algorithm instead of a bubble sort, or using binary search instead of linear search.

Macro performance issues are almost always more important than micro performance issues. Also, while micro performance issues can easily be added to code after it has been written and tested, macro performance issues must be considered from the start. Changing macro issues usually means substantially rewriting the software. So make sure you understand the problem and have chosen an appropriate algorithm and design before cutting code.

On the other hand, if a simple algorithm exists that can be implemented first to verify the operation of the device then it can sometimes be faster to get a simple (slow) driver working and later replace the key algorithms. Usually the driver/device interface will remain essentially the same and it is this interface that can be debugged during the development of the simpler driver.

One of the best methods of determining what areas of a driver need consideration is to profile the software. Profiling means measuring the amount of time spent in each routine (or portion of a routine). Some versions of the UNIX operating system provide systems programmers with the ability to profile the kernel. But unfortunately there is no built-in mechanism in most computers to measure exactly the time spent executing each routine. So most systems estimate the execution period by interrupting the CPU periodically and recording the program counter (i.e., the address of the code that was being executed at that moment). Over time a statistical analysis of these program counter values will provide an estimate of the time being spent in each part of the kernel.

The problems with this method are twofold. It is an approximation at best based on statistical sampling and it is only accurate if the sampling interrupt occurs randomly with respect to the execution of the code being sampled. But since the kernel frequently disables interrupts, and the sample interrupt is frequently clock based and many kernel routines also operate from clock interrupts, the sample will not be random and uncorrelated. Some routines will not appear at all, or will be overrepresented in the sample merely because of these artifacts. So be aware when interpreting the results that they do not necessarily represent reality.

One of the first things every hot programmer (who knows assembler) thinks of when tweaking code to improve performance is to rewrite certain frequently executed parts of the code in assembler. As everyone knows hand-coded assembler is faster than machine-generated (i.e., compiled) code.

Even if that were true (and it's not: some optimising compilers generate better code than humans in certain cases), it ignores several important facts (alluded to earlier). Writing and maintaining assembler is extremely expensive. If writing a driver routine in C costs x dollars, then rewriting it in assembler (especially tight, fast assembler) will cost at least 10x, and maintaining it over the life of the driver could easily cost 100x.

And most routines rewritten in assembler (even to take advantage of special machine instructions) only run about two to four times faster. And remember doubling the speed of the main loop of a driver is not going to double the speed of the driver as a whole. And the driver is but one small part of the system as a whole.

So when you figure it all out it becomes very hard to justify the substantial increase in development and life cycle costs with what is usually a very modest improvement in the driver's overall performance.

There are exceptions. Sometimes the only way to accomplish something is to use assembler (for example to permit an unbuffered RS-232 port to receive data at 38,400 baud). But think twice—no make that four times—before succumbing to the temptation to write a little assembler.

When considering performance improvements, do not think only of improving the performance of your driver, but also of how you can reduce the performance impact on the system as a whole. For example, every moment a device interrupt is disabled because your driver is executing code at an elevated processor priority (ie. *spl_*) is a moment some hardware device remains unnecessarily idle. Reducing the code that is surrounded by the spl_...splx calls can also improve the performance of your own driver if the interrupt you are blocking is one of your own.

Try to do as little as possible as fast as possible whenever interrupts are disabled.

Interrupts are expensive so do what you can to avoid them. And when an interrupt happens, do as much work each interrupt as possible if that will allow you to avoid another interrupt.

There are a couple of examples. Let us consider a simple terminal communications interface (similar to the one discussed in Chapter 9).

Perhaps the device has a four-character buffer on the transmit side and has options to generate interrupts either when a character has been sent or when the last character has been sent.

To minimise the overhead of handling interrupts, you ought to set the device to interrupts when the buffer is empty and transfer four characters from the driver to the device whenever an interrupt is received. While this means doing up to four times as much work each interrupt, it will result in almost one fourth the number of interrupts. The total work done by the driver will be about the same but the overhead incurred from handling interrupts will be reduced by almost 75%.

Similarly, if the receive side of the device has a buffer, don't just read a single character every time an interrupt arrives; check to see if more than one character has arrived. At the higher baud rates (where interrupt efficiency really counts) you may find that by the time you have responded to the interrupt and processed the character that caused the interrupt, another has arrived. Indeed, running the driver at a lower interrupt priority can increase the chances of this happening and result in lower overhead.

This leads to the ironic situation in which lowering the priority of the interrupts can increase the performance of the driver.

Indeed, if the buffer is large enough one can dispense with interrupts altogether and use polling. Polling involves periodically checking the device for data at a rate far lower than the maximum potential interrupt frequency.

For example, instead of responding to each interrupt as a character is received, merely poll the device once every twentieth of a second. At slow data rates (less than twenty characters per second) the overhead of polling will be higher than using interrupts, but at higher data rates (i.e., 38,400) the driver will be able to service multiple bytes of data for each poll, saving substantial overhead. The tradeoff is usually worth it. But make sure, of course, that you poll frequently enough to prevent the buffer from overflowing.

Hardware Design

Another area that is ripe for performance gains is the design of the hardware device itself. Usually the poor device driver writer has absolutely no say in the design of the hardware and must develop his driver to work with the hardware interface presented him.

In rare cases, however, you may be working with the company that is developing the hardware you are supposed to support under UNIX. In which case ask, nay, demand, to be involved in the hardware design. You may find that the hardware engineers have design choices that have little or no effect on hardware performance or manufacturing cost (the two holy grails of electrical engineers) but have a massive effect on the complexity of the software needed to support the hardware.

The best devices are almost always those that were designed by a team considering both the hardware and software engineering involved. So if the opportunity exists, or can be made, to participate in the hardware design then seize it. You will find the benefits more than compensate for the effort of having to explain software concepts to electrical engineers.

Unusual Driver Applications

The majority of this book has discussed how to write software to interface hardware to the UNIX operating system. And indeed, that is the most common use of device drivers. But there are other possibilities. As you will recall, device drivers can do things no applications program can attempt.

Drivers have access to sub-second scheduling with strict priorities. Drivers can disable interrupts and operate without pre-emption (i.e., without losing the CPU). Drivers can receive hardware interrupts directly and can access the hardware directly.

On many real-time operating systems these facilities are available to applications software but on most UNIX systems only drivers and the kernel itself have access to these features.

So when developing software for UNIX systems that need real-time features, consider migrating parts of the application into the kernel as a pseudo-device driver.

This is, of course, not a decision to be taken lightly, since developing and maintaining drivers is far more costly than for applications software. Recall that debugging and testing drivers is more difficult than applications software, and driver software is less portable than applications software because the interface is not standardized to the degree it is for applications software.

Exercises

There is only one exercise possible that illustrates the concepts discussed in this chapter:

1. Write a high-performance driver for a real hardware device. Extra points awarded for supporting a device that was designed solely by electrical engineers who have only programmed in FORTRAN (if they have programmed at all).

Chapter 15

Writing Drivers for System V Release 4

This book so far has concentrated on writing device drivers for UNIX System V Release 3.2 (SVR3), since that is one of the most popular UNIX releases around. It is also available directly from a number of different suppliers such as The Santa Cruz Operation, INTERACTIVE Systems Corp., AT&T, Microport, and Esix (Everex).

The newest release of UNIX from AT&T (the 'inventors' of UNIX) is System V Release 4 (SVR4). Although not nearly as widely available or installed as Release 3.2 at the time this book was written, it will certainly increase in popularity over the years to come.

As with the rest of this book, this chapter is not intended to be a reference but rather a guide to the topic at hand. Please consult the reference manuals for your Release 4.0 system for complete details prior to proceeding. In addition, AT&T has arranged for a generic reference manual to be published by the UNIX Press titled *UNIX SYSTEM V RELEASE 4 Device Driver Interface / Driver-Kernel Interface (DDI / DKI) Reference Manual*.

The Good News

The good news is that the changes between Release 3.2 and Release 4 from the driver writer's point of view are, for the most part, more evolutionary than revolutionary. Some of the kernel support routines have changed, many of the data structures have changed slightly, but the overall architecture of character and block drivers remains substantially the same.

The one area where the change is radical, however, is with terminal drivers. Earlier in this book we discussed two approaches to terminal drivers: the traditional approach using line disciplines as illustrated in Chapter 9 and the new STREAMS approach illustrated in Chapter 12. With almost all UNIX systems up to and including Release 3.2, the traditional approach was used, even if the system supported STREAMS. With Release 4.0 the traditional approach is strongly deprecated in favour of the STREAMS approach.

Although some Release 4.0 systems still support the traditional line disciplines for backward compatibility, all of the new terminal drivers ought to be written using the STREAMS mechanism.

The New Order

With Release 4 AT&T has defined two interfaces, the device driver interface (DDI) and the driver-kernel interface (DKI), and divided all of the kernel support routines and interfaces (i.e. entry-point definitions) into one of three categories. These are processor specific and intended to be supported beyond Release 4.0 (DDI only); processor independent and intended to be supported beyond Release 4.0 (DDI and DKI); and processor independent but not guaranteed to be supported beyond Release 4.0 (DKI-only).

Obviously the goal is to write drivers that avoid as much as possible the DDI-only and DKI-only parts of the interface in order to maximise portability. In many drivers this will not be possible but at least the division of the interface into these categories enables driver writers to recognise areas of the interface that may cause portability problems in the future.

The Release 4.0 Driver Reference Manual cited earlier provides details on the DDI and DKI interfaces. For example, the *init*, *intr*, and *start* entry points are part of the DDI-only (i.e., processor-specific) interface. So too is the *vtop* (virtual to physical) kernel support routine. None of the DKI-only parts of the interface are available under Release 3.2 and hence we have not discussed them.

Changes to the Driver Entry Points

Release 4.0 supports some additional entry points that were not available under Release 3.2.

The *chpoll* entry point permits non-STREAMS drivers to support the *poll* system call. The *poll* system call makes it possible for a user process to monitor multiple file descriptors for data and events simultaneously.

The *mmap* and *segmap* entry points provide support for devices that let user processes map some of the device's dual-ported memory directly into their memory (e.g., mapping in the video memory of a display adapter).

The *size* entry point returns the size in 512-byte blocks of the device's storage capacity.

The interrupt entry point has been renamed *int* from *intr*.

Many of the entry points discussed in this book now have additional parameters under Release 4.0.

The *ioctl* has another parameter that permits it to set the return value from the *ioctl* system call.

The *read* and *write* entry points have an additional parameter that provides all of the information regarding the transfer of data to and from the user process. In Release 4.0 character drivers there is no need to reference the *u.* structure to obtain this information (see Chapter 2).

A number of entry points (including *open*, *close*, *read*, *write*, and *ioctl*) now take an additional parameter which provides detailed information on the identity (or 'credentials' as the documentation calls it) of the user/process making the request.

In addition, several entry points that in the past indicated errors by setting u.u_error now return the error code as their function value (or 0 if no error). These include *open*, *close*, *read*, and, *write*.

Changes to the Kernel Support Routines

Many of the changes to the kernel support routines affect lesser used routines that have not been discussed in this book and therefore will not be discussed here. Refer to the references mentioned earlier for these details.

We shall confine our attention to changes that affect the drivers we have studied.

There are a number of routines that have changed their name but retain the same definition. These include *major* and *minor* (renamed *getmajor* and *getminor*); and *iodone* (renamed *biodone*).

The *physck* and *physio* routines used in Chapter 8 to handle raw (character) I/O with block devices have been combined and renamed *physiock*.

All of the routines to support clists (i.e., *getc* and *putc* used in Chapter 4) have been removed without being replaced. (Buffering within drivers is now handled either by implementing the driver as a STREAMS driver and using message buffers and queues or by implementing private buffering strategies within each driver.)

The *copyin* and *copyout* routines used in character drivers (see Chapter 4) have been replaced by a single *uiomove* routine that handles all data transfer between the driver and the user process without requiring references to be made to the *u.* structure. For single byte transfers there are the *ureadc* and *uwritec* routines.

The memory allocation routine *sptalloc* (used in the RAM disk driver of Chapter 6) has been replaced with *kmem_alloc* and many of the related memory management routines have been replaced (i.e., *ctob* replaced by *ptob, sptfree* replaced by *kmem_free* etc.).

All of the line discipline routines (such as *ttinit*, *ttiocom*, *ttyflush*, etc., used in Chapter 9) and other routines used to support terminal drivers (e.g., *signal*) have been deleted and not replaced. As mentioned earlier, all terminal drivers are now supposed to use the STREAMS model exclusively.

Changes to Kernel Data Structures

The two major changes are that the *u.* user structure is no longer supposed to be accessed directly and the support for the clist data structure has been removed.

Other minor changes to other structures such as the *buf* structure do not affect the drivers we have considered in this book.

Sample SVR4 Drivers

To illustrate the differences between SVR3 and SVR4 drivers we have ported two of the drivers presented earlier in this book: the character test data generator presented in Chapter 2 and the block test data presented in Chapter 5. In addition, the STREAMS driver presented in Chapter 12 was actually tested under SVR4 and can be considered as a port to SVR4 of the COM1 driver originally presented in Chapter 9.

This discussion considers only the differences between these SVR4 drivers and the SVR3 driver presented earlier. The reader is referred to those chapters for a description of the general functionality and structure of the drivers.

Sample SVR4 Character Driver

The prologue to the SVR4 version of the character test data generator is very similar to the one we examined in Chapter 2.

```
1   #include <sys/types.h>
2   #include <sys/errno.h>
3   #include <sys/uio.h>
4   #include <sys/user.h>
5   #include <sys/cred.h>
6   #include <sys/cmn_err.h>

7   static char foxmsg[] =
            "THE QUICK BROWN FOX JUMPS OVER THE LAZY DOG\n";
```

The *<sys/uio.h>* header file (line 3) includes the definition of the *uio* structure which is used to describe the I/O request passed to the read or write entry point.

The *cred* structure contains information on the identity and privileges of the user who made the I/O request. The *<sys/cred.h>* header file (line 5) defines this structure.

The *<sys.cmn_err.h>* header file was seen earlier when we used the *cmn_err* utility to print messages in block drivers. In SVR4 *cmn_err* is preferred to the special kernel version of *printf*.

The init entry point is the same as for the SVR3 driver with the exception that we use the cmn_err function rather that printf to display our message.

```
 8  void chr1init()
 9  {
10      (void) cmn_err(CE_NOTE, "chr1init: Test Data Driver v1.0");
11  }
```

The primary difference between the two read entry points is that under SVR4 the character driver obtains all of the information about the I/O request from the uio structure which is pointed to by the second parameter (uio_p). Compare this with the earlier driver which referenced members of the *u.* structure.

Although Figure 15-1 illustrates the uio and related structures, these details may be ignored for the most part since the kernel routines which perform the transfer (uiomove, ureadc, or uwritec) interpret and update these structures.

```
12  int chr1read(dev_t dev, uio_t *uio_p, cred_t *cred_p)
13  {
14      while (uio_p->uio_resid)
15      {
16          if (ureadc(foxmsg[uio_p->uio_offset % sizeof(foxmsg)],
                                                              uio_p))
17              return (EFAULT);
18      }
19      u.u_offset += u.u_count;
```

```
20        u.u_count = 0;
21        return (0);
22   }
```

FIGURE 15-1

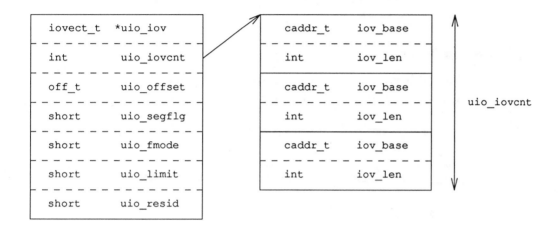

The *uio_resid* member of the uio structure tells us how much data is still to be transferred. We loop (lines 14-18) until all of the data has been transferred. To transfer a byte of data from the *foxmsg* string to the user process, we use *ureadc* (line 16). This routine is similar to *copyout* except that we pass (a) the actual character (rather than a pointer) and (b) the pointer to the uio structure which describes where in the user process the data is to be placed. Ureadc updates the uio_resid count in the uio structure (as well as other internal pointers).

If ureadc encounters a problem transferring the data, it returns a non-zero value (line 16) causing us to return the error code EFAULT (line 17). Note the different method of indicating an error. With SVR3 we placed the error code into u.u_error. With SVR4 we return the error code as the return value for the entry point.

Once the transfer is complete, we update the u.u_offset and u.u_count variables to reflect the successful transfer (lines 19 and 20). On some SVR4 systems this is done automatically from the *uio* members. On these systems lines 19 and 20 are not needed. Note that upon entry the uio_offset member of the uio structure (see line 16) is initialised to u.u_offset and is maintained during the loop by ureadc. Finally, we return with a value of 0 (line 21) indicating success.

Sample SVR4 Block Driver

The prologue to the SVR4 version of the block test data generator is similar to that seen in Chapter 5. All of the header files have been discussed previously.

```
   1   #include <sys/types.h>
   2   #include <sys/open.h>
   3   #include <sys/buf.h>
   4   #include <sys/cred.h>
   5   #include <sys/cmn_err.h>

   6   static char testpattern[4096] =
   7   {
   8         (char)0x00, (char)0x01, (char)0x02, (char)0x03,
         ....
1031         (char)0xfc, (char)0xfd, (char)0xfe, (char)0xff,
1032   };
```

The only slight difference is that our *testpattern* array is now declared and initialised as 4K bytes in size as opposed to the 1K size we used earlier. Most SVR3 systems issue strategy requests to fill 1K buffers. With SVR4, however, the system uses 4K buffers. In order to keep the strategy routine as simple as it was for SVR3 we make the testpattern array the same size as the typical strategy request.

The init entry point is essentially the same

```
1033   void blk1init()
1034   {
1035         (void) cmn_err(CE_NOTE, "blk1init: Test Data Driver v1.2");
1036   }
```

The open and close entry points do nothing (as with the previous driver). With SVR4, however, they must return 0 to indicate no errors occurred.

```
1037  int blk1open(dev_t dev, int flag, int otyp, cred_t *cred_p)
1038  {
1039      return (0);
1040  }

1041  int blk1close(dev_t dev, int flag, int otyp, cred_t *cred_p)
1042  {
1043      return (0);
1044  }
```

The strategy entry point for the SVR4 version of the driver is identical in structure to the SVR3 driver. The only change is the name of the kernel-supplied utility from *iodone* with SVR3 to *biodone* with SVR4.

```
1045  int blk1strategy(struct buf *bp)
1046  {
1047      if (bp->b_flags & B_READ)
1048          (void) bcopy(testpattern, paddr(bp), bp->b_bcount);

1049      bp->b_resid = 0;
1050      biodone(bp);
1051  }
```

The only change to the print entry point is explicit 0 return value which indicates success.

```
1052  int blk1print(dev_t dev, char *str)
1053  {
1054      cmn_err(CE_WARN, "Blk1: %s", str);
1055      return (0);
1056  }
```

Summary

As we have seen, the changes to drivers from SVR3 to SVR4 are relatively minor and easily understood. With the exception of terminal drivers (which must now be implemented as STREAMS drivers), most SVR3 drivers can be ported to SVR4 without much effort.

It is expected that with the definition of the Driver/Kernel Interface (DKI) and Device Driver Interface (DDI) it will be easier for device drivers to know which parts of the kernel/driver interface are portable and which parts are processor or UNIX-version specific.

As always, the portability and maintainability of code is dependent for the most part on good coding practices. Well-structured code with meaningful comments are at least as important as avoiding constructs known to be tied to a specific architecture or UNIX implementation.

Exercises

1. Modify the SVR4 character test data driver to transfer as many bytes as possible with each call to *uiomove* (instead of one byte per call as in the current driver). For example, if the user asked for 100 bytes, u.u_offset was 10, and the message was 44 bytes long, then the request could be satisfied by (1) transferring 34 bytes starting with *&foxmsg[10]*; then (2) transferring 44 bytes starting with *&foxmsg[0]*; and then (3) transferring 22 bytes starting with *&foxmsg[0]*, leaving u.u_offset set to 22.

The definition of the uiomove function is as follows: *int uiomove(caddr_t addr, long count, enum uio_rw reflag, uip_t *uio_p);*, where *rwflag* is one of *UIO_READ* or *UIO_WRITE*.

2. Defining a 4K array which contains all 256-byte values repeated 16 times makes for time-efficient code at the expense of memory. Rewrite the SVR4 block test data driver to define a testpattern array of only 256 bytes and modify the strategy entry point to still handle 4K strategy requests properly.

Index

Writing UNIX Device Drivers

Sample Driver Order Form

Please send me a disk containing the sample drivers from this book. I understand that the programs may vary slightly and that additional drivers may be included on the disk. I have enclosed a check or money order for US $39.95 for the disk.

Name:

_____

Address

_____

_____

_____

Please select one of the following formats:

☐ 3.5-inch disk, MS-DOS format
☐ 5.25-inch disk, MS-DOS format

☐ 3.5-inch disk, SCO tar format
☐ 5.25-inch disk, SCO tar format

Please make your check payable to Driver Design Labs and send it along with this order form to:

Driver Floppy Offer
driver design labs
1497 Marine Drive, Suite 300
West Vancouver, BC
Canada V7T 1B8